The Real Estate Investor's Answer Book

Other Business Books by Jack Cummings

The McGraw-Hill 36-Hour Real Estate Investing Course

Complete Guide to Real Estate Financing

Successful Real Estate Investing for the Single Person

The Guide to Real Estate Exchanging

The Real Estate Financing Manual

The Real Estate Investor's Answer Book

Jack Cummings

McGraw-Hill, Inc.

New York   San Francisco   Washington, D.C.   Auckland   Bogotá
Caracas   Lisbon   London   Madrid   Mexico City   Milan
Montreal   New Delhi   San Juan   Singapore
Sydney   Tokyo   Toronto

Library of Congress Cataloging-in-Publication Data

Cummings, Jack.
   The real estate investor's answer book / Jack Cummings.
       p.   cm.
   Includes index.
   ISBN 0-07-015051-6 (alk. paper)—ISBN 0-07-015052-4 (pbk.)
   1. Real estate investment.   I. Title.
HD1382.5.C854 1994
332.63'24—dc20   93-43353
                                          CIP

   5 6 7 8 9 0 DOC/DOC 9 9 8

ISBN 0-07-015051-6 (hc)
ISBN 0-07-015052-4 (pbk)

The sponsoring editor for this book was David Conti, the editing supervisor was Frank Kotowski, Jr., and the production supervisor was Pamela A. Pelton. This book was set in Palatino by McGraw-Hill's Professional Publishing composition unit.

Printed and bound by R. R. Donnelley & Sons Company.

This book is printed on recycled, acid-free paper containing a minimum of 50% recycled de-inked fiber.

*To my wife, a person who makes me feel like I
really lucked out the day I met her*

Contents

Introduction   ix

1. Investment Strategies for a Profitable Real Estate Portfolio   **1**

   1. What Makes Ownership of Real Estate a Good Investment?   1
   2. What Is the Best Investment Technique to Use?   3
   3. How Does the Technique of Economic Conversion Work and Why Is It So Important to Me as an Investor?   4
   4. How Can I Put the Idea of Economic Conversion to Work?   7
   5. What Does It Take to Become a Real Estate Investor?   8
   6. What Should My First Acquisition Be?   8

2. Real Estate Values: Keys to Why and When They Change   **10**

   7. What Makes Property Increase in Value?   10
   8. What Makes Property Decrease in Value?   12
   9. How Do I Predict Which Property Will Increase in Value, and Why Is Timing So Important?   15
  10. How Can I Determine What My Neighbors Paid for Their Property?   16
  11. What Can I Do to *Cause* My Property to Go Up in Value?   16
  12. How Can I Tell That the Value of My Income-Producing Property Is Approaching Its Peak?   17
  13. What Are Advance Signals That Indicate Property Values in My Neighborhood Are Headed Down?   18

3. Renting or Owning: Which Is Best for You?   **20**

  14. When Is It Better to *Rent* than *Own*?   20

15. What Are the Most Important *Contract Factors* I Should Be
    Aware of When Renting?   21
16. What Should I Check When Looking at Property I May
    Lease?   25
17. How Can I Negotiate the Most Favorable Lease
    Possible?   27
18. What Can I Do If the Landlord Will Not Fix What Is
    Broken?   30
19. Where Can I Find the Most Important Laws That Protect
    Me as a Tenant?   30
20. What Can I Do to Reduce the Cash Cost of My Lease?   31
21. How Can a Senior Citizen Negotiate a Super Lease?   31
22. How Can I Get *Free Rent* When Negotiating a Lease?   31

4. How to Deal with Your Real Estate Broker   **33**

23. Do I *Need* a Real Estate Broker or Salesperson?   33
24. What Is the Difference between a Realtor and a Licensed
    Broker, and Is That Important to Me?   33
25. How Can I Maximize My Benefits from Real Estate
    Agents?   34
26. What Are the Most Important Factors I Need to Know before
    I Sign a Listing Agreement?   35
27. How Does the Real Estate Law Affect My Relationship with
    My Broker or Agent?   37
28. Should I Use a Different Agent for Buying and for
    Selling?   38
29. What Is the Usual Commission and Who Pays It?   38

5. Successful Buying and Selling of Homes   **39**

30. How Can Buyers Improve Their Success When Negotiating
    an Offer?   39
31. What Should All Sellers *Know* When Negotiating a
    Contract?   42
32. What Does It Mean When a Buyer Says *"I'll Pay Your Price
    If You Accept My Terms"*?   45
33. How Should I React When a Prospective Buyer Finds Fault
    with My Property?   47
34. What Are the Most Important *Buying Signals* I Should
    Watch for?   47
35. How Do I Get Rid Of Mildew Smells?   48
36. What Are the Key Money-Making Aspects about
    Landscaping?   49
37. Should I Sell My Property Furnished or Unfurnished?   49
38. How Can I Get Rid of Dog and Other Animal Smells?   50
39. What Should Sellers Do When Showing Their Home
    to a Prospective Buyer?   50
40. What Are "Memory Smells" and How Can They Entice
    a Prospective Buyer?   51
41. What Steps Should I Follow When I Am Ready to Buy
    a Home?   51
42. What Are the "Hidden Gems" I Should Look for in a
    Property When Trying to Get the Most Value for My
    Money?   54

43. What Are the Most Common "Time Bombs" I Should Look for before I Buy a Home?   55
44. What Should I Do When I Am Ready to *Sell* My Home?   58
45. What Inexpensive Things Can I Do to Fix Up My Home to Improve My Chances of Getting Top Dollar?   59
46. How Do I Set a Price for My Home?   60
47. What Can I Do to Speed Up the Sale of My Home?   61
48. How Do I Select the Best Agent to Sell My Home?   61
49. What Is the Best Technique for Selling Real Estate in a Slow Market?   61
50. Should I Consider a Real Estate Exchange, and If So, for What?   61
51. How Is the Tax on a Sale Treated If I Buy Another Home?   62
52. How Can I Avoid the Pitfalls of a Title Closing?   64

6. The Keys to Buying and Selling Condominium and Cooperative Apartments   **68**

53. What Are the Most Important Differences between Condominiums and Cooperative Forms of Ownership?   68
54. What Critical Factors Should I Know When Buying a Condo or a Coop?   69
55. How Is the Association Maintenance Charged against the Unit I May Buy, and What Potential Problems Do I Need to Look for?   71
56. What Factors about the Apartment Do I Need to Consider before Buying?   71
57. How Should I Prepare for the Interview by the Owner's Association to Improve My Chances of Being Approved?   72
58. What Are the Most Important Strategies to Use When Selling My Condo or Coop?   72

7. Insider Secrets for Buying, Selling, and Owning Vacation Properties   **76**

59. Do I Get Any Tax Write-Offs with Vacation Property?   76
60. What Are the Eight Major Pitfalls of Owning Vacation Property?   77
61. What Is the Most Important Thing to Know before I *Buy* a Vacation Property?   81
62. What Are the Most Important Factors When Renting out My Vacation Property?   81
63. What Is a *Time-Share* Vacation Resort and How Does It Work?   84
64. What Are the Advantages and Disadvantages of Time-Shares?   87
65. What Can I Do to Increase the Value of My Vacation Property?   88
66. How Can I *Syndicate* My Own Vacation Property?   89
67. How Can I Get the Most for My Money When I Sell My Vacation Property?   92

8. Questions That Every Senior Citizen Needs Answered   **93**

    68. Why Should a Senior Citizen Look at Real Estate Ownership
        Differently than a Younger Person?   93

    69. How Much Can Retired Senior Citizens Afford to Pay for
        Their Housing?   94

    70. What Are Some of the *Options* of Ownership That Senior
        Citizens Should Be Aware of for Their Housing?   94

    71. How Can Senior Citizens Reduce Their Annual Housing
        Cost?   95

    72. What Is the Single Most Important *Estate* Factor a Senior
        Citizen Should Take into Consideration?   72

    73. What Is The Best Way for a Senior to Transfer Ownership
        of Real Estate to Reduce or Eliminate Estate Taxes?   96

    74. How Can Senior Citizens Use the *Installment Sale* to Their
        Best Benefit?   98

    75. How Can Seniors *Save Money* When They Own or Rent Real
        Estate?   99

    76. What Are The Four Best *Insider Tips* That Would Help
        a Senior Citizen in Ownership of Property?   101

9. Master Wealth Builder: Buying and Selling Land   **103**

    77. Why Has *Raw Land* Been the *Millionaire Maker* of the Past,
        and What Is Its Future?   103

    78. What Are the Key Steps to Buying Raw Land?   104

    79. When Buying a Vacant Lot, Is It True That *Location,
        Location, Location* Is the Single Most Important Factor
        to Consider?   108

    80. How Do I Compare the Differences among Different Vacant
        Tracts?   111

    81. Why Is Zoning So Important When Buying Vacant
        Land?   111

    82. What Is a *Master Plan* and How Does It Affect the Future
        Values of Property?   113

    83. What Are the Major Pitfalls When Buying Vacant Land
        and How Can They Be Overcome?   114

    84. How Can I Maximize Income from My Vacant Land?   115

    85. How Do I Entice a Buyer to My Vacant Land?   116

    86. What Are the Key Steps to Follow When I Sell My Raw
        Land?   117

**10. Income Property for the 1990s: Buying and Selling
Residential Rental Properties**   **119**

    87. How Can I Successfully Buy Residential Rental
        Property?   119

    88. What Are the Most Important *Risk Enhancers* I Should
        Avoid When Buying Residential Rental Properties?   124

    89. Which Is Better to Own—Seasonal Rentals or Annual
        Rentals?   127

    90. What Are the Key Steps to Follow When I Want to Sell My
        Residential Rental Property?   128

    91. How Do I Set My Rental Prices to Ensure Low Vacancy
        and Top Rental Income?   130

11. Buying and Selling Income-Producing Properties 132

92. How Can I Determine the Best Kind of Income-Producing Real Estate to Invest in? 132
93. How Do I Analyze an Income and Expense Statement? 133
94. What Are the Advantages When I Own an Income-Producing Property? 136
95. Why Does Ownership of the Same Property Affect Different Buyers Differently? 137
96. What Are the Steps to *Successful Acquisition* of Income-Producing Properties? 137
97. What Are the Most Dangerous Pitfalls to Avoid When Buying Income-Producing Property? 140

12. Managing Your Real Estate to Maximize Profits and Minimize Problems 144

98. What Are the Secrets to Successful Property Management? 144
99. What Can I Do If My Tenants Are Constantly Late Making Rent Payments? 145
100. What Can I Do If I Get Stuck with a Bad Check? 146
101. How Can I Reduce or Eliminate Tenant Complaints? 146
102. How Can I Avoid a Tenant's "Midnight Move"? 147
103. How Do I Evict a Tenant with the Lowest Cost and the Fewest Problems? 147
104. When Can I Use a Small Claims Court to Collect Past-Due Rent? 148
105. What Kind of Lease Should I Use? 148
106. What Are the Most Common Problems Encountered in Property Management and How Can I Solve Them? 148

13. How to Pay the Least Capital Gains Tax and Other Tax Matters 157

107. How Does Owning Real Estate Help Me Save on Income Tax? 157
108. How Do I Keep Good Tax Records That Will Help Me Survive an IRS Audit? 160
109. What Is the Tax *Write-Off* That Most People Overlook When Selling a Property? 161
110. What Is a Capital Gain? 163
111. What Is Mortgage Over Basis, and How Does That Affect My Tax Liability on a Sale or Exchange? 163
112. Should I Take the Maximum Depreciation Available? 165
113. How Does Depreciation Affect My Income Tax? 165
114. What About My Home Office—Should I Depreciate It? 165
115. Are there Techniques I Can Use When Selling That Will Reduce or Eliminate the Capital Gains Tax? 166
116. How and Why Is Real Estate Taxed? 167
117. How Can I Reduce My Real Estate Tax? 167
118. Are There Other *Tax Reduction* Methods I Should Be Aware of? 169
119. What Happens If I Do Not Pay the Assessed Real Estate Tax? 169

120. What Can I Do If a *Tax Certificate Has Been Sold* Against
      My Property?   170
121. What Happens to the Mortgage Holder When the Property
      Owner Fails to Make the Mortgage Payment as well as
      the Real Estate Tax Payment?   170

14. All about Foreclosures   **172**

122. How Do I Foreclose on Someone?   172
123. If I Get Behind in a Few Mortgage Payments, What Can I
      Do to Keep From Facing a Foreclosure Myself?   176
124. Are Foreclosure Sales a Good Buy and Where Do I Find
      Them?   177
125. How Can I Find Out about Foreclosure Property?   178
126. What Are the Major Pitfalls of Buying Foreclosed
      Property?   178

15. Buying and Selling through Auctions   **181**

127. How Does a Real Estate *Auction* Work and How Can I
      Benefit from It?   181
128. What Are the Most Important Steps I Should Take before
      Bidding at Any Auction?   182
129. Why Is the *Absolute Sale* Auction the Best to
      Attend?   182
130. What Governmental Agencies Hold Regular
      Auctions?   183
131. How Does a *Court-Ordered Auction* Differ from a Seller's
      Auction?   183
132. Why Is a U.S. Marshal's Drug Property Auction or Sale
      the Least Bargain?   183
133. What Is the Resolution Trust Corporation?   184
134. How Can I Cash in on RTC Auctions?   184
135. How Can I Select an Auctioneer to Auction Off My
      Property?   184
136. Can I Use the Auction as a Tool to Sell My Own
      Property?   185

16. Real Estate Finance Made Easy   **186**

137. What Is the Best Way To Calculate Mortgage
      Payments?   186
138. How Do I Calculate the *Yield* on an Income-Producing
      Property?   187
139. How Can I Increase *Spendable Cash Flow* from an Income
      Property?   187
140. What Is the *Loan To Value Ratio* and How Do I Calculate
      It?   191
141. What Are the Different Ways to Calculate Mortgage
      Payments and Why Is Each Important?   192
142. How Does a *Wraparound Mortgage Work to Benefit Both
      the Buyer and the Seller?*   195
143. How Does the *Cost of Living* Adjustment Work?   197
144. How Do I Calculate Real Estate Depreciation?   197

145. What Are the Most Important Steps When Making Income Projections?   199

17. Insider Secrets for Creative Investing Techniques   202

146. Are Those "*Get Rich Quick through Real Estate*" TV Programs a Realistic Way to Learn Real Estate Investing?   202
147. Is There at Least One Easy Way to Invest in Real Estate without Risk?   203
148. When Using Other People's Money, What Are the Most Important Questions I Need to Ask First?   203
149. How Can I Maximize My Negotiating Leverage with Any Seller?   209
150. What Are the Steps for Negotiating with Buyers?   210
151. What Is a *Letter of Intent* and When Should It Be Used?   210
152. What Is a Standard Deposit Receipt Contract?   212
153. What Is the Best Investment Technique I Can Use to Reduce Risk?   213
154. How Can I Use *Sweat Equity* to Acquire Real Estate with Zero Cash Down?   213
155. How Can I Use My New *Sweat Equity* to Acquire Other Property?   215
156. Why Do Real Estate Exchanges Work?   216
157. How Can I Use Exchanges to Invest in Real Estate?   217
158. How Can I Use Barter to Acquire Real Estate?   218
159. How Can I Use *Pyramiding* as an Investment Tool?   219
160. How Can I Form a Real Estate Syndication?   220
161. How Can a Syndication Be Used to Acquire Property?   221
162. What Is the Secret to Land Speculation?   222
163. How Can the *Land Lease Technique* Be Used to Acquire Property?   222
164. How Does the Lease–Option Technique Work?   224
165. What Should I Know before Getting Involved with a Joint Venture?   224
166. How Does the "*Keep Some, Sell Some*" Technique Work?   225
167. How Can I Exchange Something I Do Not Own for Something I Want to Aquire?   226
168. What Is the Quickest Way for Me to Become an *Insider*?   227

18. Finding Money for All Your Real Estate Transactions   228

169. What Is a Mortgage, Who Is the Mortgagor, and Who Is the Mortgagee?   228
170. What Are the Most Common Types of Mortgages?   229
171. How Can Wording in the Mortgage Make a Big Difference in How the Mortgage Is Paid Back?   231
172. How Do You Set Up a Wraparound Mortgage for Maximum Protection of the Mortgagor?   232

173. What Provisions Should I Include in the Mortgage When
     Using a Blanket Mortgage?   234
174. What is *Novation* and Why Is It Important?   236
175. What Key Questions Do You Need To Have Answered
     to Protect You from Random Releases of Property You
     Sell?   236
176. How Does *Subordination* Affect the Security of a
     Mortgage?   238
177. What Is *Substitution of Collateral* and Why Is It Considered
     an Insider Technique?   240
178. When Is a First Mortgage *Not* a First Lien?   241
179. Which Lender Almost Always Gives the Best Terms on a
     Loan?   242
180. How Do I Shop around for a Lender?   242
181. What Is the Key to Getting a Loan?   243
182. What Is a FHA Mortgage and Where Do I Get
     One?   243
183. Who Can Qualify for a FHA Loan?   243
184. What is a *GI Loan* and How Do I Get One?   244
185. What Are the Most Asked Questions about Veterans
     Administration Loans?   245
186. What Can You Do to Increase Your Chances of Getting
     a Loan?   246
187. Do the Mortgage Reduction Plans Really Save Me
     Money?   248
188. What Are the Insider Tips for Negotiating the Best Mortgage
     Terms?   249
189. As a Buyer Just How Creative Can I Get with
     Mortgages?   251
190. What Can I Do to Get around a *Nonassumable
     Mortgage*?   252
191. What is a "Starker" Exchange and What are the Pitfalls I
     Need to Watch out for?   252
192. What Critical Factors Should You Be Aware of before
     You Take Back a Mortgage on a Property You
     Sell?   254

19. Reducing Cost and Avoiding Problems at Closings and Deed Transfers

                                                                            256

193. What Happens at the Real Estate Closing?   256
194. Should I Use a Lawyer at the Closing?   259
195. As a Buyer, How Do I Keep My Closing Costs to a
     Minimum?   259
196. What Are the Key Steps to Keep the Seller's Closing Costs
     to a Minimum?   260
197. What Are the Dos and Don'ts I Should Know When I Am
     Getting Ready for the Closing?   261
198. How Can the Seller Legally Back out of the Deal?   264
199. Can the Buyer Legally Back out of the Deal?   265
200. What Can I Do If the Property I Bought Is Not Everything
     the Sellers Told Me It Would Be?   266

20. Planning Your Real Estate Insurance Needs   **269**

201. Do I Need to Insure My Real Estate?   269
202. What is Casualty Insurance and How Much Should I
     Buy?   271
203. What Are Some of the Special Types of Insurance Available
     for Real Estate?   272
204. Why Do I Need Liability Insurance for Real Estate and How
     Much Should I Buy?   273
205. What Is Title Insurance, What Does It Protect, and When
     Can It Be Dangerous?   274
206. If I Rent, What Insurance Do I Need to Carry?   274
207. Should I Keep All My Insurance with the Same Insurer?   275
208. How Do I Determine My Insurance Needs Before I Buy the
     Policy?   275
209. What Steps Can I Take *After* a Fire or Other Casualty Loss
     to Get the Maximum Insurance Benefits?   276

21. Avoiding the Major Pitfalls in Real Estate Investing   **279**

210. Can Being Overly Demanding or Too Soft Kill a Deal?   279
211. What Should I Do If Someone Claims to Own My
     Property?   281
212. What Are the Most Common Pitfalls to Avoid When Investing
     in Vacant Land?   282
213. What Can Go Wrong with My Zoning and How Can I Be
     Affected?   286
214. Can a Building Moratorium Really Destroy the Value of My
     Vacant Property?   287
215. What Is a *Grandfathered Use* and Why Is That So
     Dangerous?   287
216. What Are the Major Pitfalls to Mortgage Financing?   288
217. Is There Any "Easy" Way to Avoid All the Possible Pitfalls
     That Await Real Estate Investors?   290
218. What Is a *Quitclaim* Deed and Why Can It Be a Very Risky
     Form of Title Transfer for the Buyer?   290
219. What Is a *Trustee's Deed* and What Are the Limitations
     in Protection It Gives the Buyer?   290
220. What or Who Are Phantom Deal Makers and How Do I Deal
     with Them?   291
221. How Can I Know If a Property I Want to Buy Has a Defective
     Title and Why Is That So Important?   291
222. What Is an Encroachment and How Does It Affect
     Title?   292
223. What Are the Most Important Steps I Should Take *before*
     I Ever Buy Real Estate?   293
224. To Be Continually Successful as a Real Estate Investor,
     What Should I Do Every Day?   295

Key Word and Subject Index   296

Introduction

Everyone who has an interest in real estate should read this book. Buyers, sellers, property managers, mortgage brokers, lawyers, first-time property owners, senior citizens, real estate salespeople, builders, developers, people who rent and want to own, people who own and should rent. Everyone.

This book is designed as a *quick* and *easy* way to find the answers to the 224 most important questions asked about real estate. The answers to these questions are formulated to enable you to make the most of your own real estate investments so that you can take shortcuts to solve or avoid problems and to help you get started in real estate investing, or to improve your present investment strategies.

These questions have been selected from thousands of such questions that have been asked of me over the past 30 years. During that time span, I have been committed to the real estate industry in many different ways. These include being a realtor, investor, investment counselor, teacher, lecturer, author, talk-show guest and host of both radio and TV, speaker at conventions, and a real estate authority in legal proceedings. In addition to being an instructor of real estate investment techniques, I am also an avid reader of real estate books and frequently take courses and attend seminars covering tax problems and solutions, international investment potentials, and so on.

I believe that priorities and opportunities in real estate investing are constantly changing, and that to succeed in real estate it is important to be as current with the trends as possible. The answers you will find in this book are backed by years of experience, lots of *learning it the hard way*, and solid study and research and practice on what works best for which situation. Getting from point A to point Z can take a long time when you learn it out in the field. Take advantage of this experience and use this book as your crash course in getting to the nitty-gritty *quick and easy*.

With this kind of background and in preparation to write this book, I have made several personal goals important factors to the material presented. These goals are to bring you solid information that can give you the kind of answer that will enable you to make a decision, effect a change, or stick by your guns because you now have the data and background knowledge to lean on. You can profit from the experience of others in this way and avoid having to make the mistake first in order to avoid the problem the second time around.

In reading this book you will discover that the material is easy to digest, and void of that stuffy textbook kind of writing that is usually the style for "Question and Answer" books. This book, as are all my previous books, is meant to be read *and* enjoyed. The learning experience will be pleasant.

This book is much more than an accumulation of the most important questions that are asked. It is a detailed book of answers fashioned to illustrate the *why* to each of these questions. The goal of this book is to give you a fast reference to how to solve problems that may be exactly the kind you are having. The idea is to provide answers and explanations that are clear, concise, and easy to understand. Answers that have the depth to explain and to teach you about the object to which the question was directed. The advantage for you is that you won't have to ask questions; the answers are here, offered to you in such a way that you will be able to use the information for your own personal benefit. Questions touch on virtually every aspect of real estate, so it is likely that everything you ever wanted to know will be answered.

Take a look at question number 42, for instance, which asks "What are the potential hidden gems I should look for when trying to get the most value for my money?" The *answer* gives you the answer and then the *why* each of the hidden gems can pay off with profits when the time is right. The right questions and the easy to understand answers with the solid backup of *why* allow you to build your own knowledge and confidence in how to handle problems and make decisions.

You will find the question or answer that will help you most in one of two different quick and easy ways. The first is to scan the 21 chapters. In the first chapter, for example, you will find questions dealing with the fundamentals of real estate investing.

This method may be all you need to get right to the section that fits your immediate need. However, for a more detailed response to your problem or need, use the key word and subject index.

This index shows all the different answers that deal with that specific key word or topic. "Foreclosures," for example, are discussed in the answers to many different questions. By using the key word and subject index, you will find following each key word or subject, such as "foreclosures" or "senior citizens" or "mortgages," and so on, all the different question numbers where the answers touch on or deal with the specific key word or subject you may need information about.

An important part of this book are the many useful checklists, and helpful hints on how to head off problems *before* they hit you.

This book is designed to be used on a daily basis as you need help or just want to brush up on the techniques of buying and selling property. Everything about the book is designed to enable you to quickly find the questions which are most important to you.

Jack Cummings

The Real Estate Investor's Answer Book

1

Investment Strategies for a Profitable Real Estate Portfolio

1. What Makes Ownership of Real Estate a Good Investment?

The following six key factors are commonly accepted as the major reasons real estate continues to be a good investment. For most investors, these factors will be the most critical issues in investing in real estate.

The Six Key Factors of Real Estate Ownership

Is a necessity

Is a hedge against inflation

Produces income

Appreciates in value

Provides stability

Is a fundamental of wealth

To understand how each factor can affect your decisions on real estate investments, review the following brief discussion of each of the six key factors.

Is a Necessity.   Unless you are homeless, you own or rent real estate or live with someone who does. Housing, clothing, and food are three of the major necessities of life and all three can be provided from real estate.

Is a Hedge against Inflation.   Inflation is the result of an increase in the cost of living and can suddenly eat away at savings. When the cost to rent an apartment continually increases every year, a person with a fixed or limited income will find their standard of living slipping behind or the effort to keep up even harder each year. Because real estate is one of life's basic elements it adjusts naturally to the usual supply and demand economics that governs most of the marketplace.

A good example of this is an apartment building constructed 25 years ago. Then, a nice unfurnished one-bedroom apartment may have cost only $90 per month rent on an annual lease. That same apartment today (25 years later) may rent for over $500 per month. If you were the owner of that apartment over the same period of time, your "ownership costs" would not have had that same increase. Best of all, if you rented the apartment to someone else, you would have experienced a steady increase of income to "cover" other expenses that had gone up due to cost-of-living increases.

Produces Income.   The obvious cash benefit is an offset to inflation, as mentioned earlier. Owning income property is the opportunity to put OPM to work for you. The term OPM means *other people's money*. It is a cliché in the real estate industry but is a real factor in the ownership of property.

Being a landlord is a position of both status and wealth in most parts of the world. Building wealth in real estate can be as simple as acquiring property with a lot of debt and letting other people use their money to pay off your debt. Once the property is free and clear of any debt, all the income that had been going to mortgage payments now goes into your pocket.

Appreciates in Value.   As a result of the first three factors real estate has a tendency to increase in value. While this fact is not guaranteed, you will discover, by selecting wisely at the time of acquisition, planning prudently, and keeping a watchful eye on the trends in the marketplace, that it is not unusual to see real estate values appreciate greatly over a period of a dozen years or so. Even modest increases in value can produce great gains and substantial wealth. For example, because housing is in great need, well-located apartment complexes that are properly maintained should increase in value as the rents charged for those apartments also increase. A purchase price of $200,000 twenty years ago could have acquired a very nice 15-unit apartment building. In a conservative investment plan, the investor might have invested $40,000 down, with the balance being a first mortgage of $160,000 payable over a 20-year term. The obligation to meet the mortgage payment would be covered by OPM (from those who rent the apartments).

If this was your investment and it did nothing for you except provide an apartment to live in, and income from the other 14 apartments to pay the mortgage, in 20 years the first mortgage would be paid off. A very conservative approach would show the current value of these 10 units to be $400,000 or more. After all, this is only double the original investment over 20 years. While a 5 percent per year increase may not sound like a good investment, you must remember that the cash investment was really only $40,000, and that in addition to the increased value, you lived free in one of the 15 apartments. The value of the investment has increased 10 times, still not counting living rent-free and more than likely putting some cash in your pocket each year.

Provides Stability.   Real estate does not have an instant market as do other items such as gold coins, stock in IBM, and so on. A buyer must be found who has a use for a particular property or who can see the benefits it will produce. Because this is not an instantaneous market the values tend to adjust slowly on the downside. However, because real estate involves location and is not a commodity, the need for a specific location or area can cause values to go up much faster.

Is a Fundamental of Wealth.   Real estate and the items that are produced on or under it are the basis for most the wealth in the world. Wars are fought over it, divorce lawyers argue the most about it, and when you own it free and clear there is a certain soundness to your sleep at night.

2.   What Is the Best Investment Technique to Use?

The comfort zone method of investing in real estate is a proven approach to learning all you can about a specific geographic area or type of property. By having a strong focus on a narrow market area, you can quickly become an expert in the property in that area.

   For example, Able decides he will learn everything he can about the area of town where he lives. He knows that potential investment opportunities must exist there. Yet, because he does not know the marketplace, the values of property, rent potentials, etc., he is unable to recognize opportunities when they are right before his nose. To change this situation to one in which Able will begin to see the opportunities he must learn a new procedure. The best technique I have ever experienced that will work in any community and for any prospective investor is what I call a *comfort zone*.

   Able follows the checklist shown below as the basic formula to start forming an effective comfort zone for real estate investing.

The Seven Basic Steps to Establish a Comfort Zone

1. Outline on a map the exact geographic area that will become your comfort zone. It is important that you do not bite off more than you can chew. Start with a reasonable area and build from that.

2. Make sure there is a minimum of 600 properties in the area and that the total area is within one city boundary, ideally, within one subdivision if at

all possible. This concentrates your research to one city and one set of city ordinances.

3. Make a list of important governmental officials and city meetings. The VIPs will include the city mayor, county commissioners, head of the building and zoning department, head of the planning department, and other important people these people recommend as other VIPs who would be helpful or important to real estate investors. Start to attend city and county council meetings and local planning and zoning hearings. The city manager's office will assist you in finding out where and when these are held.

4. Get to know the comfort zone like the back of your hand. This means you should know *everything* that goes on in your community that can cause someone to choose or to reject a property or an area of town, and should determine how much buyers will pay for a property, what the actual market has done in the past, and where it is headed now. Some of these items include bus routes, school boundaries, locations of churches and hospitals, shopping areas, centers of employment, local zoning ordinances, and building rules and regulations.

5. Become an *insider*. This occurs without extra effort because you are getting to know the important people in the community who affect real estate values and who can be influential in helping you make a change in the value of your own property. The key is to make sure that the VIPs of the community you meet *know you* in return. This is totally within your power because you control your own follow-up.

6. Build a property value awareness file. Every time a property is offered for sale or rent, research it. Get in the habit of checking the county records on sales, and foreclosures of property for the actual sales price. Find out what people have paid by looking at the county deed records at the tax assessor's office. The office staff will provide ample help to show any prospective investor how to use the deed records.

7. Continually look for undervalued property that presents an opportunity for future profit. These kinds of property will begin to stand out as you become acquainted with your comfort zone. The property may simply need tender loving care or a change of use to make it more valuable.

3. How Does the Technique of Economic Conversion Work and Why Is It So Important to Me as an Investor?

Economic conversion is an event in which the property owner makes or creates a change in the real estate so that the net rent that can be earned from that property is increased. When this is properly accomplished the economic return on the invested capital is increased.

It is important that the investor study all options available when contemplating a change of any kind. For example, it may be easy to increase rents by making improvements to a property, but the *cost* of those improvements may actually reduce the yield on the overall invested capital. Be careful not to make a change for change's sake when the real answer to success lies elsewhere— perhaps in improved management or increased rents.

For example, Frances purchased a large three-story home that has a detached three-car garage in the rear of an oversized corner lot and a large workshop and apartment over the garage. The home has over 1400 square feet on each of the three floors, and the garage has nearly 1200 square feet on each of its two floors.

The property cost Frances $120,000, which she felt was below the market for the location. This was due to the fact the home was in need of repair—a factor that Frances did not mind, as she had different plans for the home. She was able to negotiate with the seller for a down payment of $20,000 and the seller will hold a first mortgage for the balance of $100,000. Frances has a mortgage payment that includes the real estate taxes and insurance on the property of $1,500 per month.

Frances had selected this home because she had checked the zoning department at City Hall and had discovered that the zoning laws permit several different uses for the property in addition to its use as a single-family home. These uses included professional offices, such as medical offices, insurance company offices, real estate offices, lawyers offices, and so on; a multifamily use that would allow a maximum of five separate apartments; and a mix of professional and apartment uses.

Frances's first thought was to make the needed changes in the buildings to create the maximum of five apartments. Her plan was to make each floor of the main house into a spacious two-bedroom apartment and to convert the garage and its upstairs workshop and apartment into two additional two-bedroom apartments. She studied the rental market for the area before she bought the home and had ascertained that she should be able to collect a minimum of $600 per month per apartment once the work was completed.

An architect worked up a preliminary sketch for her to take to a building contractor so she could get a price for the needed conversion. Soon Frances realized that she would need to add four completely new bathrooms and remodel two existing ones to make sure that each of the "new" apartments had at least one bathroom, and in addition completely relocate or install all the needed kitchens. The "easy thing to do" suddenly was becoming an expensive nightmare.

The builder suggested that Frances turn the home into professional offices and do some minor repair work on the second-floor garage apartment. The needed remodeling turned out to be nothing more than removal of old carpets, which hid the soon-to-be refinished hardwood floors, and general painting inside and out. The rent that would come from the offices on a triple net lease (where the tenant pays all the cost to maintain the property, including real estate taxes) was more than she could collect from all five apartments.

And there was still potential income from the garage apartment. Frances calculated that with the rent from the offices, plus a minimum of only $400 from the slightly fixed up garage apartment, she would end up with over $25,000 at the end of the year after all mortgage payments and expenses had been paid—not a bad return on her cash investment of $20,000.

Frances now had the opportunity to make the changes in the building and to find a tenant. Instead, however, she went around to local law firms and medical groups armed with several maps and aerial photographs that showed off her property while at the same time pointed out the ideal location for a prestigious office. After a week of contacting "likely tenants" she found a law firm that grabbed the opportunity Frances was offering. The lawyers realized that if they made the improvements, they could have a much lower rent, and that over a period of five years they could save considerably over what they were currently paying and moreover, have a landmark office facility.

Frances was maximizing her use of OPM by giving the lawyers something important in return. The final economic conversion of this property into a lawyers' office did not cost Frances more than a few weeks of scouting potential tenants.

Economic conversions follow many different paths. An old-style motel might be converted into small shops, a drive-in theater might be given added income potential as a flea market by day, a vacant lot might become a parking lot or a "U-Pick-It" strawberry patch.

Sometimes the economic conversion is very subtle, such as when a strip of 18 small shops is converted to 18 antique boutiques. The shops still exist, but because of a change in concept and the development of a *theme*, the rents to be charged can be increased—and the tenants would willingly pay for the opportunity to be at that location.

Every real estate investor who wishes to *build wealth* should look to economic conversion as a logical process to follow. This means that every prospective investment should be considered only if additional income can be created from the property so that the total yield on the investment is increased.

Very small changes in income can make very large changes in value. This occurs because most real estate investors buy an income-producing property based on the yield or return they will get on their investment. When an investor wants a 10 percent return on his or her invested capital, that means that for every additional $100 of net income per month there would be $1,200 of net income for the year, and an increase of value of $12,000 (10 percent of an additional $12,000 in sales price).

If, as in this example, a buyer wanted a 10 percent return on his or her cash invested, a property that has $25,000 of income left over at the end of the year after all payments and expenses have been made would be worth $250,000. As Frances's conversion was destined to have that kind of year-end return, she could see a potential sale of a property that cost her only $20,000 out of pocket and that would return her $150,000 (after payback of the $100,000 mortgage to the original owner).

4. How Can I Put the Idea of Economic Conversion to Work?

The best kind of economic conversion for any real estate investor to attempt would be one that was selected after following these four steps.

The Four Steps to Economic Conversions

Homework.   Do detailed homework of the existing real estate market and all options available. Any economic conversion should not be attempted until a detailed study has been completed of all the alternatives that are allowed under the current zoning or that could reasonably be accomplished through a change of zoning or variance of city ordinances. Once the investor sees what can be accomplished, the next step is to determine what is most likely to succeed. Only by knowing the market area can this be determined with safety.

Stay within Your Comfort Zone.   Work within your own comfort level. Given several viable options, each of which shows promise for economic gain, the best economic conversion would be a change that suited the investor's ability and capability. This extends well beyond the level of competence in property management or business acumen. The total comfort level also should include the financial responsibility that will come with the project as well as property management.

Know the Lender's Preferences.   It is good to know what type of real estate the lenders like to give loans for. Even if you have all the cash necessary to accomplish the project, you should find out where the "smart" loan money is going. This can be a good indicator of which kinds of business operations or real estate properties are going to maintain their value the most. Today, lenders are very conservative, and following their example will produce an equally conservative investment portfolio.

Learn How to Avoid or Overcome Pitfalls.   Be aware of all the potential pitfalls when going to contract on the property. Far too many investors divulge their plans too early. Your great idea might just be picked up by someone else if you are not careful, so make sure you have a firm contract to purchase the property before starting to talk to a local building official, a banker, or even a friend.

Every investor should realize that time can be both a friend and an enemy when making any economic conversion. The smart investor asks for ample time in the purchase contract to accomplish everything needed.

5.   What Does It Take to Become a Real Estate Investor?

The most critical of the four elements that a real estate investor should possess is *determination*. However, having all the determination in the world may not be enough to succeed without three other elements. These are a *positive attitude, strong goal orientation*, and *self-confidence*.

The mixture of these elements can provide the foundation for a success in any chosen path. I started with determination: the *will* that can keep you going against all adversity. This single factor is essential to all those success stories of people starting with nothing and ending up wealthy beyond their dreams.

A positive attitude is harder to obtain and often even harder to maintain. The world is full of adversity, and it is easy to accept that failure is the opposite of success. This is not true: the lack of desire for success is the opposite of success. Failure is simply readjustment time. Try again, or try a different approach, but try. This is where both determination and positive attitude work together.

Add the next to last element, a strong goal orientation, and the plan to succeed has focus and direction. Proper goal development must be learned, however, as it is not acquired overnight. The key to the whole effort is seeing an intermediate goal as a stepping stone to a longer-range goal and then working bit by bit to attain that step before proceeding.

If you build a ladder to success by doing tasks that have the greatest possible chance of success, your overall goal is eventually obtained and self-confidence is maintained at a high level. An example of this process is becoming an *insider* in real estate investing. One step is to get to know as many VIPs as possible. You have absolute control over this process because the VIPs are highly visible, and you can ask one to recommend you to another. By simply having the right attitude about meeting them and then making sure you follow up properly so that *they* get to *know you*, your ultimate goal of becoming an insider is ensured. The *right attitude*, by the way, is not to try to speed up the process. If your first positive event is just to have met a VIP, and the second positive event is to follow up, then you are functioning in a solid, positive mode.

Building one simple success on top of another is the secret to accomplishing anything. To write a book, write one page, then another, while keeping the overall goal in mind. The process of simple successes piled on top of others builds something all the money in the world cannot buy: self-confidence. Once you achieve self-confidence and mix in the other three elements, the world and success are yours.

6.   What Should My First Acquisition Be?

The first acquisition should be a property that helps you move closer to your goal. This is not sidestepping the issue, as the answer must come from you as you establish your own plans for the future.

Goals Dictate What You Should Buy

Because most people do not set proper goals it is critical that you understand that without proper goals your efforts toward any dream can become a series of frustrations and disappointments. To acquire a property simply for the sake of owning something may be a boost to your ego for the moment, but will do little or nothing to move you closer to your goal. The wrong property can and most likely will move you farther away from your goals.

If you are renting where you live now, one of the first aspects of real estate ownership should be to consider owning your own place to live. While this concept may not be ideal for everyone, if you are settled in an area and expect to remain there for five years or longer, then in the absence of any kind of goal at all, this should be your first consideration. But what should you buy: a home, an apartment, or an apartment building? Each has its advantages and disadvantages, and your own ability to deal with the complexities of these properties will help you make a meaningful choice.

Clearly, a very handy person, someone who is able to fix up both the inside and outside of a property, may consider a small apartment building that needs a bit more than some tender loving care. Satisfying two intermediate goals at the same time, a place to live and added income to cover debt service, is a sound way to go. On the other hand, a great interior decorator may find that taking a condominium apartment and redecorating it to be more in line with that investor's abilities. Investors must ultimately develop the comfort zone of expertise that will work best for them.

2
Real Estate Values: Keys to Why and When They Change

7. What Makes Property Increase in Value?

Every circumstance that can cause real estate to increase in value can be attributed to one or more of the following critical factors. Each will be discussed in detail.

Why Property Values Increase

Inflation

Improved infrastructure

Economic conversion

Increased bottom line

Capital improvements

Supply and demand

Inflation.   Inflation is the increase in the cost of any item or service due to the increased cost to reproduce the item or provide the services. In real estate these increased costs occur because of many different circumstances. One area of such cost increase occurs in bureaucratically imposed costs, for example, the overall cost to obtain building permits, to meet environmental standards, and to construct roads and sewer facilities. As new buildings cost more, old buildings become more valuable. Because real estate is tied to a specific location, older, already improved properties may not be directly comparable other than the cost of replacement. This occurs because the value of a highly sought after location often increases above the effect of inflation alone.

Improved Infrastructure.   Infrastructure is the total of all elements that make up a community. This includes the roads, the public and private facilities, shopping centers, theaters, banking systems, sewer and water facilities, schools, airports, ports, jails, hospitals, and so on. Improving or expanding the infrastructure of a community can have a major impact on the value of properties. Generally there is both a positive and a negative impact and some properties may go up in value while others go down.

This dual potential of improvement to infrastructure requires all real estate investors to be very watchful of proposed community changes or improvements. A long-range benefit may cause a sudden drop in value due to temporary construction or road detours. A property owner or tenant who is operating on a tight budget may find that even a slight decline in revenue can mean economic disaster. This type of situation can present a great opportunity to an investor who can endure the temporary drop in value.

Economic Conversion.   Economic conversion has been discussed in question number 3 and is any change of use of an existing property. Not all change produces a positive effect, however, and the overall effect of an economic change should be carefully weighed.

Economic conversion is one of the best ways for an investor to control the ultimate increase of value. The more you know about the local real estate market conditions and trends, the greater your prospect of making a successful economic conversion. A very simple example of an economic conversion would be to take a vacant lot and convert it into a used car sales lot. The lot is converted from a non-income-producing property to one with a positive cash flow. If the income from the car lot warrants a greater price than you recently paid for the lot, then the value has increased due to your conversion of the property.

Increased Bottom Line.   When you increase the annual cash flow of an income property, you will most likely increase the value of that property as well. Many factors may cause this increase, such as your improved management, decreased expenses, increased rents, and so on. Because the value of an income property can be a multiple of the net operating income (the net operating income is the total rents collected less total operating expenses but not depreciation or debt service), small increases in the bottom line can mean much greater increases of value. For example, a property that would be valued at 12 times the net operating income (NOI) of $80,000 per year would have a value of $960,000. Increasing the NOI to $88,000 (only an $8,000 increase) will boost the value to $1,056,000, giving a total increase of $96,000. This is how fortunes are made.

Capital Improvements.   Just as improved infrastructure in a community may have a positive effect on value, so can improvements made directly to the property. However, for income property these capital improvements should have a direct effect on increased rents for this added cost to increase the value. As an investor, the key is to distinguish between costs needed to restore a property to the value you have paid for it and improvements that increase value. Almost every property on the market will need capital to be spent just to maintain it or, because of deferred maintenance, to bring it up to standard. You should not expect that improvements will increase the value of your property unless you have taken into account these costs and have already discounted property value at the time of acquisition.

Supply and Demand.   The supply of and the demand for any item will have an effect on its value. Because of the fixed nature of real estate, supply is tied to specific areas of the country or of town. Generally, the resulting supply and demand will be closely tied to the community infrastructure and its rules and regulations. Local zoning may limit certain kinds of businesses to specific areas, and the inability to increase the area size limits the supply dramatically. When the cost in an established area climbs too high for new businesses to locate there or for the needs of existing businesses, new communities may compete with the old location, causing a rise in value in these new areas.

Supply and demand theories of real estate are very local in nature. With the exception of the availability of financing, which is a function of banks and less geographically connected, the market trends in one city may not have any consequences on what happens in your town, which may be only a hundred miles away.

8. What Makes Property Decrease in Value?

Property values decline for seven principal reasons. They are listed below and briefly discussed.

Why Property Values Decrease

Decline of neighborhoods

Adverse effects of infrastructure change

Governmental controls and regulatory changes

Economic obsolescence

Supply and demand

Lack of proper maintenance

Urgency to sell

Decline of Neighborhoods.   When a neighborhood begins to decline, for whatever reason, the values of property within that area will fall. It is important to realize that the decline occurs first, and then values fall. Over a long period of time, this fall in values may ultimately cause the area to undergo a readjustment of value such that new investors see the advantage of making new investments in the area. However, the time from the start of the decline to the rebirth of the area can be very long.

Neighborhoods decline for many different reasons, one of the most obvious and predictable being the lack of building upkeep and maintenance. When this happens, tenants move out, rents are reduced in an attempt to provide some income flow from the property, and the next step is a downward spiral of less maintenance, lower rents, and ultimately, slums. Tenants move out for many reasons but usually because of an event in or near the area that makes the area less desirable as a location for a business. This might begin as a temporary situation, such as a long-term road project or other improvement to the overall infrastructure of the community, but this area becomes cut off and isolated and businesses move out. With lower rents in place a lower economic element moves in and takes over vacant business and residential properties.

Real estate investors are well warned to stay away from urban renewal projects. These projects are best left to the community itself and to large corporations that can afford to spend and lose a lot of money before a profit is made.

Adverse Effects of Infrastructure Change.   This is the opposite side to the benefit a new hospital or an expanded airport can bring. All major infrastructure change is likely to cause some properties to go up in value and others to decline. New roadways, especially superhighways, may require new rights-of-way that have the end result of cutting nice neighborhoods into two less desirable areas. Increased traffic, noise, pollution, etc., are all negative side effects of almost any infrastructure change.

Governmental Controls and Regulatory Changes.   Every bureaucracy has a tendency to expand and become more complex. In real estate terms this complexity usually increases the cost to build and/or maintain real estate. Often building permits and other city requirements may become so expensive that it is not economically feasible to build or continue to operate a specific type of business or rental property. For small construction jobs it is not uncommon for the cost of meeting all the rules and regulations and obtaining all the required approvals and permits to be more expensive than the actual construction itself. When this occurs the value of predevelopment property can decline, while already improved investments increase in value.

It is common for communities to establish building moratoriums or impose expensive impact fees for new construction. These events occur partially because of the natural willingness of the existing residents of a community to pass on costs of the needed infrastructure improvements to the newcomers. The end result is that the new buyer must pay more simply to cover the costs the developers must pay to hold on to the property during the moratorium or to meet the requirements.

Economic Obsolescence.   A large part of any modern building will become economically obsolete over a period of time. Eventually the day comes when major expenditure of new capital must be invested to support desired income levels. The best economic option may be to demolish the building and start over.

Many property owners do not properly maintain their buildings. They manage to get by because of other positive factors in their favor, such as great location, heavy demand for the area, etc. However, the point of no return will eventually occur, and without added investment the property will eventually decline in value.

Supply and Demand.   Overbuilt situations occur as a natural part of the real estate cycles when builders overestimate the number of units or the amount of square feet being constructed to meet the present demand. The result is too much for too little demand. When this happens the market goes into a tailspin because most builders and developers operate on other people's money (OPM), and when the sales or rental predictions fail to materialize they get in trouble financially and scramble to meet debt service. The sudden results can be a sharp decline in rental rates in brand new properties as these developers attempt to get all the cash they can. In the end the lower rents reflect lower values, and if the builders can just barely meet their expenses and debt service, a further decrease in rents hastens the lender's foreclosure sale and bargain prices for new investors.

Lack of Proper Maintenance.   Improper maintenance is a slow deterioration of the property and the property value. This usually is a result of poor management or lack of management. For example, a professional person, such as a doctor or lawyer, owns an apartment building because his or her accountant said it would be good for tax shelter. However, this professional has no time to think about the property and hires a firm to "look after it." And *look* after it is about all they do. Soon, repairs and maintenance that should be done on a regular basis are not done at all. The professional looks at the bottom line, the cash he or she gets after the manager's cut, and realizes it is not increasing. Shortly, a long list of expensive repairs that need to be done to maintain tenants and rents develops. The owner must either commit to these delayed expenses or watch the property decline in value.

The biggest problem with lack of maintenance is the fact that the cost to restore the property to the condition it should be in will be far more expensive than if general maintenance had been done regularly.

Urgency to Sell.   If you want the value of your property to start to decrease immediately, put up a sign in the yard that says "Owner Must Sell—Moving Out of Town." Wolves, i.e., aggressive buyers, seem to smell blood suddenly and hone in on the potential bargain.

All property owners should review their long-range goals on a frequent basis to see if their investments are working properly for them. This kind of planning will allow the investor to avoid potential situations that may ultimately require dealing with a pack of wolves.

9. How Do I Predict Which Property Will Increase in Value, and Why Is Timing So Important?

The best way to predict the future is to study the past. In real estate terms this is much easier, for example, than looking into a crystal ball and predicting whom you will fall in love with tonight. Nearly everything that can happen in your area has already happened in some other location. Even though the final value of any property is best determined by the price a person will pay for it, the reasoning that goes into the buyer's decision-making process is predictable.

People buy because of location, use, cost, emotional appeal, and pride of ownership and to make a statement. All of these are human motivations. All are predictable. In fact, selecting a property that is likely to go up in value is pretty easy. The problem is knowing when that will happen.

Having the right timing is the maker of fortunes in the real estate market. For example, if you attend a city council meeting where a new highway is proposed that will open up areas outside of town, you could presume correctly that this new road will have the potential of increasing the values of the new area to be accessed. If the property is currently farmland and priced accordingly, and is in an area that will allow, or could allow (with proper rezoning, for example), a mixture of commercial and residential zoning, then the ultimate profits to be made by buying this property could be tremendous.

However, enter timing: from the day a city council talks about a new road to the day this road opens for traffic can span many years. Worse yet, the actual pathway of the road may vary slightly or be dramatically altered. The value of the land you rush out to buy will indeed go up...but when? Will it increase while you still own it, or long after your mortgage was foreclosed and you lost everything?

Short-term speculation is much safer than long-term anticipation, and one of the quickest turnarounds is to find a property that is suffering under a temporary adverse effect of infrastructure enhancement, and then wait out the short term. What is an example of this kind of investment? A bridge is being widened to make way for the anticipated expanding of traffic over the next ten years. Businesses on or near the approach to the bridge may suffer tremendously during the two years of construction...so much so that tenants move out, owners need to sell, and prices of real estate that are actually destined to jump in value decline...making the profits that much greater later on, all as a result of timing.

10. How Can I Determine What My Neighbors Paid for Their Property?

The sale of real estate in most parts of the world is strictly regulated and documented. The chain of title (ownership) of any specific property is likely to be maintained in one or more governmental bureaus or departments not far from the property itself.

Virtually every area has a local tax assessor's office. In the United States this task is left to the local county tax assessor's office. A visit to the local tax assessor's office would be the first place to find the details on any property.

If the tax assessor's office does not have the needed information, then the property records office of the clerk of the circuit court may. It is in this county department where information on property transfers are maintained and deeds are recorded.

Every public department and records office is open for you to review almost any public document of record. The people who work in these offices are trained to be helpful and to assist you in getting the most from the data that they can provide.

11. What Can I Do to *Cause* My Property to Go Up in Value?

Change the zoning

Make an economic conversion

Obtain a variance

Paint and fix up

Relandscape

Change the Zoning. Because value to a prospective buyer is based on two main factors, location and use allowed, a change in zoning can dramatically affect the use allowed. A farmer sells his strawberry patch to Sylvia. She then goes to the local governing authorities and after properly filing a petition to rezone obtains authority to build a shopping center and a hotel on this land. Through the change of zoning Sylvia has created a new use; land that will support a shopping center and a hotel is more valuable than a strawberry patch.

Make an Economic Conversion. This concept may also include a change in zoning, but in general refers to a change in use that is already permitted. Discussed in question number 3, this technique is one of the best methods to increase values in real estate. It is also safe and relatively risk-free when properly handled, as you can enter into a contract to acquire a property based on obtaining all the required permits and approvals to make the desired change.

Obtain a Variance.   Sometimes the only thing necessary to increase the value of a property is to get someone to bend the rules just a little. When a property owner is faced with a building regulation or city ordinance that will not allow something to be done, there are times that the city or other governing body will grant a *variance* to permit the desired construction or other use, despite rules to the contrary.

For example, a new backlighted sign that is built closer to the road than the rules allow might attract the right tenant who will lease the property for more money than the present tenant. This higher lease supports a greater value.

Paint and Fix Up.   Giving a fresh coat of paint and fixing everything that is clearly broken are good steps to increasing property value. Some properties have several years of poor maintenance but are structurally sound and in good locations. All that need be done is cosmetic work.

There are some key factors here: Do not scrimp on important and highly visible items such as front doors and door knobs. Quality paint does not cost that much more than the cheap stuff.

Relandscape.   Existing landscaping often is either too much or not enough. Sometimes all that is needed is to move some plantings around or sell off the excess and plants that are too big for the property (thereby getting top dollar from builders who want mature plants), and to put in a more modern look that allows you to show off the newly painted property.

12. How Can I Tell That the Value of My Income-Producing Property Is Approaching Its Peak?

The critical word in this question is *approaching*. The actual moment when your property has reached its top dollar will be an unknown. It is doubtful that a prospective buyer would say, "I'll pay you one million dollars...uh oh, on second thought, I'll only pay half a million dollars."

Every investor should keep track of the local market to take advantage of a potential sale, if it fits the investment plan, before the market turns downward and property values decline. The three key signs that a property's value is approaching its peak are usually quite visible if you look for them:

Continuing strong real estate market

Getting top income with little room for improvement

Approaching economic obsolescence of major items

Continuing Strong Real Estate Market.   There are a number of local indicators that you can check. I stress *local indicators* because national statistics on real estate are often tied to *housing starts*, which is an average from the whole nation or wide areas of the country and can be misleading. Your area may have zero housing starts while the national statistic is on an upturn, and obviously the opposite can just as easily occur. The best local indicator can be obtained from the local Board of Realtors. They keep track of the sales of their members, and a strong number of sales and a high volume of property moved is a good sign. By keeping in touch with the board you can track the local statistics on a monthly basis. For example, a steady three-month drop in sales during a time of the year that normally shows brisk business can be a definite sign that the market is going soft and may be headed for a decline. The local building departments keep track of the housing starts in your area and can provide you with statistics. Because a decrease in building permits often precedes the actual market decline, by the time you see them drop this may just be a confirmation of what you already expected. The market may be softer than you thought.

Getting Top Income with Little Room for Improvement.   If a rental property is at the top of its rental potential, if a hotel is already doing better than any other hotel in the area, or if a restaurant has reached its maximum without expanding, then only inflation can increase the gross revenue without added capital investment. Investment property buyers look at such situations and realize that there is no likely direction to go but down. The top value for the moment has been reached. Without some other event occurring, such as an expansion of the facility or a restructuring of debt expense that would contribute to an even greater bottom line after refinancing, the maximum value has been reached.

Approaching Economic Obsolescence of Major Items.   Even though your income is up and promises to go up a bit more, your property is facing major expenses due to economic obsolescence.

Building items such as roofs, elevators, air conditioning and heating systems, boilers, carpets, furniture, electrical wiring, and plumbing, all have their useful life. In addition to their useful life there comes a point when the maintenance of the item exceeds, in the long run, the replacement cost.

13.   What Are Advance Signals That Indicate Property Values in My Neighborhood Are Headed Down?

Rather than discover that no one is willing to pay you the same price you paid for your property, watch for the signals showing that your neighborhood is already in a decline. If you and your neighbors act quickly it may be possible to reverse the trend.

Four Advance Signals Indicating
Property Values Are Headed Down

Increased crime

Increased vacancy factors

Abundance of "For Sale" signs

Drop in the level of property maintenance in the area

Increased Crime.   If you close your eyes to what is going on, you will be oblivious to increased crime in your comfort zone. Newspapers are quick to point out where crime is taking place, and a visit to the local police department will provide you with eye-opening details.

Increased Vacancy Factors.   If you have not yet seen any vacancies, but begin to notice "For Rent" signs in places where they never were before, then this is a very good indicator that the economic climate is shifting. Checking with the owners of those properties may also produce another grim fact: rents asked are dropping as well.

Abundance of "For Sale" Signs.   This may be a seasonable trend, so check with the local Board of Realtors before you jump to conclusions. The Board of Realtors can tell you about rentals too, and if there are other downward trends, the "For Sale" indicator can mean that people are financially strapped and looking for a change of lifestyle, which is a sure sign of decline.

Drop in the Level of Property Maintenance in the Area.   When a good market shifts downward, the drop in the level of property maintenance in an area can be the last signal to appear. This is not, however, an indicator that the down market is on the upswing.

In a previously well-maintained area, it may take a while for the declining market to begin to affect the pocketbook of these property owners. When the cash flow pattern begins to slip and there is a question of either making the mortgage payment or painting the building, the building does not get painted. A continued decline in the level of property maintenance has a domino effect of causing tenants to move out and requiring even lower rents to be offered to attract any tenants at all. The whole demographics of an area can slowly change from one economic strata to a lower one and values will be reflected through their steady decline.

3
Renting or Owning: Which Is Best for You?

14. When Is It Better to *Rent* than *Own*?

Even if you can easily afford to own, there are times when it may be much better for you to rent. To make this decision you first need to carry out an honest study of what your total costs would be in either situation and compare those costs with your goals.

For example, if the local real estate market is such that a property can be leased on a long-term annual basis for between 4 and 6 percent of the real value of that property, then the economics will point to the lease as a possible benefit over ownership.

Are there markets like this? Yes—in moderate- to higher-priced residential properties it is not unusual for rents to be unrepresentative of the value of the property. I recently leased an apartment in New York City and paid $950 a month ($11,400 for the year) for an apartment that had been sold to a Japanese investor for over $200,000. His combined taxes and building maintenance exceeded the rent I was paying. In another situation a friend of mine has a home that was appraised for $950,000, and the most he could get from an annual rent was $3,500 per month. This amounts to $42,000 for the year and is less than 5 percent of the value of the home.

If you were to buy that $950,000 home with $200,000 cash down and get a very accommodating loan from the bank, your annual payment of interest only on the debt could exceed $70,000 per year, not including any principal reduction. Moreover, you would owe annual taxes ($12,000 for the year), insurance ($2,200 for the year), and general upkeep ($3,500 for the year). If you wanted to live in this house, which would you chose: to rent or to own?

Your age and lifestyle influence greatly the determination to own or rent. If you know that you will be firmly established in one geographic part of the world for a long time, then ownership can have its obvious advantages—provided that you can afford the economic commitment. One way to make sure you can afford the cost is to acquire property that also produces income to offset some or all of your costs.

If you are retired, have a lot of free time on your hands, or have nothing to tie you to any single location in the world, then ownership can become a real burden. This is another ideal situation where becoming a tenant can be the right choice.

You cannot afford to buy, so you *think* you have to rent? Stop for a moment. If this is the reason you became a tenant, then change your attitude about buying property and learn how to own real estate. Unless you are solidly on welfare and cannot see any way out of this situation, chances are there is real estate that you can buy.

15. What Are the Most Important *Contract Factors* I Should Be Aware of When Renting?

The following is a list of the important elements of any residential lease. In a commercial lease many of these are equally important. Each will be discussed in detail.

The Twelve Most Important Rental Contract Factors

Cost of living and other rent increases

Default

Hidden costs

Improvements made to the property

Penalty for late rent payments

Property inspections

Property insurance

Repairs—who does them, who pays for them

Right to renew

Security Deposit

Signs

Utility costs

Cost of Living and Other Rent Increases.   When a lease will tie the landlord into a commitment greater than a one-year term, a cost of living increase provision causes lease payments to adjust upward to reflect an increase in the cost of living. This type of increase may be simply called COLA (cost of living adjustment). A phrase in the contract similar to the following may be used:

> ...and therefore, at the beginning of each new year of this lease, the rent will be adjusted according to any increase in the All Items cost of living index as is published by the United States Department of Labor, or in the advent that index is no longer published, by the commonly accepted replacement for that index. The adjustment will be made by taking the increase in the All Items index over the previous twelve months, and increasing the last adjusted *base rent* of this lease by that same percentage, the new amount will then be the *new base rent* for the next 12 months.

The base rent of any lease is usually a net amount that does not include other charges. Your lease may or may not have any other charges, but if it does, those costs could include the following: sales tax (when charged on residential leases—check with the state sales tax office in your county or area); common-area maintenance (CAM) charges, which are usually a percentage of your total square footage; electricity, water, and other utility charges; late payment charges; damage assessments; pest control; security alarms and protection; doorman cost; and cable TV. Any or all of these additional charges may also be tied to the cost of living increases, and you may find your monthly rent increasing faster than you thought.

One way to limit the increases is to limit the amount your lease can be increased over a year's term. It would be a good idea to contact the Department of Labor in Washington, D.C., or call the nearest federal building in your state and ask for the nearest Department of Labor office where you can get labor statistics and most specifically the cost of living index. This office can put you on a mailing list to receive the most recent indexes every month. This free service will also include (if you ask for it) a booklet on how to interpret the list.

The staff members in these offices are used to getting phone calls from real estate owners and tenants and are usually very helpful in giving you data over the phone.

While you are getting ready to negotiate a lease you may discover that the All Items index may have averaged a 4 percent per year increase over the past three years. It should be an obvious benefit to you if in the negotiation of a lease you can tie your first few years of increases to one half the actual increase to the All Items index.

Default.   Review carefully anything in the lease that would cause you to be in default. Not everything may be specifically spelled out. For example, the lease may state that any violation of any city, state, federal, or building rule or regulation will cause your lease to be in default. The key phrase here is *building rule or regulation*. If you are leasing an apartment in a condominium building, you will be expected to abide by all the rules of that building. Make sure you know what those rules are before you sign the lease. They may include rules you do not want or cannot abide by.

Events that occur once you are already in default may become a function of law, and the landlord-tenant laws may vary from state to state. This is one of the very good reasons why you would be advised to have a lawyer look over any legally binding document.

Hidden Costs.   Some of the hidden costs have already been mentioned, such as increases to rent above the base rent due to cost of living adjustments. Other hidden costs can be repairs and replacement of items in the apartment. Most leases provide that you are to keep the property in good repair and in the same condition as when it was delivered to you for occupancy. However, did you check out everything? Had you done so, you might have found that all the appliances were over 15 years old and not working well. You should not be obliged to pay for the replacement of a 15-year-old refrigerator a week after you move in, but your lease may give the landlord the right to demand that you do.

There are property inspection companies that will inspect the property prior to your moving in, and although these companies are generally used by a buyer, there is no reason you cannot have them do a minicheck on any of the items that might become an expense to you. Before you go to the expense of having this inspection, make sure you have a fully executed lease with the provision that it can be canceled (before you move in) if you do not like the inspection report for any reason, and that if anything is found not to be in good working order, the landlord will fix those items or allow you to do it and then deduct the cost from your next rent due.

Improvements Made to the Property.   If you plan to make any improvements to the property you should have a clear understanding in the lease that you are permitted to make the improvements and that you are not required to return the property back to its previous condition at the end of the lease.

If you plan to add something that may be "fixed" to the property, such as a heater for the swimming pool, an electronic air filtering system that is built in to an existing air system, or any other expensive apparatus, be sure that you have the option to remove those items simply by making sure the connections or construction necessary returns the property to its original condition. You may want to take those expensive items with you and would be prohibited otherwise.

Penalty for Late Rent Payments.   Most leases have a penalty for late payment of rent. Be sure you understand how this penalty is applied. I have seen leases that allow the landlord to subtract the late charge automatically from the security deposit. You may not be aware that this is happening until the end of the lease when you ask for your security deposit back. It is a good idea to have a provision that requires the landlord to give you advance notice prior to making any debits to any deposits you have given them.

Property Inspections.   Landlords want the right to inspect their own property from time to time for several reasons. First, they want to make sure that the property is being used according to the lease and is kept in good repair. Second, they may want to show the apartment to a prospective tenant as your lease draws to its close.

Make sure that the landlord must give reasonable notice prior to making the inspection (be specific about how many days—usually two working days), and feel free to restrict the weekends and evening hours.

Property Insurance. Property insurance is a two-way street. First, as a tenant you want to be sure that the landlord has sufficient insurance on the property to cover any damages in the event of fire or windstorm or other natural causes. Also, does the owner of the building have liability insurance to cover you for any negligence on his or her part?

Second, tenant insurance is a must, because even if the owner of the building has more than adequate coverage, your personal property will not be covered if you are robbed or suffer a casualty not covered by the owner's insurance.

Repairs—Who Does Them, Who Pays for Them. Every tenant should know exactly what their responsibility is with respect to the repair of an item in the property that is being leased. However, it is one thing to have a provision that gives that obligation to the landlord, and another to get the work done and paid for. For this reason I suggest the following clause or something similar be included in your lease:

> ...and in addition, should any of the electrical or mechanical items that are listed below, all of which are owned by the landlord, malfunction or fail to operate properly, it will be the obligation of the landlord to promptly cause the item to be returned to its good operating order, and if not repairable to be replaced with another item of similar nature that does operate properly. Should a period of time in excess of 48 hours pass from the first notice to the landlord of malfunction or improper function of any listed item without a service call by a qualified repair person to repair or replace the item, then the tenant may hire a locally licensed repair person to do the needed repair or replacement. The cost for work ordered by the tenant may be charged to the landlord or paid for by the tenant, and if paid for by the tenant would become a *credit in full* off the next rent and charges due until which time that the payment by the tenant was completely offset.

Right to Renew. Every tenant should ask for a right to renew their lease, even if at the time the lease is negotiated there is no thought of extending it beyond the initial period of time. There are several reasons for asking for this right. The most important is that without having some clear understanding about a renewal, the landlord could refuse to renew the lease even though your circumstances changed such that to move at the end of the lease would be very costly or at best inconvenient. Another good reason is that by locking up the terms for future rent, at least to a formula (say, adjusted to one half the increases of the cost of living index), you can better budget your expenses in an area of town that may suddenly become in vogue, where rents skyrocket.

Security Deposit.   The first step in dealing with a security deposit is to understand what the state law says about these deposits. Many areas of the country have laws that require the landlord to keep security deposits in interest-bearing accounts; other laws may not be so specific. Even if the state law does not require the landlord to maintain the deposit in an interest account, you can make that a provision to the lease.

It is not uncommon for the landlord to have the right to deduct penalties or assessments for damage from the security deposit. Make sure that no such deduction is made without notice being given to you prior to the deduction so that you can contest the deduction if you feel it is unreasonable or unwarranted. Otherwise, you may find that your total security deposit has eroded over a long-term lease.

Signs.   Some leases have a provision that allows the landlord to place a "For Rent" sign in the window or on the property as your lease draws near its termination. Such a sign may draw unwanted and uninvited visitors to your door at all hours of the day. If any signs are allowed they should be placed so as not to indicate which apartment is for rent and to direct attention to some other place.

Utility Costs.   When the lease provides that you pay all the utility costs, it is likely that not all those costs are being divided equally among all the tenants in the building. You need to find out if there are separate metering systems for each apartment for each of the utilities. It is not unusual for an apartment building to have one water meter, and if other services, such as garbage collection, are calculated by the amount of water used, then you should see who the other tenants are before you agree to a *pro rata* division of the water bill. If one of the rentals is a restaurant or a laundromat, you will definitely end up paying for part of their water and garbage collection service.

16. What Should I Check When Looking at Property I May Lease?

In general, the following will help you ensure that you have done your homework prior to signing a lease.

Ten Critical Inspection Points to Check before Leasing

Authority to make a lease

Building rules and regulations

Condition of all furniture and fixtures

Condition of appliances

Condition of plumbing

Garbage collection

Lease restrictions

Pest control

Security

Smell test

Under certain circumstances there may be factors that may be more important to you than those listed above. Do you need wheelchair ramps, sturdy rails on stairways, elevator sound signals to indicate floor levels, or some other specific need?

Authority to Make a Lease. Is the person with whom you are dealing authorized to sign your lease? If you are dealing with an agent and not the owner, ask that the owner execute the lease as well as the agent, or at least give you proof that the agent is authorized to sign the lease. If this is not done and there is a problem in the future, you may discover that the agent did not have the authority.

Building Rules and Regulations. Many rental buildings and most condominiums and cooperative apartment buildings have very strict rules and regulations. Make sure that you are given a current set of these rules and regulations to review prior to signing the lease. You may discover that the rules and regulations prohibit certain things the agent or landlord said otherwise…such as having a pet, letting your grandchild visit for a month, permitting you to sublease while you take a four-month vacation, and so on.

Condition of All Furniture and Fixtures. Whatever is in the property you are about to lease should be examined by someone capable of determining if it is sound, in need of repair, and in good working order. Otherwise, you may be liable to fix it later at your own expense.

Condition of Appliances. Appliances may look good and work fine but be 15 years old. If this is the case, it is a good idea to exclude them from the provision of the lease that indicates that you are to keep everything in good working order.

Condition of Plumbing. The condition of the plumbing is important because of the time it takes to repair a broken water pipe, not to mention the damage caused by the gushing water. Check the following: test each faucet to make sure both hot and cold water is available—and that the hot water is hot enough; fill all the sinks and tubs—then see how quickly water drains; flush each toilet after you have put several tightly rolled balls of paper in the water (no more than half an inch in diameter) to see that they evacuate. If any of these situations are not up to your standards, then the problem needs to be fixed prior to signing the lease.

Garbage Collection. What do you do with your garbage? Is there a chute on each floor or in each apartment? Do you and everyone else leave it outside your door at night? These and other questions about garbage need to be answered; you may be neat and have sweet-smelling garbage, but your neighbors may not.

Lease Restrictions.   Much like building restrictions, some specific restrictions may be in your lease that you do not like or agree to. If you do not like them you may be able to negotiate them out of the lease. Ask the simple question: "May I see a copy of a sample lease that would contain all the rules, regulations, and restrictions I would have to abide by?"

Pest Control.   Is there any? What kind is it? Who pays for it? These are just three questions you need to get answers to. If there is no pest control, then why not? In any event, check around for signs of pests. Pull out a bottom drawer in the kitchen and look below it to see if roaches have been living there. Live pests are a quick turnoff, but dead ones may simply indicate that the place was insecticide-bombed just before you got there.

Security.   Security should extend well beyond the front door or lobby of the building. Do the windows close securely? Are there dead-bolts on each exit in addition to the main locks? Are there fire alarms? Be sure to check them to see that they work. Are there fire exits? Does the building have a modern fire sprinkling system? When was it last tested?

A check with your local fire and police departments will tell you if there have been any recent problems in the building or area. It is a good idea to know what kind of other tenants are in the building too. Are you safe from them? Stop by the building early evening on a Friday and mid-morning on Saturday; you may discover children everywhere even though there were none at noon when you last visited.

Smell Test.   This is the supreme test of all, that is, if your olfactory glands are working properly. Start being aware of the smells as you first approach the building. Then test the lobby or hallways. Do you smell food cooking? Is there a garbage smell? What about mildew or dog or other animal smells—do you notice any?

When you enter the premises, check for odors as you first step in the door. Does the carpet smell? What about the closets? Shift your attention to the kitchen. Smell the inside of the oven. Do you notice rancid butter or grease? Now the refrigerator—I can tell horror stories about the insides of refrigerators.

Unless the lease is a bargain, do not rent a place that fails the smell test. Bad smells may be a clue to something worse.

17. How Can I Negotiate the Most Favorable Lease Possible?

Getting ready to meet the landlord or his or her agent should be an event you plan for. Your attitude should be that if the property is right for you, then you want to be in a position to negotiate the best lease possible.

Nine Steps to Help You Negotiate Favorable Leases

Make a good impression

Have excellent references

Demonstrate your financial ability

Negotiate in person

Negotiate soft terms—one at a time

Ask for "clean up time"

Get "move in time"

Lock up renewal rent terms up front

Get approvals on leasehold improvements you will make

Make a Good Impression. A neat personal appearance, a freshly washed car, and polite manners contribute to establishing a good foundation to negotiate a lease. Every landlord is looking for a solid pillar of the community—even if you are not one, act like it.

Have Excellent References. The word *excellent* is relative of course, and all you really need is a few local people to say something nice about you. If you had a good relationship with your last landlord, get a letter of recommendation from him or her.

Demonstrate Your Financial Ability. If you start to hedge about paying the rent while you are negotiating the lease, you will *not* be setting a good stage for the rest of the negotiating. However, you should never agree to anything until everything has been agreed to by the landlord. For example, when the landlord asks, "Can you afford the first month plus the last two months rent, and a security deposit?" a good reply would be "I'm sure you will be satisfied with my financial ability, and if you want, I can give you the telephone number of my banker. Now, can we go over the conditions of the lease?"

Negotiate in Person. This gives you the opportunity to look people straight in the eye. If you do so and smile at the same time, this can make you look more sincere.

It is too easy to say *no* over the phone, and you want to use every ounce of your charm and neat appearance to win the landlord over to your side. Remember, the landlord truly wants you to be a wonderful person.

Negotiate "Soft Terms"—One at a Time. When you are negotiating a lease, it is best to deal with the decision maker. In this way, you can get affirmation on each "soft term" as you go along without ever having to commit until you see the final lease. The following are a few of the soft terms that you may want to negotiate for.

Move in date

Date when first month's rent starts

Security deposit split over several payments

No security deposit at all

Barter for the rent instead of money

Free month's rent at the end of each new year you renew

Property repainted inside, outside, or both

Part of the furniture at an unfurnished rent

New carpet

Clean the carpet

New kitchen appliances—all or part

New air conditioning unit(s)

For example, you have seen the home you want to rent and are talking to the owner. You like the property very much, so you begin getting the owner's okay on several "minor details." Make sure you have a note pad to write these down. Go down the list of things that you would like to have. But most important, ask for some things that you do not mind the landlord rejecting. It will be the overall balance of agreements versus objections that makes the negotiation process work. When you get a rejection, go immediately to an item you would like and say, "Well, if you will not replace the air conditioning system, how about a new refrigerator? After all, this one must be over 10 years old anyway." If you get an "okay" for the air conditioning system, then ask for something you could accept not getting. A key to good negotiations is not to commit yourself until you have gotten all the "okays" possible. Then go over your list of items the landlord has approved and get a blanket approval.

Ask for "Clean Up Time."　Clean up time is another way of saying *extra free rent*, but it comes at the start of the lease. If the apartment needs even the slightest cleaning, then ask for an extra two weeks or more just to get the place ready for you to move in.

Get "Move in Time."　This is more free rent time, but you never call this free rent. It is customary in the rental business to offer a tenant time to move in; after all, there is apt to be an overlap of leases between where the old tenants move out of and where they move into. Some landlords even offer to *pay* your moving expenses if you move to their property—do not overlook this.

Lock Up Renewal Rent Terms Up Front.　The reason should be clear, even if you do not anticipate ever renewing your lease, that a year from now things could be different. Tie up the renewal term as much as you can; it is just an option for you to take if the market is stronger a year from now. If the market has not gotten any stronger and in fact weakened, and you have decided you would like to renew your lease, you are under no obligation to follow through with the option agreement and can ask for a reduced rent.

Get Approvals on Leasehold Improvements You Will Make.   No matter how minor the remodeling or additions you think you might want to add to the property, try to get everything agreed to in advance of signing the lease. One step to consider is to make sure you have the right to return the property to the same condition it was in before the lease in case you want to take with you, for example, that newly installed hot tub and the special (and expensive) security system.

Landlords like to hear their tenants talk about improving the property, and as long as the additions would not be a detriment to the property, just the fact you asked about this can improve your chances of getting other requests approved.

18. What Can I Do If the Landlord Will Not Fix What Is Broken?

It is a good idea to have a provision in the lease that will allow you to fix anything that is broken at your own expense and then deduct it from your future rent. This provision should not come into effect until after a reasonable time has been given for the owner to remedy the problem and should only be a safety step for you.

If you do not have such a provision already in a lease, and you are faced with a broken refrigerator and the landlord cannot be reached or will not respond, then you may have no choice but to fix the broken refrigerator yourself and hope for the best.

Before you have that problem, write the owner or his or her agent and ask for the policy on such matters—be sure it is given to you in writing.

A good tip is to ask the landlord for an emergency repair number for really important problems, such as plumbing and electrical repairs.

19. Where Can I Find the Most Important Laws That Protect Me as a Tenant?

State laws that govern the landlord–tenant relationship may vary slightly among states, but usually they follow general standards that seem to be logical. However, you should not assume that this logic is always in the favor of the tenant because it is not. Call your state senator or state representative and ask the administrative assistant who answers the phone to assist you in obtaining a copy of the state laws that deal with the landlord–tenant relationship. While you are on the phone, ask to be put on the state official's mailing list for any new changes in laws that affect you as a landlord or tenant.

20. What Can I Do to Reduce the Cash Cost of My Lease?

Try barter or "sweat equity." Barter is a simple approach where you give the landlord something other than cash for all or part of your rent. This form of exchange can be anything from cleaning supplies or other products that come from your own business or use of a time-share you own in Orlando, Florida. If you do not own anything you can barter, become creative. Make a deal with a travel agency to sign you up as an outside agent, then barter a $12,000 deluxe cruise to Europe for a full year's rent. Of course, you will have to pay for the cruise, but you may get back a big commission as some cruise lines pay hefty fees to agents in the slow time of the year—often over 30 percent. If your cut of the commission was 70 percent, this would equate to nearly three free months of rent (30% commission equals $3,600; your cut is $2,520.00).

Sweat equity is similar to barter but instead of a product or item, you actually perform a service or do work for the landlord: sweep the halls, pick up trash, cut the lawn, do bookkeeping for the landlord, collect rent, paint walls, fix the plumbing, etc.

The success of these two techniques may depend on your attitude and presentation to the landlord. For example, indicate that you might be having a rough time over the next few months, and then suggest an alternative method to reduce your monthly outlay; at the same time, show that you are conscientious and do not want to get behind.

21. How Can a Senior Citizen Negotiate a Super Lease?

In areas of the country where there is a reduction of the real estate tax through a homestead deduction, it is likely that such a deduction is increased for a senior and/or handicapped citizen. If the tenant would be able to get a better tax break than the owner of the property and the circumstances were right, the landlord would profit by having the title of the property put in the tenant's name.

A friend of mine owns 16 apartments that are actually condominiums. They are assessed around $35,000 each, and if each were owned by the resident living in them (instead of being leased), there would be a homestead exemption of a minimum of $25,000 per unit, which would reduce the assessed value to $10,000 each or $160,000 for the whole building. The tax due at this assessed value would be around $4,000 for the whole building. The tax actually levied against the building is $14,000. Were my friend to put the title to each apartment in the name of the existing tenants, there would be a savings of $10,000 in real estate taxes, which is cash in the pocket.

22. How Can I Get *Free Rent* When Negotiating a Lease?

Asking for free rent is like getting any of the right kind of favorable lease terms: it takes proper timing and knowledge of the rental marketplace.

If the market is such that there are dozens of available rentals, then offering the owner a long-term lease could be predicated on he or she giving you a substantial "clean up", "move in" free rent period.

There are some special things you can do that can encourage the owner to grant you free rent. Several are listed below:

Offer your space as a temporary office for the property manager

Use your professional influence to attract other tenants

Do some of the CAM at the building

Put on your letterhead and advertising "the best location in town"

Act as a rent collection agent for the owner

Manage the property

Agree to a list of improvements you will do for the owner

4

How to Deal with Your Real Estate Broker

23. Do I *Need* a Real Estate Broker or Salesperson?

If you are buying or selling property, you do not need a real estate broker or salesperson. However, members of the real estate profession can save you a lot of time and help you sidestep problems. In the end, either as buyer or seller, you most likely will benefit from their services.

As a professional realtor for over 30 years I can vouch from experience that it is very difficult to sell your own property yourself. After some bad experiences representing myself, I now use another broker or an agent to represent me as the seller. As a buyer I work extensively through agents who bring me properties. Because I am candid with them and let them know exactly what I want, where I am headed, and what my goals are, they know they can spend the time to help me find what I want.

24. What Is the Difference between a Realtor and a Licensed Broker, and Is That Important to Me?

The National Association of Realtors is an organization made up of licensed real estate brokers and associates from many different states. This association has its own code of ethics and functions through the hundreds of Boards of Realtors located around the United States. These Boards of Realtors are local branches of the national association and each has a membership from a specific geographic area.

All the members of any board function as a marketing unit, and several boards combined (say south Florida or southeast Texas) make up a nucleus of members who cooperate with each other in their marketing efforts. To assist those efforts, the Board of Realtors operates a multiple listing service (MLS) in which the members can list the properties they represent. This MLS varies depending on the size of the board, and can be a monthly or more frequent book or series of books that contain information on thousands of properties offered for rent, exchange, and sale. Most interestingly, only other realtors are supposed to have access to this listing service. These are some of the advantages that a prospective buyer or seller has when using the services of a realtor.

A licensed broker or associate who is not a member of a Board of Realtors cannot use the term *realtor*. This person may be equally qualified to serve your needs, depending on what those needs are. The fact that this person does not have the networking available to realtors may not be a disadvantage to you. Many real estate brokers and salespeople choose not to join the Board of Realtors (and become a realtor) not because they would fail to qualify, but because they see no benefit to them nor the type of clientele they handle. Often these real estate firms are far more selective about the number of properties they market and can devote more time and attention to their clients' needs than a national association. The true test of whom you should use will depend on your interviewing several brokers to find the agent who best relates to your needs and one you have confidence in.

25. How Can I Maximize My Benefits from Real Estate Agents?

Step 1. *Show the agents how they will benefit.*   Agents are in the real estate business to make money, not to be your tour guide. If you are sincere about your dealings and can express that you are a buyer or seller and that you want to use their services, but you demand their willingness to work and expect them to do everything they can to help you attain your goals, the result can be very rewarding for all.

Step 2. *Be sure the agents understand your goal.*   They have to be working in the right direction, and this will depend on the signals you have given them. If you are a buyer, the agent will ask questions that will help them look for the right kind of property. If you are vague about what you want, which might indicate that you have undefined goals, then the effort the agent spends can be frustrating because nothing will seem to fit what you think you want. Formulate your goals; then clearly express them to those you want to help you.

Step 3. *Help the agents become creative.*   If you are going to delve into real estate, then you should do all you can to learn some of the creative techniques for buying and selling. You should not rely on your agent or anyone else to take you by the hand. You should take the lead; this may mean you have to express the willingness to use creative ideas and techniques to reach your goals. Most agents are not assertive in making creative deals because they are not trained to be.

Step 4. *Discover the agents' energy zones.* Everyone responds to praise and appreciation, so do not wait until the property you want has been found and the deal closed to praise your agents. The life of a real estate agent can be filled with frustration and disappointment. It is, generally, a life dependent on commissions, and when deals fall apart there is no income despite the fact that all the work and effort has already been spent. Pat your agents on the back from time to time if they are working hard on your behalf. They will respond with a positive attitude toward you and their task to help you.

Step 5. *Make them a part of your team.* You should have a team of people who assist you in all your legal, accounting, business, and other important aspects of your life, even if you are an expert in that same task. The idea of working for a team is a natural tendency and it can build loyalty from agents who, after all, are insiders to the real estate industry. Insiders like to deal with other insiders, so having them on your team is a benefit.

26. What Are the Most Important Factors I Need to Know before I Sign a Listing Agreement?

The following seven factors are critical whenever you place your property in the hands of an agent through an exclusive listing agreement. This document is a legally binding contract that binds both you and the agent for a period of time.

The Seven Most Important Prelisting Agreement Factors

What is the real estate firm going to do for me?

Does the agent understand my goals?

Is the agent willing to work hard for me?

Does the agent have enough time to devote to my property?

What is the commission I am expected to pay?

How will the listing firm split the commission with a co-broker?

What is the term of the listing?

What is the Real Estate Firm Going to Do for Me? The firm should do whatever they promise to do: advertise, keep the property open, network the property, make a color brochure, put a sign in the frontyard, or whatever. Make sure you have these commitments in writing and get a timetable of when you can expect these events to happen. If the items are important to you (they should be) insist on the right to withdraw the listing if the agents fail to keep their promise and timetable. Let them suggest the timetable: most agents will be overly eager to impress you and are apt to cut short the actual time they will need. Review that schedule and add on a reasonable period to take account for the lead time it takes to put any good marketing program into effect.

Does the Agent Understand My Goals?   The agent who works toward the wrong goal may well end up there, at no benefit to you. Explain to your agent exactly what you are trying to accomplish. For example, if you want to build your real estate portfolio to the point where you eventually own 100 apartment units, and now own none, be sure the agent knows you want to start slowly with 20 units or so and not to jump right to that end goal. If you have a change in your plans and goals, be sure you let the agent know so he or she can shift the property search accordingly.

Is the Agent Willing to Work Hard for Me?   You cannot just take the agent's word on this—you have to look at his or her past record in job performance. Following through is the key to success as a real estate salesperson, and that takes persistence and the ability to overcome frustration. Do you have an agent who can handle that? If not, find another one who will meet those roadblocks head on and win.

Does the Agent Have Enough Time to Devote to My Property?   Some agents use their charm to get listings but end up with too many and are never able to sell them. They can become successful, however, because if they can keep the listing long enough some other agent may sell the property and they will still get a commission. You really want an agent who is an aggressive *seller* and not the charmer who can get listings but then ends up with too many properties to work with. Some real estate firms have already figured this problem out and work their agents in a team. If you find a team that combines charm with aggressive marketing, you may have found a team you that will take you to great wealth.

What Is the Commission I Am Expected to Pay?   Due to the illegality of price fixing, there is no standard commission. Each brokerage firm is allowed to establish its own guidelines, and many are flexible within those individual guidelines. The key to remember is when you pay a commission you are only paying for results. Thus it is not unusual for real estate commissions in the United States to be as high as 10 percent for vacant property. Residential properties may vary between 4 and 7 percent. The listing agreement should be very specific as to the price you are offering and the percent of the selling price you will have to pay as a fee. Be sure that the listing agreement is specific about whom you pay the fee to. You do not want to get into a situation where you start talking directly to other brokers who do not know you already have a listing agent, because you might end up being obligated to two commissions.

How Will the Listing Firm Split the Commission with a Co-Broker?
If you are using a realtor who will list your property in the MLS, there is a

good chance that an agent from another firm will actually sell your property. The selling agent will be paid a percent of the fee you are paying. It is customary for the two firms to split the total commission in half, but this is not always the case. Some listing firms simply show the percentage of the selling price the selling office will get and not what the division between the offices actually is. It is my opinion that if the division is not a 50–50 split between the offices, there should be an advantage in favor of the selling office. You want the best effort to sell your listed property, so insist that the listing firm not get more than the selling firm.

What Is the Term of the Listing?   How many months did you tie your property up with this real estate firm? The listing should be very specific about this and should show the actual date the listing expires. Say that the property was not sold by the expiration date; the agent will ask for an extension. If you are satisfied with the efforts and wish to continue the listing, be sure the extension is valid only with your approval. Avoid any listing that has a provision that allows for automatic extension for a specific term if you fail to withdraw the listing by a predetermined date.

27. How Does the Real Estate Law Affect My Relationship with My Broker or Agent?

There are five forms of business relationships you can have with a real estate agent. In the following situations both the buyer and seller must be informed as to the form of agency that exists. Some state laws are more strict about the method of notifying the parties, and as a practical matter consider that as a buyer or seller you should *ask* the question and get the answer in writing as to exactly which of the following relationships exists. Then find out how your state law governs the agent's fiduciary responsibility to you and the other parties to the transaction. Call the nearest Board of Realtors in your area and ask them to put you in touch with your state bureau governing licensed real estate brokers and associates.

The Five Forms of Real Estate Agency

1. *Subagents* are licensees acting for other real estate firms as coagents (as through the Board of Realtors MLS). Even though your listing agreement is with company A, salesperson working for company B may become a subagent of yours by attempting to sell your property.

2. *Single agents* are licensees who act as either a seller's agent or a buyer's agent but never represent both parties in the same transaction. These agents may adopt the policy not to become subagents when working with other brokers.

3. *Seller's agents* are licensees who are employed by and represent only the seller in a transaction. In this situation the agent owes total loyalty to the seller.

However, state laws may require the seller's agent to make certain disclosures to buyers of known property defects, etc. This is a form of a single agency.

4. *Buyer's agents* are licensees who are employed by and represent only the buyer in a transaction. This is another type of single agency. This form of agency occurs when the buyer delegates to a licensee the right to act on his or her behalf in a real estate transaction, regardless of whether the commission is paid by the buyer directly or by the seller through a commission split.

5. *Dual agents* are licensees who attempt to represent both the buyer and the seller in the same real estate transaction. This is the usual type of agency and, with careful notice to all parties, is legal. This form of agency places a great deal of pressure on the broker to maintain a proper fiduciary relationship with both parties of the transaction. Because of potential problems, either as a buyer or seller due to the agent accidentally and unintentionally violating the fiduciary relationship with you or the other party, it is a good idea to insist that your agent act as a single agent and represent you as either a buyer's agent or seller's agent depending on your status at any given time.

28. Should I Use a Different Agent for Buying and for Selling?

Review the previous question (27) to refresh you with the five different forms of agency. My recommendation is that as a seller you always insist that your agent represent you as a single agent—a seller's agent, and that if you are a buyer that the agent become your buyer's agent. This will require the agent to notify all other agents or property owners with whom you deal of this situation.

The same broker can represent you in each situation provided they maintain the status of single agency each time.

29. What Is the Usual Commission and Who Pays It?

There is no "usual" commission according to anti–price fixing rules and regulations; however, within any community there will be a common range of commissions charged. From a practical point of view the commission will range from 4 to 10 percent. International transactions may be higher.

When a seller lists a property with an agent, the seller usually pays the fee in the event of a sale or other disposition (exchange, lease, lease-option, etc.). However, the seller may elect to list *net* of commission, indicating that the seller expects to get a certain price and the agent can add on whatever commission he or she wants. While the idea of a *net* commission sounds attractive to a seller, agents are reluctant to agree to this kind of commission because they have no control over what the seller will actually take nor can they control what a buyer offers. Agents who are savvy in real estate brokerage will not work on a net listing.

5

Successful Buying and Selling of Homes

30. How Can Buyers Improve Their Success When Negotiating an Offer?

The following steps will enable you to approach the entire spectrum of acquiring real estate with self-confidence, knowing that you are well prepared for the negotiating process. Success in a one-on-one negotiation depends on this inner confidence, both for your own sake and to impress the other parties. Everyone likes to do business with a successful person; at the end of the deal, everyone can go away from the closing feeling good about that person. This process builds good reputations. Make this one of your goals.

The Buyer's Ten Steps to Successful Contract Negotiations

Be positive about everything you do

Know your goals

Find properties that move you closer to your goals

Set financial and personal ceilings—then expand them

Do your homework

Discover the seller's motivation

Learn how to handle timing

Get started on the right foot

Understand the fundamentals of motivation

Establish a deadline on the deal

Be Positive about Everything You Do.   If you have a negative attitude about anything, then your whole outlook on everything you do will be slanted. You cannot be a positive person if you allow negative thoughts or negative people to become part of your life. Positive people attract other positive people. The more positive you are, the more difficult it is to say no to you.

Know Your Goals.   You should have your goals written and posted where you can see them every day. I know this sounds overly simplified, but only you would have to see them, no one else need to. By keeping your goals in clear sight they will also be clearly in focus when it is time to negotiate that contract to buy or sell. By knowing where you are going, you will be less likely to over-pay when you buy or hold on to a diminishing benefit when you sell.

Find Properties That Move You Closer to Your Goals.   This is easier said than done, but if you follow a plan and get to know your investment area and local market conditions, you will begin to see the opportunities that were there all the time, but that you did not recognize before. Everything you do that is directed toward your goals should fit a pattern and be attempted in a logical order. The key to success is to avoid being sidetracked from your main purpose. Determination is, after all, only one of the necessary attributes to success; a clearly focused goal, self-confidence, and persistence round out your chances for success in everything you attempt.

Set Financial and Personal Ceilings—Then Expand Them.   You only have so much money and economic strength, and your personal abilities will carry you only so far—that is, for the time being. As your confidence increases you will be able to raise your investment sights. Your success in raising your goals will be your honesty with yourself. Take periodic self-reviews of things you should be doing to increase your abilities. For example, if you are struggling with accounting or have a hard time understanding the income and expense statements sellers show you, then sign up for a night course in book-keeping. Most communities have adult education programs that cover just about every aspect of real estate. Take advantage of these inexpensive and mind-broadening programs; they will pay off.

Do Your Homework.   Doing homework in real estate is called *due diligence*. It is critical if you want to avoid risky mistakes. No one said that making a fortune in real estate was going to be easy. There is a lot of information that you need to gather and then learn. The local marketplace is dynamic and the person who learned everything two years ago and did not keep up to date is dealing with yesterday's news. Get into the habit of carrying a notebook around with you at all times, and when you see a "For Rent" or "For Sale" sign, write down the phone number, the address of the property, and what type of property it is. Then call and get the details. Even if you are not interested in the property, ask if you can see it. This allows you to learn more about property in the area, and also to meet either an agent or the owner. Either can be a good source of information if you take the time to ask for it.

One very important aspect about due diligence is the *greener grass syndrome*. You have experienced it many times before: the sensation that the grass looks greener over there, on the other side of the fence. Often, even the smartest real estate investors forget that more than location changes as you go from one part of town, state, or country to another. A buyer used to the high prices at home in New York City, or San Francisco, for example, can come across a home in Georgia or a thousand other places for one-third the price it would bring back home. Without due diligence that investor has no valid perspective on the real value of that "away from home" property. Do your homework.

Discover the Seller's Motivation.   Everyone has a reason for selling their property. Knowing what has prompted the seller to dispose of the property you would like to own can be very helpful to you in how you structure your offer. You will discover that sometimes the reason is based on a wrong premise. For example, a person moving out of town who must now find another place to live elsewhere may not know that he or she could exchange the property, give a long-term lease with an option to buy, etc. The key to discovering the reason is to find out what "benefit" the seller is seeking. Sometimes you acquire a property by helping the seller achieve his or her goals through helping them gain the benefit they want.

Learn How to Handle Timing.   All salespeople know that timing can be the single element that can ruin a deal if not properly handled. You have heard the saying, "strike while the iron is hot"; this is certainly true when negotiating a sale. Both the buyer and seller can become colder than a block of ice if the deal does not progress. It can be very easy for either party to become "fatalistic" about the transaction if the other party seems to be throwing unwarranted delays into the transaction. It is a good idea to use an agent for that purpose, however, as this removes anxiety about the transaction. However, make sure your real estate agents understand that you expect them to keep on top of the deal until it has been accepted by all parties.

Get Started on the Right Foot.   Good communications skills are very important when dealing with other people. In real estate negotiations these skills are best used to make sure that you give the right signals to the other party and do not disrupt a transaction that was moving in the right direction. In the very beginning of any transaction it is a good idea to express your feeling about the property and make sure the other party understands how you feel. For example, "Mrs. Seller, I think your home is absolutely perfect for me and I hope that we can get together on price and terms because I know my wife and children will just love this neighborhood." Later on, as you close the gap on those price and terms, you can continue to let the seller know that you and she are on the same side of the fence. After all, you both want the seller to sell you the home.

Understand the Fundamentals of Motivation.   There are many reasons people are motivated to do what they do. Your task as a buyer is not to attempt to motivate them to do what you want but to allow their own motivations to arrive at a decision that is mutually agreeable. Motivation plays a strong role because many people cannot make a decision. A decision as critical as accepting an offer on their home or other property can often be put off so many times that the buyers give up and move on.

The importance then of dealing with motivation is to *help* the seller come to that mutually agreeable decision. A good salesperson can be worth his or her weight in gold in this part of the negotiation process, but if you are dealing directly with the other party yourself, continually look for that benefit they are seeking and the real reason they want to sell. Eventually, you may find that the real reason is a pending divorce, a health scare, or financial problems. Work within the scope of the seller's goals whenever possible by opening options to them that they may not have realized.

Establish a Deadline on the Deal.   It is a great feeling to negotiate a deal and finally come to a successful conclusion. However, if you let yourself get bogged down in endless meetings and countless back-and-forth offers and counteroffers, then you have not given the right signal to the seller or perhaps to yourself. Every deal should have a deadline for the current negotiations. I say *current* because even if you are not successful this time, you can, as long as the property is still for sale, come back again. But you should not let the seller know this…and in fact, if you break off a deal this afternoon, by tomorrow you may have found something you like even more, which may take you out of the picture altogether as a buyer. So set a deadline. Put it in the contract: "If this offer is not accepted by noon of the 7th day following the date executed by the buyer, then this agreement shall be considered null and void and each party hereinafter released from further obligation to each and the other." In counteroffer situations this provision can be modified or removed. However, the initial posture is to make sure everyone knows that you are a ready, willing, and able buyer and that if you cannot acquire this property you will go elsewhere, and soon.

31. What Should All Sellers *Know* When Negotiating a Contract?

To win any game, you must know the rules and techniques, and most of all, whom you are playing against. In the heat of negotiations, each party to the transaction may assume that the adversary in the deal is the other party—buyers against sellers and vice versa. In reality this could not be farther from the truth. The buyer wants to buy the property. The seller wants the buyer to buy the property. Is that an adversarial relationship? Actually, the two parties sometimes forget that they both really want the same end result. The problem then is not negotiating an agreement on the end result but simply how to get there. For the buyer the end result (I want to buy—I know the seller wants to sell) was decided the moment he or she told the salesperson to write up the offer.

When the seller approaches a transaction with this nonadversarial frame of reference the whole negotiating process will be less traumatic and far more successful for both parties. After all, they both want the same thing.

The following checklist will help the seller keep the end result firmly in focus while keeping the negotiations moving toward that destination.

The Seller's Negotiation Checklist

Never be insulted by an offer

Review your goals

Know what benefits are given up

Can you use the benefits gained?

Avoid saying "no"

Help the buyer to become an owner mentally

Keep all options open

Be creative

Let the agent absorb the heat

Look for "win–win" situations

Take a look at each of these factors. If you have been a seller before, did you go over any of these prior to entering into negotiations?

Never Be Insulted by an Offer. As a broker for nearly 30 years I have heard hundreds of sellers toss the buyer's offer back into my lap and tell me how they are insulted at the offer. Their insult may have been prompted by the low price offered, or the terms, or a dozen other things that "rubbed" them the wrong way.

It does little good for me to suggest that if they are insulted at an offer, how do they feel about all the people who did not even like the property enough to make an offer?

The point is, there are ready, willing, and able buyers who want to win points in the deal. If they do not win points, they will not buy. It is simple as that. However, before jumping to conclusions that it is *you* that must lose points, think back at a time when you may have walked out of a store when you had in your hand exactly what you wanted to buy. For some reason, however, you felt slighted and you left, perhaps to drive all the way across town and buy the same thing, for more money, just to prove something, win points, or not to lose face. This idea about losing face may sound silly but it is not.

So, why does the buyer have to win points? There are dozens of reasons. Here are some of them: to impress someone (e.g., girlfriend, neighbor, the agent) that they are capable of getting a good deal; to play the game they "think" they are supposed to play; to try to get a steal; and to be lead by others because they are a novice at real estate.

The initial offer from one of these people may indeed appear too far off your target. However, if you throw the offer back or counteroffer with a price and terms exactly matching the listing terms, then you have removed the potential of any points being won, and the game may be over for you.

Review Your Goals.   You should review your goals every day, so to be thinking about them before starting to negotiate with a buyer should not be an exception. It is a good idea to pay very close attention to the reason you decided to sell the property in the first place. This will help you keep in clear focus where you want to go after the sale.

Know What Benefits Are Given Up.   The property you own may have some very positive benefits to you, despite the fact that you want to dispose of it. As you go over your goals look at the positive factors of the real estate you own. You would not be the first seller that has decided to keep the property after he or she found out the benefits could not be replaced by the price a buyer was willing to pay.

Can You Use the Benefits Gained?   Circumstances of a sale may seem to solve your problems or move you closer to your goals. But do they? Take a hard look at the bottom line, the end results after you make the sale, pay your taxes (if any to pay), and then move on with your life and investment planning. This would be particularly important if you were to take another property in exchange to facilitate the transaction. Can you use the other property, or does it now become a bigger problem?

Avoid Saying "No."   You should never commit yourself, no matter how much the buyer or the agent may press for a commitment, until you understand the total offer being made. Once you have a clear understanding of the total offer you should not say "no" even if the offer is not acceptable as presented. Instead, you should adapt the offer to terms and conditions that are acceptable to you and make the counteroffer. There are many ways to change the agreement, allowing the buyer to win some points that have little or no effect on your end results. The better approach is to say "Yes, Mr. Buyer, I think we can get together on this deal, and I do appreciate your interest in this property. I think your family will love this neighborhood and your children, as have my children, will enjoy this home. I have made a few modifications in the offer and have accepted it."

Help the Buyer to Become an Owner Mentally.   The quicker the buyer begins to see him- or herself as owners of your property, the smoother the negotiations will go, and the quicker you will have a firm and binding contract. Sellers can aid this process by giving the buyer positive signals that all is going well in the negotiation process. Let the wife come over to measure for new carpets and drapes, ask or have the agent ask bonding questions such as, "Will you move in right after the closing?" or "The seller said he will have the rooms repainted right after he moves out, would you like to select the colors?" This kind of question can be a closing question for a salesperson, because it allows the buyer to say "yes" (to buying the property) by agreeing to a small item.

Keep All Options Open.   No one knows everything, so do not enter negotiations with a closed mind or with such a narrow focus that you will not explore something new and innovative. A buyer or an agent may have an idea of how you can attain your goal, and the buyer his or hers at a price or terms that you may not have agreed to before.

Be Creative.   There are many books written about creative real estate. You might enjoy learning some of the different techniques that can make a deal work for you. There are perfectly legal tax angles that can save you thousands of dollars or give you a fast deal if you will just open up and be creative.

Let the Agent Absorb the Heat.   In the usual situation the real estate agent is working for you, so you should let that agent absorb the heat of any anger or frustration thrown off by either side without passing that onto the other party. There is no reason for the agent to tell you what uncomplimentary name the buyer called you when your counteroffer was presented. An agent can be anxious to make a deal because of the commission they will earn, and can be determined to get the deal signed up even if it means going back and forth a dozen times until midnight or later, rather than let the deal "rest" over the weekend and the buyer "go cold". Far too many deals collapse because each side attempts to be so unanxious that someone else beats them to the draw, or "fate" enters the picture and minds change.

Look for "Win–Win" Situations.   When you keep your eye on the goals and benefits you want to gain, and those you are happy to eliminate (because they no longer help you), then you will find more win–win situations are possible. To some degree negotiations are "give and receive" processes. Only in the hottest of real estate markets will sellers be able to sit back and wait for their exact price and terms. But remember that waiting is time, and time is money. You may win now by taking a slight modification in your price or terms than by holding out.

32. What Does It Mean When a Buyer Says "*I'll Pay Your Price If You Accept My Terms*"?

To some degree it means, "there are other ways to skin the cat." Assume a seller sets a price for a vacant lot, say $100,000 payable, $54,000 cash to a mortgage of $46,000. Along comes a buyer who says "I will pay your price of $100,000 if you will accept these terms":

BUYER: I will assume your mortgage of $46,000.

SELLER: Agreed.

BUYER: I will pay you $5,400 per year for ten years—that totals $54,000. Okay?

This offer totals what the seller wanted, almost. The difference between what the seller wants and what the buyer is offering is only *time*. Time then becomes one of the fundamental negotiating elements in real estate. If I can pay you want you want, but not exactly when you want it, then perhaps we can negotiate not on money but on time. This works most of the time but is not the only factor to consider.

The amount of money the seller will have to reinvest after the transaction can also be used by the creative buyer for negotiations. Consider this same seller who, 15 years ago, paid only $10,000 for this vacant lot now worth $100,000. There is a mortgage outstanding of $46,000 on the lot, which is $36,000 more than what was paid for the lot. So far the seller has had the use of this extra capital ($36,000) without having to pay any income tax on that amount. However, when the lot is sold, everything above the book value (called *basis* in real estate) will be treated as a capital gain—including the $36,000 that the seller has most likely already spent. If, because of other income and expenses in the year of the sale the seller's overall tax rate was only 26 percent, the amount of tax to pay on the gain would be $23,400. This would leave the seller with $22,600 (not taking into account any closing costs or real estate commissions). This is a drop of over 50 percent of the amount of cash the seller thought he or she would end up with.

What was the seller going to do with the money anyway? The lot is being sold because the seller sees no benefits from it…in fact, it is a liability because there is a mortgage on it that requires payments. What are the seller's goals? Or is the seller like so many others who have no real goals in sight and is just trying to unload a problem?

A creative buyer may present an alternative: "Let me give you my six-unit apartment building in exchange for your lot." The details on the apartment building are as follows: price, $180,000; existing first mortgage, $120,000. If the seller holds the second mortgage of $6,000, the equity in the apartments is $54,000, an even swap for the lot equity.

Does this new benefit help the seller of the lot? It may not, but it does present an alternative that may not have even been considered. This kind of exchange would likely qualify as a tax-free exchange under IRS Code 1031, so there would be no loss of reinvestment power. If the apartments are capable of paying off the total debt of $126,000, then that will be a future benefit, and if there is income now, then this is much better than the seller having to make payments on the previous $54,000 mortgage.

Successful deal making in real estate depends on both the buyer and seller not getting bogged down in a price battle. Each party can look for other ways to skin the cat.

33. How Should I React When a Prospective Buyer Finds Fault with My Property?

Rejoice and be happy. Most real estate agents know that the moment a prospective buyer starts to find fault with a property, that is a buying sign. Of course if the buyer makes a statement such as, "This place is like a pig's pen" and the reference is valid, then this may not be a buying sign.

The signals are often very subtle and at the same time can be taken as an insult by the sellers if they are listening. The prospect says "I can't stand the color of that carpet." The seller, in his or her mind, adds "What idiot picked it out?" and is insulted. In reality the prospective buyer was thinking "This is the first thing I will change when I buy."

34. What Are the Most Important *Buying Signals* I Should Watch For?

Every person who inspects your property will give off some signals that can give you a clue as to how they feel about the property. However, some of these signals can be misunderstood by novice agents or by the sellers who may be present. The following are some positive signals that are solid buying signs.

The Seven Most Important Buying Signals

Nitpicks

Starts to talk about redecoration

Asks about structural items

Asks about hidden factors

Wants to know the seller's motivation

Introduces time to the negotiation

Comes back several times

There is no order in which these signals may be displayed, if at all. Some buyers are very warm and open, others cold as ice; each may be a real buyer for your property or may hate the place. Anytime you start to see one or more of these seven signals, both you and your agent should start to close in on this buyer...and not let him or her get away.

Nitpicks. When buyers start to pick apart a property, this can be a sign that they are attempting to appear disinterested. One or two nit-picking statements may not give a clear signal, but four or more does.

Starts to Talk about Redecoration. A strong buying signal is hearing "Can my decorator come over?" or the comments about where they would place their furniture, what color to paint the walls, etc.

Asks about Structural Items. Unless there is some interest in the property, there is no reason to get into technical details. Any such questions are strong buying signs.

Asks about Hidden Factors. Hidden factors can be anything from "What is behind this wall?" to "Have there ever been any termites?" It could be that the buyers are looking for a hidden gem that will help convince them to buy, such as "Are there hardwood floors under this carpet? (Please let there be so I can say "yes" right now and close tomorrow)."

Wants to Know Seller's Motivation. These questions indicate that buyers are thinking how to structure an offer. You have to look beyond the casual "Why are they selling?", because that question might simply be raised to pass the time during the visit. Once the buyer starts to ask for more information about the seller's motivation, some solid interest is being manifested.

Introduces Time to the Negotiation. This can be a very strong buying signal. "How soon could you move out?" is about the strongest question dealing with time.

Comes Back Several Times. This sign is hard to assess because it is both a buying signal as well as an unsold signal. Buyers who have not made up their mind may revisit several properties several times and then not buy any of them. It is clear that these people are having a hard time making up their mind and thus may not make a decision without some help. A good agent should make an effort to resell your property rather than push for a decision.

35. How Do I Get Rid of Mildew Smells?

The keys to getting rid of musty mildew smells in any property are shown below.

Get Rid of What Is Holding the Smell. If it is old carpets, or other fabric material that has imbedded mildew or other smells, then get rid of the source of the smell. When the mildew has found a home behind a wall, perhaps in insulation between the wall studs, there may be no simple solution. If this is the case you need to contact a professional cleaning firm that has equipment to fumigate the mildew to kill it within the walls.

Stop the Cause of the Mildew. Mildew is a plantlike life form that grows almost anywhere in an environment with some humidity, warmth, no circulating air, and little or no sunlight. Leather is a good place for mildew to get started, such as shoes and jackets in a dark, warm, moist closet. The interiors of walls may be soaked every time it rains from an undetected leak such that there is no water in a room, but you notice the smell of mildew and other unpleasant smells. The best way to handle this is to repair the leaks, air out rooms frequently, and have circulating fans to keep the air moving in a room tfhat is closed up for any period of time. However, make sure you kill the old mildew by washing down the area with a chemical made just for that job. Any hardware store will have several fine products from which you can chose.

36. What Are the Key Money- Making Aspects about Landscaping?

Landscaping can be one of the best improvements you can make to any property. Because of this it is important that you landscape your property with a plan according to how long you anticipate you will keep the property. If you are a builder and plan to sell the property as soon as you can, then you would invest in mature plants to best show off the property. On the other hand, if you are like most homeowners, you may keep your home longer than 10 years, perhaps for a lifetime.

The key time factor is seven years. Even a modest landscaping program should be planned with a seven-year maturity in mind. Naturally, the plant material will continue to grow, but except for certain kinds of trees (such as palms, most pine trees, and a few others) at the end of the seven-year period you would be maintaining the growth at that status quo.

If you want the best return possible from landscaping, have a professional lay out your plan. Explain to him or her about your seven-year plan and provide the economic budget you can work from. This will enable the landscaper to design an overall master plan, for implementation now or staged over a period of time. The most critical concern should be the slowest growing of the plants. Get them in the ground as soon as you can, and buy plants that will reach the desired size within the time allowed.

Work on the front and the living areas of the backyard first, mainly because you want to enjoy the home yourself and not just be a slave to your master plan. Fill in the rest of the landscaping as you go.

Ask the landscaper to include as many different kinds of plants that provide edible produce...but only if these plants fit the overall plan. Citrus, mangos, avocados, bananas and plants complement property in tropical areas, whereas pecan, walnut, apple, plum, peach, almond, and other trees can be used in cooler areas to produce a beautiful and functional yard that may attract just the buyer you will be seeking years from now.

37. Should I Sell My Property Furnished or Unfurnished?

If the question of keeping the furniture need not be considered, then my recommendation is to offer the home for sale unfurnished. When you list your home for sale unfurnished, *do not* state in the listing that the furniture is also available. Such statements automatically encourage a buyer (who likes the furniture and wants to buy it) to ask you to throw it in. What really happens is the buyer makes an offer that includes the furniture. You can always discuss the furniture in the negotiations, but it is best to require the buyers to ask for it. This is another buying signal: "Would you include the baby grand piano?" Your answer should be: "Are there any other conditions to your offer to buy my home?"

38.   How Can I Get Rid of Dog and Other Animal Smells?

The first step is to accept the fact that there is a dog or other animal smell in the property. The human nose has a wonderful fail-safe ability that eventually accepts an odd or even distasteful smell as normal. People who have lived near paper mills for a few years do not even notice the smell that you might find very unpleasant. The same goes for any smell, including old damp dogs, kitty litter boxes, and even your household llama. However, your agent knows the smell is there, and so will any prospective buyer.

Like the mildew problem, you first must get rid of what is holding the smell. That means cleaning the dog bed well, changing the kitty litter daily, and bathing the dog and the llama more often. Then wash the area the animal most frequents with fresh-smelling soaps, and use odor-killing sprays.

In cases where puppies and other animals have wet the carpets a number of times, the carpets may have to be replaced. A rug shampooing cannot totally solve the problem—but if the carpets are in good shape, contact a carpet cleaning firm that will give you references (that you check) and ask their advice.

39.   What Should Sellers Do When Showing Their Home to a Prospective Buyer?

The following are the most important steps you can take when you know a prospective buyer is coming to see your home. Take into consideration other seasonal items—make sure that the snow is cleared off the drive and walkways, that the air conditioning is adjusted to be cooler in the middle of the summer, etc.

Six Sales-Producing Steps to Take When the Buyer Is Going to Inspect the Home

Yard neatly cut and trimmed—shows pride of ownership

Front door clean and polished—the first impression is most important

Bathrooms neat and clean with new towels—important in closing

Kitchen spotless—sink clean and empty and refrigerator uncluttered

All lights on—bright homes are happy homes

Pleasant "memory smells"—drowns out "old" smells

40. What Are "Memory Smells" and How Can They Entice a Prospective Buyer?

Memory smells can be both good and bad. Everyone has some of both, and the idea is to introduce one of the "good" smells into a property when prospective buyers are coming to inspect the property, for example, when brokers hold open houses or when you have been notified that a prospective buyer is on the way.

Each of the following smells can be created in relatively short time, if you plan for it. There are many variations on the following smells and many others are not mentioned at all. The idea is not to produce the smell that you find pleasing, but a smell that is safe and generally accepted as having a high percentage of success as a good memory smell for most people.

The Top Seven Good Memory Smells

Bread baking in the oven

Cookies baking in the oven

Pies baking in the oven

Turkey baking in the oven

Freshly brewed coffee

Heated hot chocolate

Candy as It Is Cooked

To top off the delightful smell, having a sample of the food to taste can be a real winner. It works for supermarkets—why not for your home?

41. What Steps Should I Follow When I Am Ready to Buy a Home?

Most successful people work hard at obtaining their goals. The key word in this sentence is *goals*. The unfortunate fact for many people is they have no real goals in focus. Many people function on a day-to-day basis with dreams and not with well-formulated goals. They do not know exactly where they are going, do not have a timetable to get there, and do not do all the right things to ensure they are equipped and capable of getting where they want to be. In essence, setting and obtaining goals are hard work that is directed toward one final result.

With no clearly defined goal there is no purposeful plan, and actions tend to be random and often without any real satisfaction because there is no way to judge what progress has been made, if any.

The process of buying a home is not an everyday event. Your approach to this task should be taken very seriously and the more deliberate your approach, the greater your success will be in making the right decision. The following are twelve steps that will help you organize this important event.

Twelve Steps to Follow When Buying a Home

Write down your needs

Discuss the plan with all family partners

Review your financial capability

See if there are preliminary matters to deal with

Select the area where you want to live

Check the life-style values in the area

Firm up your plans and start looking

Select one or two agents to work with

Inspect a minimum of a dozen properties

Check the prices of recent sales

Get prequalified for a loan

Be ready to act

It is possible that your specific needs may add several steps to this list, so do not limit your advance work to just these twelve items.

Write Down Your Needs.   Study them for a few days; you are bound to make some changes. Goals take time to develop and need to be adjusted to the current situation from time to time. Your needs differ from your *wishes*, however, so start first with the basics and work from there. If you can afford to go beyond your present needs, then you should definitely have those extra comforts. After all, you worked hard to get them.

Discuss the Plan with All Family Partners.   This is an important decision and everyone who will either live in the home or help you pay for it should be involved in the plan.

Review Your Financial Capability.   Are you ready to make this financial commitment? You may discover that you may have to go back and make changes to the list of needs in the first step. One approach might be to look for a home that includes income potential, such as a duplex with two units or a small apartment building, to add to your financial stability.

See If There Are Preliminary Matters to Deal with. Do you have a home you might have to sell first, or can you exchange it for the property you want to buy? Do you need to get settled in your new job? Plan ahead and anticipate the time it will take.

Select the Area Where You Want to Live. Think ahead—think about schools for the kids, hospitals for health problems, closeness to work, if this is a benefit, etc. Check out several areas of the town you plan to live in. You may discover new areas that you like better than your first choice.

Check the Life-Style Values in the Area. A neighborhood you drove through while on the way to work might seem like a paradise. But drive through on a Saturday morning and you may find many children playing, numerous sporty cars parked on the streets indicating the presence of many teenagers, street parties of friendly neighbors, police cars driving up and down the streets because of a crime problem, unwanted people at street corners, etc. It does not take long to find out what a neighborhood is like if you do some leg work. Ask around: check the police department, the fire department, etc. Are there any problems you should know about? Ask the neighbors—"Hi, I'm considering buying a home on the next block and, well, would you mind telling me, will I like living here?" This question might just give you all the right answers to help you decide for yourself.

Firm Up Your Plans and Start Looking. There is no better time than the present, so once you know what you want to do, go do it! Looking to find a property to fit your needs should be both a fun time and a learning experience. As with everything you do, however, map it out, and keep records of what you see.

Select One or Two Agents to Work with. Real estate agents know most of the other agents who work a specific area of town, so it will be counterproductive for you to work with more than one or two agents. Even though the agent technically works for the seller in most cases, you will find that each agent has many different sellers. Also, if the agent is a member of a local multiple listing system, they will have access to the vast majority, if not all, of the listings in the area.

Inspect a Minimum of a Dozen Properties. Do not worry if you miss an opportunity while you are learning about the area. It is much better for you to be aware of what is going on in the local market, and this requires you to do homework. One of the most important steps in this process is to see as many properties as possible that are for sale so that you can begin to get a feel for two important aspects of this search: to find out what you can get for your money, and to adjust your needs to what you can afford.

Check the Prices of Recent Sales. Most areas of the country have easily understandable property records that indicate what the current owner paid for

3224

24474

the property and how much other properties have sold for in the recent past. This information allows you to see a pattern of values in this specific area. Keep in mind that prices for property that sold in other areas and neighborhoods may have no real relationship to prices where you are looking unless you know the areas are very similar in the most important aspects.

Get Prequalified for a Loan.   Most banks and mortgage brokers will take you through the process of getting prequalified for a loan. This will enable you to know exactly how much you can afford, unless you have some extra cash hidden somewhere. If you are looking for income-producing properties this prequalification may not be that accurate but can give you a good idea of how much you can borrow. Keep in mind that if you are going to use seller-held financing, then you may find a far more motivated lender in the seller as you are solving his or her more important problem—buying his or her property.

Be Ready to Act.   Once your plan is made and you have a good feel for the market and what you can do, do not let any opportunity that comes knocking get away.

42. What Are the "Hidden Gems" I Should Look for in a Property When Trying to Get the Most Value for My Money?

Even in homes that are only a few years old, some of the valuable aspects of the property may be covered over and eventually forgotten. In older properties it is not unusual for the existing owner to be unaware of some of the hidden gems that can exist. These gems will vary by area of the country, and there are many others not mentioned below, such as a wine cellar or root cellar that was boarded up long ago and forgotten. The following are the top seven hidden gems you should look for.

The Top Seven Hidden Gems You Might Find in Homes

Solid brass fixtures

Hardwood floors

Slate or tile floors

Hardwood tongue-and-groove paneling

Copper plumbing

Copper roofing

Crawl spaces

Solid Brass Fixtures.   Years of paint may have covered up these beautiful fixtures, and they may now be not only very valuable but irreplaceable. Scrape some of the paint away with a knife where it will not be noticed—after asking permission, of course.

Hardwood Floors.   Peek under the wall-to-wall carpet. If you spot hardwood do not assume that is everywhere nor that it is in good condition where it has been installed. It is possible that the carpet is there just to cover up the places where the good hardwood has been removed and replaced with plywood. If the hardwood is viable you may find it worth refinishing. Always make a thorough inspection of any hidden gem to be sure it is not partially fake. If restoration is needed, be sure to get the advice of an expert before you assume you got a bargain.

Slate or Tile Floors.   If you do not see hardwood floors, you might find slate, tile, or who knows, even marble floors. Most of these types of floors can be refinished, and if they suit your preferences, you may have found a real gem at last.

Hardwood Tongue-and-Groove Paneling.   If the wall appears to be wood but has been painted or papered over, it may be worth checking to see if you have genuine hardwood tongue-and-groove paneling. This can be very expensive to install (unlike the much less expensive thin sheet, plywood-backed paneling), and while it is costly to remove layers of paint, it might be worthwhile.

Copper Plumbing.   When you have the property inspected this can be a very pleasant find. When the seller knows the plumbing is copper it is a good idea to make sure the buyer is told of this valuable asset.

Copper Roofing.   If you find copper sheeting over the whole roof, you have made an important discovery, as this can be the best kind of roof you will ever have. Copper scuppers and drains are a plus, even if the roof is of more conventional material.

Crawl Spaces.   Some homes and commercial buildings have crawl spaces either under the building or between walls for access to the plumbing and electrical installations. This may be very important to the buyer of a motel or hotel and is good news to any home buyer of property that is 10 years or older.

43. What Are the Most Common "Time Bombs" I Should Look For before I Buy a Home?

Do not assume that the following list is the total of all potential time bombs that you might encounter, because it is not. Each area of the country has some special problem that is likely to be more critical than any of the following, and you need to know what those special problems are. They can include, for example, the potential for sinkholes, a phenomenon caused by an underground cavity that had been eroded hundreds of years before finally collapsing. Such sinkholes have been known to swallow up whole houses. Earthquake zones, tornado areas, falling rocks, avalanches, rising rivers, etc., all pose threats to life, limb, and property. The list provided below covers the more likely problems of which you should be aware.

Eight Property Time Bombs You Should Be Aware of before You Buy

Termites

Broken plumbing

Roof leaks

Property line encroachments

Environmental hazards

Code violations

Pending special assessments

Title problems

Termites.   There are several kinds of termites; all are preventable and their damage can be kept to a minimum when encountered early. However, termites may come and go, and leave behind substantial damage. It is important in most areas of the world to check for termites and their damage. The question "Are there any termites?" may not disclose their damage. Have a professional check all property to ensure that neither termites nor their damage exists. If either are found, then it should be up to the seller either to make the necessary repairs and have treatments done, or to adjust the price accordingly.

Broken Plumbing.   Only your plumber can tell if the plumbing is in need of repair. One of the signs of a potential plumbing problem is a large water bill. Water charges for amounts over and above presumed use can signal a broken water pipe underground. Even a steady flow of water from a pipe several feet underground may never be noticed above ground. If the pipe is under a building, the damage may be undetected until the building falls into the hole that was eaten away by the flow of water. Plumbing repairs can be very expensive.

Roof Leaks.   If you buy in the dry season it might be several months before you find a leak. You can, however, look for ceiling or wall stains, which indicate that there was a roof leak at one time. Of course, these stains can be painted over and hidden, or the roof could have been fixed. It is a good idea to make sure a complete roof inspection is a part of your prepurchase checklist.

Property Line Encroachments.   Not all property line encroachments are visible and not all property lines are obvious. Underground septic tanks or drain fields may extend from one property to another, from the neighbor's or from your own property. In either case problems can arise. A recent survey can help prevent most of the property line encroachments but not all, because not all underground installations may show up in public records. One key is to make sure the survey marks all the corners of a property. Make a physical inspection of these corners. Are they what you thought them to be? Draw lines between the corners—use a heavy cord or colored surveyor ribbon where buildings or landscape allows. Ask each neighbor if he or she knows of any underground installations from either property that cross under or near these boundaries. Check the local building codes to be sure that all buildings on the property do not encroach setback lines.

Environmental Hazards.   There are several important environmental problems that you may want to check. The most important is radon gas inside a home or apartment. This gas occurs in a natural state as the result of the decay of uranium, radium, and thorium. This gas is found in minute particles in the air, dissolved in some spring water, and within certain minerals that contain uranium, radium, or thorium. Because this gas is colorless and odorless and is the heaviest gas that exists, when it seeps into a home or apartment the concentration can quickly build up. This gas is highly radioactive and can be very dangerous. Test kits are available at most well-equipped hardware stores, and all property inspection companies are capable of testing for this gas.

Outside the home, hidden underground time bombs are toxic chemicals, oil products dumped into the ground, and other unpleasant items that simply await your shovel. A check into the usage and recent geologic histories is helpful and may show that the site was once a landfill area, that an oil refinery once occupied the site 50 years ago, or that there is a deep burning coal fire two miles under that very spot.

Code Violations.   Past, present, and future code violations should be checked. A visit to the local building departments that have jurisdiction over that property would be the place to start. If any violations have been recorded against the property you should check to make sure that the problem has been corrected. Are there any present violations? You can ask for an inspection; this may occur automatically if the property being purchased is commercial in nature and you are attempting to apply for a business license. Future violations do not require a crystal ball. Often laws are passed that give property owners a lead time to prepare for the code change. No violation may exist now, but a law may be in place that will require you to do something soon—something that might be very expensive, such as provide interior fire sprinklers in every enclosed space, fire alarm devices, and new enclosed fire exits. These future violations might be the very reason the property is offered for sale at such a "great" price.

Pending Special Assessments.   Like future code violations it is possible that pending special assessments are planned but have not yet been implemented. This is more likely to occur with a condominium or cooperative apartment than a single-family home, so check with the building association. Is there a plan being discussed or already passed that will impose a special assessment on the property you are considering purchasing? If so, find out how much, and take that into consideration when you make an offer.

Title Problems.   In the United States many properties have a clear chain of title that is evidenced by an abstract of title. This is an actual history of recorded documents that shows the chain of title as far back as legal action requires. In Florida, for example, an abstract of title starts with the Land Grant from Spain. If an abstract of title is not available, the history of title can be checked through a title search. This requires a manual review of recorded documents to see if the present owner was given good title and still has it to pass on to you.

Problems that occur with title are often nothing more than an improperly executed deed or mortgage satisfaction, or a lien that had been discharged but not properly documented. Death of a partner or of a spouse of a past owner can also pose complications and require the seller to take legal steps (not always expensive, but some problems can take years to clear up) to produce good marketable and insurable title.

44. What Should I Do When I Am Ready to *Sell* My Home?

All prospective sellers should follow these five important steps in their decision making before they list their property for sale.

Five Important Steps to Follow before You Put Your Home on the Market

Review your present benefits

Balance those benefits against future needs

Examine all other options

Weigh those options against your goals

Establish your timetable and price accordingly

Review Your Present Benefits.   Take a hard look at what you are about to give up. Are you ready to do that, or do you plan to add to those benefits with your next property? Do you need those added benefits? This reminds me of the seller who calls the listing agent and comments that "After reading the advertisement you placed in the newspaper about my home, I didn't realize how wonderful my property really was...so take it off the market, please!"

Balance Those Benefits against Future Needs.   Once you have taken a good look at what you are about to give up and have examined what your finances will be after the sale, are you able to meet your goals for future needs? If so then proceed; but if not, and if you are not forced to sell, then you may want to take a harder look to see if your goals may need adjustment or just your plans.

Examine All Other Options.   Many people wait until they are overcome by problems and have few options to follow. Even if you did wait to the point at which some options are no longer available to you, there still remains more than one avenue to follow. Most sellers think that the only way out of debt is to unload what they have by selling it at any price, which may be the proper course. However, under the right circumstance a gift to a charity can solve the problem and offset future income at the same time through a deductible contribution. Alternatively, perhaps a real estate exchange to put your equity into another kind of property would be better.

Weigh Those Options against Your Goals.   This emphasizes the point that has been stressed throughout this book. Goals are the focal point of everything positive. If your goals are correctly set, that is, written down, set in intermediate, easy to reach steps that are attainable by you, clearly in focus, and reviewed on a regular basis, your decision process will be easier, and options open to you more abundant.

Establish Your Timetable and Price Accordingly.   Time is both friend and enemy of the real estate investor. If you use time properly, you will allow it to give you the lead time necessary to accomplish the maximum benefit in the sale or disposition of a property. If you do not manage time well, you will become overly anxious or worse, a desperate seller.

The key is to know what your timetable is and to work according to those needs. For example, if you know that by the end of twelve months you will be moving to another state, put your property on the market now. Agree to rent it back for up to a year to aid a prospective buyer to move now, even when they may not need the home right away. Start looking for a property where you are going to move and be an aggressive buyer in that area via an exchange of your old property. Be active…let time work for you.

45.   What Inexpensive Things Can I Do to Fix Up My Home to Improve My Chances of Getting Top Dollar?

Naturally you will have to do whatever is necessary in the following list within your budget. If money is not a problem, then go through the home and make sure that everything that you have been putting off that you *know* should be done, gets done.

When you list your home, ask the agent to make a detailed list of anything he or she feels would be helpful to the sale of the house if it was fixed, changed, cleaned, moved, or thrown away. You might be surprised that if your agent is very candid with you, you may have a very big garage sale soon. By the way, it is best to get rid of all this unwanted, unnecessary stuff right away because it will make your home look less cluttered. The following list contains what I feel are the top items.

Twelve Inexpensive Things to Do to Maximize Your Property Value

Paint the front door

Make sure every door functions properly

Trim lawn and landscaping neatly

Fix all obvious broken items

Plant new landscape

Paint walls

Clean—clean—clean

Remove all clutter

Put new brass street numbers on the house

Have a clean and neat refrigerator

Install closet expanders

Get rid of bad or offensive house smells

46.   How Do I Set a Price for My Home?

Ask at least two prospective real estate agents to give you a competitive market report (CMR). Some agents may have different names for this report, but the report will be a compilation of all the listed properties and those that have been sold in your area. A well-prepared report will stress properties that are similar to yours and show the actual listed price, the actual sales price (if already sold), and the time the property has been on the market (which should also include previous listings that were unsuccessful).

Based on this report the agents will suggest that your property falls within a price range and will recommend that you list your property at the middle to upper end of that range.

This kind of report is usually accurate on the high side, that is, rarely do homes sell at the price they are listed at anyway, so no matter what price you list the property at, buyers will offer less, and sellers generally build in some buffer for negotiations.

With all this in mind, you should go with the best property report or analysis, trust in the agents you have developed rapport with, and let the agents help you arrive at a fair market price.

47. What Can I Do to Speed Up the Sale of My Home?

There are many things you can do to aid in the sale of your home, and these four are proven over the years to be the best at producing results. They are as follows:

Keep your goals clearly in sight

Work at the offer/counteroffer process

Keep the house open for inspection when the agent cannot

Be realistic about your price

48. How Do I Select the Best Agent to Sell My Home?

Drive around your neighborhood and nearby areas (two miles in all directions should do) and see which real estate firm has the most listings. Also, make a list of all the firms in the area advertising property for sale. Put check marks by the firms that represent properties that are similar to or more valuable than yours (rather than less expensive). Call the firms you have indicated with check marks and talk to the agents about the houses they are representing. Do not tell them you live in the area and want to sell. What you want to do is find out how they deal with a prospective buyer. If any of them irritate you, cross them off your list. When you find one you like, make an appointment and meet in person. You should meet with a minimum of three agents before you decide which one is for you.

Insist that the agents go over all the details of the listing agreement and put in writing all that they are going to do for you.

49. What Is the Best Technique for Selling Real Estate in a Slow Market?

The very best technique to sell any real estate is to become an aggressive buyer for some other property, for which you are going to offer your property in exchange. To do this effectively you must have a strong focus on your own investment goals and then seek only property that will move you closer to those goals than the property you are trying to sell.

50. Should I Consider a Real Estate Exchange, and If So, for What?

A real estate exchange is a very good way to increase your end-result benefits. The answer to question number 32 illustrated one example of how an exchange could introduce a benefit that the seller had not thought of before.

Saving on taxes that would be due in a sale can be strong motivation but should not be the principal reason you would take a property in exchange. The key to exchanges is to think and act as though you are a cash buyer. It is possible that in the right transaction the seller of the property you end up with can also get cash out of the transaction as well as other benefits.

For example, say you have a home in Chicago you have been unable to sell. It has been on the market at $175,000 for some time and is free and clear of all debt. You cannot afford to buy a home in Tampa, where you want to go, until you sell your Chicago property. Therefore you are stuck in limbo—or are you?

You take a trip down to Tampa and start looking for what you would like to own. Because you are going to retire, you want to get a place to live and also have some income property. You find several small apartment buildings you would like to own and start making offers. One such building is a 10-unit property that has a nice owner's apartment. The fair asking price is $400,000. The seller has a first mortgage of $100,000 on the property. You offer your Chicago home plus $125,000 cash. The deal looks like this:

The apartment complex:	$400,000
Less the existing debt:	100,000
Seller's equity:	$300,000
Your Chicago home:	$175,000
Plus your cash:	125,000
Your equity:	$300,000

You get the $125,000 in cash by casting a new first mortgage on the apartment building of $300,000 (a reasonable 75 percent loan-to-value ratio). After you pay off the first mortgage of $100,000 and give the seller $125,000, you are left with $75,000 less some closing and loan costs.

The sellers of the apartment building may or may not want your Chicago home, but because they have solved a major problem, they may be in a much better position to absorb the Chicago property by making it easy for a buyer to acquire it. They do not have the same problem you had...after all, they got rid of their Tampa property and got cash on top of that. They might be satisfied to hold a low-interest or "soft" mortgage (easy terms) or trade the Chicago home for a blue-water sailboat and head for Tahiti.

51. How Is the Tax on a Sale Treated If I Buy Another Home?

The Internal Revenue Section 1034 governs the sale of your primary residence and allows that under certain circumstances, there will be no gains tax due if you reinvest the proceeds of the sale in a new home. The rules of Section 1034 are as follows:

1. The property you sell must be your legal residence at the date you enter into a contract to sell.

2. The new residence can be a property you already own provided you acquired it within 24 months from the date you deed your old residence to its new owner, or, the new residence can be a property you buy within 24 months following the date you deed your old property to its new owner.

3. The tax consequences (if any) are found using the following check sheet:

Residence-for-Residence Check Sheet

Adjusted sale price of old property
1. Sale price of old property   _____
2. Less fix-up cost   − _____
3. Less selling expenses   − _____
4. Adjusted sales price   _____

Basis, old residence
5. Original cost   _____
6. Plus improvements made   + _____
7. Less depreciation taken   − _____
8. Basis of old residence   _____

Realized gain
9. Sale price of old residence, line 1   _____
10. Less selling expenses   − _____
11. Amount realized in the sale   _____
12. Less basis of old residence, line 8   − _____
13. Realized gain on old residence   _____

If new residence cost is less than line 4
14. Adjusted sale price of old residence, line 4   _____
15. Less cost of new residence   − _____
16. Gain recognized (taxable) from sale   _____
17. Total realized gain, line 13   _____
18. Less line 16   − _____
19. Gain not allocated to new property   _____
20. Cost of new residence, line 15   _____
21. Less gain not allocated, line 19   − _____
22. New basis of the new property   _____

If new residence cost is more than line 4
23. Cost of new residence   _____
24. Less line 13 (gain of old residence)   − _____
25. Basis of the new residence   _____

52.   How Can I Avoid the Pitfalls of a Title Closing?

Closing is the term used for the event that occurs when the buyer and seller actually transfer funds and the deed. At this time mortgage notes and mortgages and all other necessary and important documents are signed and executed. Most of the time these events take place without any problems, but not always.

The Buyer's Ten-Item Preclosing Checklist

Reinspect property

Verify the survey

Verify the legal description

Check for good title

Ask questions about hidden time bombs

Review and verify inventory

Question all repaired damage

Have closing agent go over the procedures with you

Read and understand all documents you are to sign

Understand your legal rights and options if problems occur

This checklist is not something you should attempt to do solely on your own. Obtaining professional advice in any legal transaction, especially one as important as the sale or purchase of real estate, can be the least expensive part of the whole transaction. It is much better to avoid a problem than to fight your way out if it in court.

To help you properly deal with this checklist each item is briefly discussed below.

Reinspect Property.   Prior to the closing, and as close to the actual time and date of the closing, you should have a detailed walk-through of the property. The sellers should be aware that you are going to do this well in advance so that there will be no last-minute delay or difficulty getting into the property. The reason for this is to ensure you that the property is exactly what you expect it to be. Are all the furniture and equipment you contracted for still there? Has any of it been replaced with cheaper items; are all the trees and other plants still there (don't laugh)?

As you go through the property it is a good idea to have a copy of the property inspection report, which you had arranged for some time prior to the closing. If there were items to be repaired or replaced, check to be sure the work was done as ordered.

Verify the Survey.   Do the property and the recent survey match up? To find out, as you take your reinspection tour make sure that you locate the survey markers. It is a good idea to have ordered them marked by the surveyor who did the survey in the event they may have been accidently moved or hidden by landscaping. Check the measurements. Are they the same as the legal description and survey indicate? Does the survey show any encroachments? If so, this must be dealt with before you close on the property.

Verify the Legal Description.   If the legal description is given in metes and bounds, the actual property border dimensions will be given. Do they match the survey and your actual measurements? Does the legal description match the actual property dimensions as would be shown on a city subdivision plat? Errors do happen, and you would not be the first person to buy a property next door to the property you had seen and thought you were buying.

Check for Good Title.   This is a job for your lawyer, title insurance company, or escrow closing agent. They can review the history of title transactions and can tell you if there is a possible problem with the title. Most of the time these matters are rather simple to clear up and are nothing more than an unsigned deed or a death not properly recorded. However, other problems can arise that are very serious and expensive to clear up...or that may not be able to be cleared up at all. Do not close unless you know the title is good.

Ask Questions about Hidden Time Bombs.   Be sure you discuss with your agent, lawyer, accountant, and insurance agent any possible hidden time bomb that might occur after the closing. It is possible that you may overlook something important that might initially seem to be insignificant, but that later can require you to pay more taxes than you need to, to have a potential legal action filed against you, or to jeopardize your rights to file legal action against someone who wronged you.

Review and Verify Inventory.   Checking inventory can be a tedious job, but it is important and should be done. It is not unusual for an inventory list that is made when the property is first put on the market to differ greatly from a final inventory taken or checked on the day of the closing. Often the differences are accidental or the items are misplaced, in different rooms, but sometimes the items have already been taken off the property.

Question All Repaired Damage.   If you do not question it, who will? Some closing agents will suggest that you close, even though the damage has not been repaired, by putting a sum of money equal to the estimate for repairs in an escrow account. I do not recommend this procedure unless you have other plans for the area that would need the repairs. For example, if there is damage to the concrete decking around a pool, and your plans are to remove the concrete anyway and put pavers over most of the backyard, why do any repairs at all? Take the money.

Have a Closing Agent Go over the Procedures with You.   Find out what is going to happen the day of the closing before that day arrives. It is not necessary for you and the seller to be at the closing at the same time; in fact sometimes it is advisable that you *not meet* that day. Why? Lots of strange emotions are going on when a home is sold and even the smallest problem seems to blow up into something much bigger. Good friends can become life-long enemies.

   The actual procedures of the closing are simple, and the buyer can arrive before the seller and complete all the documentation needed, deliver the check or other items necessary, and leave. The seller then comes along and signs the deed, the documents are recorded, and the closing is finalized. Some closings take place entirely by mail.

Read and Understand all Documents You Are to Sign.   Some of the best closing agents will actually read the document to you and explain every item without your having to ask questions. I like this kind of closing agent because he or she wants to make sure that no person is intimidated by anything that goes on at the closing.

   If your closing agent does not do that, ask them to. If there is anything you do not understand about any part of the documentation, then ask. In fact, ask a lot of questions until you are comfortable that you understand not only the document you are about to sign, but also the potential problems that can occur as a result of the document and what your obligations and liabilities are because you have executed that document.

Understand Your Legal Rights and Options If Problems Occur.   What can you do if there is termite damage after all? Who can you claim damages from in that case? What do you do if you find out that the agent lied to you about something important, something that you relied on when you decided to buy? What about the mortgage you signed, only to find out later that there was another mortgage already on the property that the lawyer did not discover when he or she checked the title, and that the agent and the owner did not tell you about? Who do you sue?

You should go over these and ensuing questions with the closing agent, and make sure you are comfortable with the answers they give you.

6

The Keys to Buying and Selling Condominiums and Cooperative Apartments

53. What Are the Most Important Differences between Condominiums and Cooperative Forms of Ownership?

Condominium properties take many different forms of construction and range from what appears to be "normal" single-family homes to more conventional high-rise apartment buildings as well as professional office space and other commercial and industrial types of buildings. The method of condominium ownership is not new and resembles a form of subdivision of ownership that has been popular in Europe for hundreds of years. In essence, the building is divided up into segments, generally apartments or office space, and each owner gets a deed to that specific space—along with ownership and the obligations of ownership to a portion of public space (halls, stairs, entrance area, meeting rooms, recreational space, etc).

Cooperative properties make up a building that is owned by a corporation where the shares in the corporation give the holders of that stock rights to certain space in the building. This usually relates to apartments but can also relate to commercial space. One share or a block of shares, depending on how the corporation is set up, gives the holder the right to occupy a specific apartment. Upkeep cost is divided by all owners based on a percentage of the space owned. This form of ownership can be found in various parts of the country and is very common in New York City. There are no specific advantages to ownership through a cooperative, and in light of the advantages that exist through condominium form of ownership, few cooperatives are being developed.

54. What Critical Factors Should I Know When Buying a Condo or a Coop?

When you buy a home or business that is part of an association such as a condominium or cooperative, there are several aspects that need to be carefully checked. The following are five of the most important.

The Five Critical Factors When Buying a Condominium or Cooperative

Association rules and regulations

Annual assessments and charges

Debt and mortgage obligations

Building association balance sheet

Potential neighbors

Each of these items must pass your test or you might be headed for trouble. Review each below.

Association Rules and Regulations. The building owner's association has very distinct rules and regulations that may differ from any other property you have looked at. State law may regulate the extent of those rules and regulations, but usually there is ample flexibility within the law for rules to be imposed that may not be to your liking or may be too lax to suit your needs. These rules may govern simple things such as furniture being moved in and out of the apartment and hours when trash and garbage can be thrown out, and stricter aspects such as rental of your own apartment, and the age of who can rent or live there.

Annual Assessments and Charges. The cost to keep up a big building, with 24-hour security, swimming pools, meeting rooms, workout rooms, saunas, steam rooms, and all the other facilities that can come with such a life style need not be as expensive as you might think. By the time the cost to maintain all those facilities is added up and divided among the owners, the annual fee may not be any more than you are used to paying for a gardener and pool cleaner to come to a private home. However, sometimes special charges that cost small fortunes are incurred to take care of the replacement of major items such as elevators, central heating or air conditioning, or building painting and roof work. Usually such costs are not levied without advance notice, and more often than not, such assessments follow a year or more of political infighting within the association of owners. Make sure that such an impact is not about to be slapped on the property you just bought. You have a right to ask questions of the building management, but the best way to get this information is to contact the owner and his or her agent, ask directly the following questions, and get the answers in writing:

- Are there any possible building repairs or improvements that are being discussed by management or the building association board of directors?
- Have any assessments been planned but not levied?
- Does the building have a reserve for replacements, and how much is it?

Debt and Mortgage Obligations. If the property is a condominium, then mortgage information can be checked in the same way as a home. All mortgages of record would be recorded in the public records under the legal description of that property, and any liens against the owner would be recorded against the owner by name. Potential problems of unrecorded mortgages can be circumvented through a careful title search by your lawyer or title insurance company. A land lease or recreational lease (where allowed by state law) would also be recorded in the public records and should be checked. All such documents should be read to find out the fine-print terms. Leases and mortgage interest can escalate, balloon payments can come due tomorrow, e.g., and options to buy come and go without your knowing about them.

Cooperative mortgages usually come in two stages. First there may be an overall mortgage that covers the entire building. When this is the case, each of the apartment owners would be obliged to pay a share of that mortgage. A default on their share may ultimately cause them to lose the shares they own in the cooperative, and with them their rights to the apartment. However, everyone understands that a mortgage must be paid or they will suffer the consequences. It may be difficult to get information on the amount of the total mortgage owed and what your share of that mortgage would be once you owned the apartment. You should insist on knowing how much the mortgage is and not just assume that because the monthly maintenance charge includes the mortgage that the $700 dollars a month charged now will continue that way forever. You may find that six months after you close the underlying mortgage balloons ("Oh, you didn't read the mortgage document? It's in the public records"), and that your share of the payoff is $50,000. Remember, when you buy a property that has outstanding debt, the total debt must be added to the cash and other equity you pay to find out exactly the price you really paid. Coop owners in New York City have frequently quoted me prices to buy their apartment without even knowing what their underlying debt was…"Oh, it's just in the monthly maintenance payment."

Building Association Balance Sheet. Every well-managed building should have a reserve for replacements. If you are looking at two apartments in two different buildings and cannot make up your mind between the two, look at the balance sheet of the building management. Do they owe six months of contract wages? Is the building replacement and repair account at zero? If one building has been accruing funds over 10 years for a major building replacement, and the other has nothing in the bank but a major replacement just around the corner, then choose the building with better management.

Potential Neighbors. It is important to check the neighbors in any community you may move to. After all, the people who live around you can make your life either pleasant or troublesome. When selecting a home, I recommend prospective buyers to walk around the area at several different times of the day and night. Saturday at midmorning can present a different picture than noon on a workday.

A condominium or cooperative presents a different problem, but the need to check the neighbors is even more important. These people not only will live in your neighborhood, they will have something to say about how you must live.

If the building has recreational facilities, such as meeting rooms and swimming pools, then visit the building several times during the hours when these facilities will be most likely in use. This may be the only time you will see your potential neighbors. Feel free to talk to them and ask them about the building and the management. Ask what they dislike most. You might find something very important.

55. How Is the Association Maintenance Charged against the Unit I May Buy, and What Potential Problems Do I Need to Look For?

Association charges for maintenance may be charged monthly, quarterly, or semiannually. Rarely are the usual charges collected on an annual basis, but special charges can be.

The hidden time bomb comes in the form of special assessments either that are about to be levied, or worse, one that is already past due but not yet paid by the seller. Lax management may not have gotten around to placing a lien on the apartment, so when your lawyer or title insurance company checks the title they do not find a lien. However, this assessment can be charged against you anyway, after you have closed on the unit.

56. What Factors about the Apartment Do I Need to Consider before Buying?

The overwhelming answer is another question: Do you really want to live there?

Many people move from a home or other kind of private residence into a condominium or cooperative. These same people may have, at some time in their past, lived in a rental apartment and may relate to that experience. However, living in a condominium or cooperative that you own is not the same as living in an apartment that you rent, for the following reasons. When you rent, there is always a "temporary" feeling about living there. You learn to live with the neighbors because they too are just temporary and if you want, you can move. When you own your apartment, the temporary nature of living in a rental apartment disappears. If you are used to coming and going as you please, working in your own yard, taking a skinny-dip in your own pool, then your life is in for a change. Are you sure you want to live there?

57. How Should I Prepare for the Interview by the Owner's Association to Improve My Chances of Being Approved?

When you buy into a condominium or cooperative, it is usual for you to meet before a review board prior to your contract becoming valid. This is just one of those difficulties that makes association ownership different and annoying. On the other hand, the idea of not letting just anyone live in your building has its advantages too.

The review committee could come under much scrutiny from potential legal actions should they violate someone's rights. The problem is that some committees spend most of the time looking for ways to reject you legally. Forestall such action by not giving them any legal reason to reject you.

You should prepare yourself by knowing the state laws that govern such home associations. Ask your real estate agent to get you a copy. Also, get a copy of the building rules and regulations if you have not done so already and be familiar with the rules you are expected to abide by once you live there. This will give you a clue as to what kind of questions the review board will ask. After all, they want you to like the same things they like.

Use political pull if you have it, or get your agent to pull some strings within the review board. These associations have their demagogues, and bureaucracy can be a critical part of living and surviving in a condo or coop. It is often better to flow with the tide than fight it. And most of all, dress conservatively, no matter what you normally like to wear.

58. What Are the Most Important Strategies to Use When Selling My Condo or Coop?

Selling any property is simply a question of letting the property meet the expectations of the prospective buyer and satisfy the buyer's needs. Some properties will do that all by themselves...all the agent has to do is introduce the buyer, "Buyer, meet your new property." However, this is a rare event, so take a look at the following proven sales strategies that work.

Eight Proven Sales Strategies for Condominium and Coop Apartments

Stress the security

Highlight all the benefits

Name-drop important neighbors

Show off party rooms during a party

Discover the buyer's motivation—then use it

Introduce the buyer to compatible neighbors

Be creative

Have all important facts in writing

Review each in detail.

Stress The Security. Many people buy an apartment because they no longer feel secure where they presently live. The idea of 24-hour security, banks of television monitors that telecast views from a dozen hidden cameras, armed uniformed guards roaming around the building to protect life, limb, and property can be very appealing. Therefore this factor should be stressed. No matter how lax the security is in your building, it may appear to be a sanctuary to the buyer. Enforce this by showing the buyer all the special security features such as hidden cameras and one-way doors that allow people out but not back in unless they have the right passwords, and stressing the number of guards on duty at any time.

Highlight All the Benefits. It is not unusual for people who live in a condo or coop to be unaware of some of the benefits their own building offers. You will need to know them all and build on them. For example, mail is usually a closely awaited event in many large apartment buildings, so much so that when mail arrives it becomes a social hour. I have seen buildings that will hoist a flag in a courtyard that is visible to all apartments the moment that mail has been put into the boxes in the mail room. Turn this normal event into a special benefit. Mail is collected for you and kept safe, even if you are out of town for a week, or a month, or more.

Health facilities, exercise rooms, tennis courts, swimming pools, etc., are all bonus features, but there is probably more to offer. For example, there could be yoga classes where the teacher comes to the building instead of you having to run across town, private tennis lessons just outside your back door, or scuba lessons in your own Olympic-size pool. These benefits might be the little thing that motivates the buyer.

Name-Drop Important Neighbors.   "Oh, Mr. and Mrs. George Bush live across the hall, and did you know, the head of cardiac surgery from the Cleveland Clinic lives two floors down." Note the subtle nature of not mentioning who lives higher up. Use that approach when possible. You should not just drop names of famous people, but names of the kind of people you think the buyer would relate to. This might require a quick judgement call on your part, unless you have a clue from the agent, or it is the agent who is dropping the name who already knows the client.

In general, it is best to play up the benefits of the building through the names you drop. "Oh, Jimmy Connors lives here, and it is not uncommon to see him out on the tennis courts…or in the sauna afterward."

Show off Party Rooms During a Party.   As a realtor I have taken prospective buyers through some of the most elegant condominium buildings and visited absolutely beautiful party rooms that left everyone disappointed because the rooms were not designed to just be beautiful, they were designed to be enjoyed during a party. It takes a party to see them put to their intented use.

Brokers can arrange a special cocktail party and invite likely prospects or invite other brokers to bring their prospects to this very private showing of your property. If that is not possible or timely, and you know there is a party planned, then try to schedule a showing of your apartment when you can also take the prospective buyer through the party room in the midst of a social gathering of neighbors (if the neighbors are friendly).

Discover the Buyer's Hot Button—Then Push It.   When buyers look at the apartment and all the other amenities that go with it, watch their eyes, listen to their questions, and pay attention to their body language. All that they do will lead you to their motivation. Questions about the depth of the pool, for example, might be a sign of interest in scuba lessons or a fear of drowning (themselves or a child), so be careful not to react the wrong way. Be safe and stress the security at the pool, then find out why the question was asked.

Too many agents rush through the building part of a property, showing and stressing the apartment itself. This is wrong. People do not buy an apartment, they buy a life style. Somewhere the motivation can be uncovered, and it may manifest itself with approval of the apartment, such as saying "what a beautiful view," but what they really are thinking is the view is beautiful because they can sleep with their windows open at night since they are 20 floors up.

Introduce The Buyer to Compatible Neighbors.   This is a very good closing technique and is generally saved for the second visit, unless you are lucky and run into someone you know is compatible with everyone while walking around the building.

On that second visit, invite a friend in the building over for coffee at the same time the prospective buyer is coming over. Tell the buyer you thought they might like to meet one of the neighbors to ask about the building from the standpoint of someone who will still be living in the building.

Be Creative.   Already you have seen some very creative techniques, most of which have rarely seen used by agents. However, there are many other areas where you can be creative in finalizing a deal. You can create a successful negotiation by being open minded and letting the prospective buyer mentally transform into a buyer. This happens if you give strong but not desperate selling signals.

Take the posture that you and the buyer both want the same thing: that they buy your apartment. Once they are sold on that prospect, the only business that will remain between you is defining the terms of that sale. The more the buyer thinks of him- or herself as owner, the smaller that gap will become. You can drive buyers away by not responding to their need to own that apartment.

Have All Important Facts in Writing.   If your property is listed for sale, the agent will have a copy of the listing to give to the prospective buyers. This is okay, but it may be just like every other listing the buyer has seen. You want to give them not only the facts but do so in such a way that they will remember the elements that count. Reinforce everything that has been mentioned earlier by giving the technical details on all the benefits of the building. If you have cable, stress the top-of-the-line wiring system and that the building also has satellite antennas with over 200 extra channels (if it does, of course). Also, mention the security system, which is not an ordinary security system but one with state-of-the-art equipment. Remind buyers that the tennis courts are of special construction. Remember what Elmer Letterman stressed: to sell the steak you sell the sizzle.

Have a photograph of the apartment, and if you really want to make sure they never forget the building, take a Polaroid snapshot of them as they try out the grand piano in the party room.

7

Insider Secrets for Buying, Selling, and Owning Vacation Properties

59. Do I Get Any Tax Write-Offs with Vacation Property?

At the present writing of this book, the IRS still allows certain expenses of a second home to be deductible from income. The two basic expenses allowed are real estate taxes and mortgage interest, both of which are deductible as they would be on your primary residence.

All mortgage interest is subject to certain limitations that come into effect based on the date you became obligated to the debt and what the proceeds of the loan were used for. For example, if the mortgage is taken out after October 13, 1987 and the proceeds are used to buy, build, or improve your home, and the amount of the mortgage plus any other mortgages you owe on that property that were taken out prior to October 13, 1987 (when it did not make any difference what the money was used for) and the combined total debt does not exceed $1 million dollars (the limit is $500,000 if married filing separately), then you can deduct all the interest. Other variations of dates of the mortgage or use of the funds will require you to check with your accountant as to the disposition of that interest.

Real estate taxes are fully deductible from either your primary or vacation property.

If you rent out your property, then you can deduct certain "business expenses" as you would from any income property depending on the rules and regulations that apply to passive or nonpassive income. Generally, rental property falls into the category of *passive income*. The importance of this is that expenses that exceed income may have some restrictions as to the amounts that can be deductible against other income from nonpassive income sources. The Clinton tax package of 1993 has made some important changes in past tax law in this respect and may go through fine tuning in 1994.

There is a fine line drawn between your ownership of a vacation home as an income property and as a second residence. If you, any member of your family, or another person with whom you bartered or exchanged time for your own use at another residence uses the property for a combined total of 14 days or more, then the property is deemed as a residence or second home by the IRS rather than an income property, and you must divide expenses based on the number of days you used the property and the time it was rented out at a fair rent.

There are other aspects to proper and full accounting of income and expenses of a second home that only your accountant can provide during the year you file your tax form. The key to getting the maximum benefit from allowable deductions is for you to keep copious records of dates the property was used, who used it, and the amount of rent charged (if rented). In an audit, the IRS may ask for a statement from a qualified party to verify the rent you charged to be fair and not below rates for the area. You should build your case in advance by having two or more real estate firms quote you, in writing, the amount of rent (weekly, monthly, and annually) that would be reasonable for the different rental seasons of the year.

Even if you are not allowed to take expense deductions or to apply a loss against present or future income, keep very detailed records of all expenses and maintain those records for as long as you own the property. It is possible, under certain situations, that you can deduct these expenses from your profit at the time of a sale.

60. What Are the Eight Major Pitfalls of Owning Vacation Property?

Every vacation homeowner has or will experience most of the following eight pitfalls of owning vacation property.

The Eight Major Pitfalls of Owning Vacation Property

Location

Keeping up with the maintenance

Absentee management of rental use

Long-distance problem solving

Undetected crime

Financing

Extra record keeping for tax purposes

Being out of your comfort zone when buying or selling

Your ability to deal with and in some situations avoid the pitfall altogether will be enhanced if you review each in detail.

Location.   The location of the vacation home is the very reason you wanted to own it and is apt to be the very reason you will want to sell it. To some degree this will depend on your attitude about the property and that location. If the area is a part of the country where your family has been going to for years, and you have lots of vacation time and friends who either live or visit the area the same time you do, then you are likely to continue going to that location for a long time. However, many people fall in love with the warm winter sunset from the wraparound balcony and buy the property without realizing they might become bored looking at that sunset night after night when there is nothing else to do.

People buy whole-ownership vacation property thinking that if they owned it they would go there more often. The same rationalization is often given by the owner of a boat, which may end up tied to a slip at a marina, growing sea grass on its bottom.

If you can afford whatever you want to do, then none of this may matter to you, but if you are looking for a good buy and an investment you can use and eventually profit from, then use this following tip: Find a nice property in the area you think you want to own and rent it for 12 months. This will cost you much less than the property you are about to buy and will give you all the time one year can provide to slip away to that vacation hideaway and enjoy your life as you envisioned you would. Also, it will give you time to try out other seasons of the year to see just how well you like them.

If all goes well, then take part of that 12 months and look for a real bargain that will serve your needs and meet your goals for years to come.

Keeping up with the Maintenance.   When you live in a home on a long-term basis you may take for granted the little things that you do to keep the place in good working order and as clean as you like it to be. Add a second home to this scenario and problems start to multiply.

First, during the time you are not there, dust settles everywhere, and while you can cover almost everything with sheets, the floor, walls, tops of counters, edges of frames and door jams, and in general everything not protected by dust covers can accumulate a thick layer of dust, which, for some reason, seems to harden.

That is, it all seems to harden except the dust that has settled on the sheets you have used to cover the furniture. Now you arrive, it is late in the evening, your flight from Chicago was delayed 32 hours and all you can think about is a warm fire in the fireplace and a good night's sleep. You start to pull the dust covers off the sofa, chairs, lamps, etc., and suddenly clouds of dust blossom everywhere. Welcome home!

Oh, this is just the start, too. A winter water pipe that has broken due to an ice blockage floods the house as soon as there is a thaw (the heat from that roaring fire in its hearth). While you sleep, neighbors (who arrived for a weekend visit to their vacation home down the hill from yours) realize that there is a waterfall coming out from under your front door, and that the water has completely flooded their home too.

One tip that will help you survive such problems is to buy a second home that is no more than three hours distant from where you live. Then you can run over there a couple times a month just to do some cleaning and general upkeep maintenance. If that is not possible, then make sure there is an adequate maintenance service available in the area that you can rely on to keep watch over your property and be available to solve any problem that comes up. If the cost for such maintenance is too expensive, then perhaps you really should not buy the second home.

Absentee Management of Rental Use.   Distance may make the heart grow fonder, but when it comes to having a vacation home that you hope to rent out when you are not using it, distance can create some very special problems.

The most critical is that a potential tenant may destroy your property. This does not happen with every tenant, but sooner or later, unless you are very careful, it will happen.

Absentee management of rentals is very difficult, so you will then be forced to use a local rental office. If you get the right one and give them some very strict rules to abide by, then you may have no problems. But remember, when your prospective tenants are on vacation they are less likely to treat the property with tender loving care.

Long-Distance Problem Solving.   This is a two-way street. When you own a vacation home you feel obligated or compelled to spend time there that you might not have spent if you were just off on a holiday. This means that because you are at your vacation home you may have additional problems where you normally live. Distance is the reason for the potential problems, not at which end of the road you are located at any given moment.

Distance problems can be kept to a minimum, of course, by trying to be logical and practical about your purchase. That hideaway on the top of the mountain or on a rocky shoreline on Costa Brava might have taken your breath away and the breathless emotion may have caused you to sign the contract, whereas *reason* would have made you stop and think: "Hey, what am I doing?"

If you cannot live without being in the area and having a second home there, then start looking at each of the pitfalls listed here and find the solutions to them, or find a property that does not have such a high probability of potential problems.

Undetected Crime.   There is a criminal element that loves vacation time for two reasons. When you are on vacation you are not at home, and when you are at home your vacation place is empty. These criminals have the best of all worlds—because they constantly travel in the off season, they can get two shots at you for the price of one.

Becoming a victim of burglary is not the end of the world. It can happen when you are sleeping or going out to a movie. The problem, however, is that you might not know about the criminal act until you arrive, say, at midnight after driving 44 hours straight in heavy snow, on icy roads, to find that every stick of furniture as well as the central heating unit has been removed. This can be an economic blow as well as an inconvenience.

Security becomes a major factor that you should consider when buying a second home. Alarms may not be enough, however, so strong door locks, storm and burglar-preventative shutters or decorative bars may be necessary. The best solution is to buy property in a secure community, such as the twentieth floor of a condominium with 24-hour doormen and roving armed guards with attack dogs.

Financing.   One of the most difficult residential investments to finance is the second home. Because of this you may be required to put more cash down than you might be comfortable doing or look around for that seller so desperate to sell (they are going through all of these eight pitfalls) that they will hold soft paper with easy payback terms and take a low down payment.

When you buy you should take out insurance that you too may want to sell this property, sooner than you think. This insurance is to make sure that any mortgage you assume or take out when you buy will be assumable by a prospective buyer when you sell. Otherwise, you might find that to sell you have to reduce or worse, pay off the existing mortgage you owe just to entice a buyer.

Extra Record Keeping for Tax Purposes.   Any property you own adds to your own administrative process. Not only will you need to keep copious records to get the maximum benefits from the IRS, you will have to keep track of those monthly expenses that must be tended to: mortgage payments, association fees, management costs, light, water and phone bills, annual taxes, etc.

A tip that will make record keeping easier is as follows. First, have a record book where you can keep notes on every obligation, expense, payment of income, etc., that pertains to that property. If you have several other properties, either keep separate record books or have a journal with dividers to separate each property. Second, on the first page of the journal make a list of every reoccurring expense for that property. Be sure to record the usual payment due dates, amount owed, account numbers, names of persons and address to mail the payment to, and their phone numbers. Write this *in pencil*, because this information is apt to change over a period of time. Third, have a large master calendar for the year—one with a full page for each month with squares for each day that are big enough for you to make notes of those and other obligations. In addition to being a reminder of what you need to do at a quick glance, such planning enables you to free up brain cells for more productive things than worrying about meeting deadlines.

Being out of Your Comfort Zone When Buying or Selling. This is the worst pitfall of them all—making an investment of something you know nothing about. For example, I have seen people come to Florida who are accustomed to prices in New York City and pay far more than they should for a second home, simply because their point of view of value was based on what they knew—New York City—and not the actual market in Florida.

It can happen to anyone, and I have been tempted by what I thought were bargains in foreign countries or in other cities in the United States by looking at prices that were one-half or one-quarter of what the same kind of property would bring if it were in my own backyard, within my comfort zone.

Any prospective buyer can do the necessary homework to create a comfort zone in any location in the world. However, this takes time and effort, which most people do not want to spend when they are on a holiday.

61. What Is the Most Important Thing to Know before I *Buy* a Vacation Property?

When you start looking for a vacation home, there is one question that you should write in big bold print on a 5 × 7 inch card. Every time you see a place you might consider, pull this card out and read it very slowly out loud: *Do I really want to live here?*

Play the devil's advocate with yourself and push for a detailed explanation to any positive reply you might give to that question. Think about the pitfalls mentioned in question number 60, and try to dissuade yourself from buying. If you survive this test and buy, well, at least you have done so with your eyes open.

62. What Are the Most Important Factors When Renting out My Vacation Property?

The following factors can make the difference between a well-operated rental program and constant worry. As any property manager will attest to, the real key to a well-maintained rental property of any kind will be the kind of tenants you cater to. When it comes to vacation properties, this can be very important because of the attitude that often prevails when people are on holiday. I call it the "take the hotel towel, ashtray, and television home with you" syndrome. Do not let that problem become yours.

The Six Most Important Factors When You Rent out Your Vacation Home

Know the tenants

Have strict rules about occupancy and enforce them

Get a sufficient damage deposit

Check inventory before and after

Check utilities before and after

Check for damage before and after

As with any list there may be something unique about your property that should also be on your list. I can think of several items that might apply to some situations, such as being sure that storm shutters are put up in storm areas. However, these six factors will take care of most situations, and they are discussed in detail below.

Know the Tenants.   I do not mean you should just know their name, but make sure you have copies of picture identification, home addresses, their home and office phone numbers, names of references, type of car (if it is owned and not rented), auto license, and so on. The more data you get and the earlier you get it, the better equipped you are to do some homework and check to make sure you know who these people really are. One simple but comprehensive rental application plus different identification cards placed face down on a copy machine can give you everything you need.

I know some property owners that will let anyone rent their property as long as the tenant pays a rather expensive security deposit. Keep in mind that it will be impossible for you to charge anyone sufficiently to make up for the damage they can do. Even a grandiose deposit for damages will not compensate you for what *could* happen. For example, when the renters head back to Jiddah, Saudi Arabia and they have left your mountain cabin empty of furniture and the central heat turned to 110 degrees with all the windows open and no one will be there for two months, you will understand what I mean.

Have Strict Rules about Occupancy and Enforce Them.   A list of your rental rules and regulations should be given to the prospective tenants prior to their arrival, with the understanding that if they do not like them or feel that the rules are restrictive, then they need to either discuss the problem with you or make other arrangements. It might be possible to bend one or two rules slightly for the perfect tenant, but by maintaining strict rules you may actually attract other people who respect what you are doing.

What goes into the rules and regulations? The first and most important is the actual rental contract. That agreement should be properly designed to protect you to the maximum. Do not use one of those "standard rental forms" you can buy in an office supply store. Those forms are too evenly balanced between the tenant and the landlord to serve your needs to obtain the maximum benefit. Get a good one from your lawyer or at least from the rental management company you may use. Be sure you understand everything in that contract, because even if you do not sign it yourself, your management company may bind you to any agreement they execute in your behalf.

Once you fully comprehend the rental contract you can start to list any rules that are imposed by others on you, such as association regulations or condominium rules. After that, the best rules you can impose will regulate the following: total occupancy; pets; smoking; cooling and heating temperature; use of phone; check-in and -out times; security deposit conditions; your rights to inspect with reasonable but short notice, or at specific times and dates predetermined; use of facilities; off-limit rooms or closets (if any, keep them locked if possible); and whatever you feel is important to you.

However, it may be difficult to enforce your rules. After all, you might be 5000 miles away and totally dependent on local management. Regardless of how you operate your lease program or how well you know the people who are renting your property, make sure you have someone who can do the check-in and -out procedures. It is an unfortunate fact that some of the worst offenders of your rules and regulations may be your "friends," because they will assume that those rules are not for them but for people you do not know.

Get a Sufficient Damage Deposit.   *Sufficient* is a relative word in this situation. As has already been mentioned, it will be impossible for you to get a deposit that will cover any possible loss. There is a limit to the amount you can effectively charge someone and keep them as a tenant. One way to soften the security charge impact and increase your security is to get some money up front in addition to rent, then have the tenants sign a credit card slip, which you properly validate and then hold pending any damage. Rental car companies do this, and many rental management companies have the facilities and arrangements with major credit card companies to accommodate this service. A very good rental contract is essential to cover all the obligations the tenant has in the event of damage to any of your property or loss of items they previously checked off during check-in as being part of the inventory.

Check Inventory Before and After.   Everything that is available for tenants to put their hands on, from the teaspoons to the television set, should be listed on the inventory checklist. You will expect these items to be left in like condition when the tenants check out.

This is usually the most lax of all management obligations, and you should stress this as critical. You can go so far as to pass the obligation for replacement of stolen or missing items onto the management company if they did not follow the procedures of check-in and -out properly. Nonetheless, things will disappear anyway, but at least you will have some way of tracking down blame, and you will have an opportunity to deduct the cost from the damage deposit or take legal action if needed.

As a part of the check-in procedure, it is important that tenants sign a statement that they have checked the inventory list against the actual inventory in the property and verified that everything listed is there and working or listed what is missing or not working. From that moment on tenants can and should be held responsible for missing or broken items.

Check Utilities Before and After. Did someone leave water running or the heat on? This might seem to be overly simple, but a full checklist of all the things that someone should check both before tenants arrive and after they leave is essential. After all, airline pilots who take off and land hundreds of times a month still go through a checklist every time they pilot an aircraft.

In addition to the logical questions, "Did they leave the pot of water boiling?," or "Is there propane gas in the tank outside?," make sure that unauthorized phone calls have not been made. This might be difficult if there is no way to control the phone usage until you get the phone bill several months later. If you do not want to restrict the phone use completely, and you cannot do so through equipment controls, then be sure that your rental contract allows you to charge the tenant for any phone calls made during the period of their occupancy. Phone bills usually show the exact time and date of any long-distance phone call, so having the tenant record the exact time they check in and out will give you an opportunity to collect for such charges.

If you rent your vacation home on a regular basis, you may want to invest in a phone system that can be coded not to allow phone calls that begin with 1 or 0. If your apartment or villa is part of a complex there may be a way to have all the outgoing phone calls channeled through a central operator.

Check for Damage Before and After. This is another very important check that should be a regular procedure. Many property managers may overlook the check-in procedure, feeling that if the property was okay when the last tenant checked out, then why bother checking for damage when the next tenant checks in? The reason why is because the cleaning team, a repair person, or someone sent to check something else might have caused damage.

63. What Is a *Time-Share* Vacation Resort and How Does It Work?

The development of time-share vacation properties is one of the fastest growing kinds of real estate properties. A time-share, interval ownership, or vacation time (three names for the same thing) usually consists of a resort-style property that is made up of apartments, villas, hotel rooms, or a combination of all three. The form of ownership can vary from outright ownership 100 percent of the time (with or without limitations of the owner's personal use) to ownership of a specific week of the year called *the interval* or a nonspecific week of the year, called *floating time*.

Some vacation time resorts are set up so you do not actually own the real estate but have a lease-hold interest for a specific period of time, say 30 years. Others located in some foreign countries may have other kinds of ownership less common to those in the United States.

Most of the vacation time resorts are members of one of the two exchange associations that have made time-share ownership a truly interesting phenomenon. The largest of such organizations is Resorts Condominiums International (RCI), and the other major company is Interval International (II). Each of these organizations provides time-share developers with the opportunity to participate within their system. Each has high standards that the associations insist the developer or the resort management maintain. If the resort does not keep those standards in force, then it is dropped from membership. This has major consequences for the property and other members of RCI. When a resort is a member of RCI or II its time-share owners, who are members of the appropriate association, can deposit their time into a space-bank operated by the association. This allows any other member of that organization to swap into the unit. This format of vacation ownership allows the owner of one vacation time condominium to go to any of the thousands of locations around the world, paying only the modest administration fee.

When you purchase a one-week period of time in a resort, for example in Orlando, Florida, that time period may be a set week of each year. As most check-in days are Saturday, the ownership may be recorded as week 27 of unit 216 of Orlando International Resort. Week 27 would begin the 27th Saturday of that specific year.

As the Orlando International Resort is a member of RCI, if you also joined that organization you would be able to deposit your vacation time in the RCI space-bank. This would allow you to draw against your banked time by making an exchange into available resorts around the world. According to RCI their current fee is $89 for an exchange from a U.S. property to another U.S. resort. International exchanges through the space-bank cost $119. A new service they have does not require you to bank your time (you can use it *and* get another vacation). The RCI Great Escapes program can get you a confirmed week in many selected resorts within the system for $219 if booked 61 days to a year in advance. Another program, called RCI Last-Minute Escapes, must be booked within 2 to 60 days of the check-in time, and only costs $179 per week. Bonuses allow extra weeks for the regular charge and in some areas of the world allow two weeks for every one week you bank.

The time-share industry has taken much criticism for many years due to the investigation of dishonest developers. Most states have very strict marketing laws that govern the sale of time-share resort properties, and in general the concept is a good one.

There are many pitfalls, however, that a prospective buyer should be wary of. The following are three of the most important:

The Top Three Time-Share Pitfalls

Inability to say "no"

Fees too costly

Resale problems

Inability to Say "No."   There is a saying in the time-share business that no one ever wakes up in the morning and says, "Today I am going to buy a time-share apartment." Sales are made in the millions of dollars each week across the country to people who are glamorized and emotionalized into buying, but virtually none of them thought they were going to buy anything that day. The salesperson does not have to be smooth or overly slick, as many are not and yet they still produce large sales. What works is the technique, the sales pitch, the beauty of the product, and the idea of a life style of traveling around the world where you can stay in beautiful accommodations that are deluxe apartments for the cost of a small hotel room. Time-share vacation units are a very good example of the "sizzle" being the key. If you are a salesperson or want to learn a lot about selling, visit a time-share resort and pretend to be a prospective buyer (but be careful, you might end up being one).

Fees Too Costly.   Paying too much for a week is a frequent argument of owners who start to add up what the total cost is at the end of the year. It is possible to pay as much as $30,000 for a week, although that would be rare, and have an annual charge (for your one week) of $400 or more by the time you take into consideration your RCI or II membership. This might sound like a lot of money, but that cost must be balanced against all the benefits that *you could* take advantage of. As for overpaying when you buy, this will happen in any real estate if you do not shop around. There are bargains in the time-share market if you look for them.

Resale Problems.   Problems in resale do occur with many resorts. This happens for several reasons, and if you are careful you can limit your risk of experiencing this pitfall. First, take a look at the size of the project. If it is a very large complex, which would be any resort with 100 units or more, then the developer can have control of the market for that facility for a long time. There will be little opportunity for resale anywhere near your purchase price until the developer is out of the project. However, if you are creative you can attempt to get a good price if you want to sell even while the developer is still around by offering your available week to other owners who own the week just prior or just after your week. This is called *double loading*, and a happy owner may want to increase his or her vacation time at that resort by another week. I have sold some of my weeks at very good prices in this manner.

National newspapers such as *USA Today* and *The Wall Street Journal* often display advertisements from marketing companies that resell vacation time resort weeks or that represent lender foreclosure sales of this time. Often these are prime sources for buying an inexpensive week that will allow you access to the entire space-bank system. Keys to look for are the following.

Is it RCI approved? While Interval International is not a bad second choice, it is still in my opinion a second choice. If you are bargain hunting, stick with RCI properties.

Stick with "red time." Red time is the code for prime season at the resort and when you plan to use the space-bank system you will find that in a normal long-advance reservation exchange (one you plan for usually three or more months in advance) you can exchange down to a less active season of the year, but you cannot exchange up. Keep with red time.

Watch out for high maintenance charges. It is not uncommon for a vacation time resort to have an annual charge for maintenance and taxes of over $400 per week. Your key is to find a resort that meets all the requirements of these tips and will not cost you over $300 per year *including taxes, maintenance, and your annual RCI dues.*

Pick units that sleep a minimum of four. The number of people the facility will sleep is also part of the space-bank exchange criteria. Both the color code and the number of people the unit will sleep affect the long-range reservations, so this aspect can be very important. With a long-range swap you can exchange down to a smaller unit, but you can rarely exchange up to a larger unit. A unit that sleeps four would usually be a one-bedroom apartment with a living room that would convert to a sleeping room for two people. A unit that sleeps four *in privacy* would have two distinct sleeping areas and may actually accommodate a total of six. Because you are going for the bargain, price the units that sleep the most *in privacy*. If there is little difference in price, go for the larger unit.

Do not pay the price the seller asks. Negotiate, negotiate, negotiate. You will find a seller willing to meet a reasonable offer sooner or later.

Whenever possible buy directly from the owner. Look in local newspapers. Keep in mind that if you want to own a unit in Orlando, then look in an Orlando newspaper. If the owner still owes on the purchase mortgage, then you might make a deal just to take over the debt. If you do, make sure that you get a letter from the lender stating the exact amount owed that might include all past interest, maintenance charges, and taxes. This may be a small deal, but there is no reason you should be lax about checking title.

When you buy, make sure the future time has not been traded in the space-bank and already slotted to someone else. Because the owner could have banked his or her advance time, and as that time might already be taken in exchange by another RCI member, your ownership of the week would not give you that time back. By knowing the owner's name, RCI account number, and the legal description of the vacation time unit, you can call RCI and find out the status of the future time.

Resorts Condominiums International (RCI) can be reached by phone at (317) 876-8899. Interval International (II) can be reached by phone at (305) 666-1861.

64. What Are the Advantages and Disadvantages of Time-Shares?

When discussing the advantages and disadvantages of time-share vacation resorts, it is important that you compare apples to apples. When you own your vacation home, you may use it only for a very limited time of the year. However, you pay for that facility 100 percent of the time and generally have a substantial sum of money tied up in the real estate. You can rent it out of course, but that presents many problems, and when you do want to use it, you have to go to that location, whether you like it or not.

Time-shares have taken much of the sting out of vacation ownership. Now you need only own the time you want, and in fact, if you use some of the special programs such as space-banking and bonus weeks, you are not limited to either a specific time or location. The world can indeed be yours.

I would not be the person to tell you not to buy a time-share vacation resort apartment, because I own a dozen of them myself. However, what I will tell you is do not buy one without shopping around, and then buy to fit your needs rather than your emotions.

For example, I own five weeks at the Orlando International Resort. It is a nice facility, but in the 10 years or more of my ownership, I have only used them a total of four times. Is that a bad deal for me? Not at all. I space-bank most of them, and because Orlando is one of the most requested areas in time-share locations, my banked weeks are taken by another member almost as soon as my weeks are listed in the database. This in turn gives me a computer-calculated advantage over people who own time-share weeks in remote parts of the world or in nice areas during tornado season. If the owner of a resort in Tierra Del Fuego (at the tip of South America) for a week in July makes a request the same day I do for a resort in San Francisco, I will get it and the other owner will not.

My weeks have cost me anywhere from $4,000 to $8,000 for the week. By using the space-bank exchange I have traveled around the world and have stayed in resorts where the weeks may have cost as much as $30,000 per week. The key then is to own a week that will allow you to maximize the space-bank system rather than pay top dollar for a location you will rarely visit.

65. What Can I Do to Increase the Value of My Vacation Property?

Landscape according to the area

Enhance "fun areas"

Start with or convert to maintenance-free living

Provide quality in relaxation zones

Do preventative maintenance—and keep it up

Plan for an eventual sale

Landscape According to the Area. Proper landscaping can be the single most effective dollar spent to increase the value of any residence. When your vacation property has land and grounds that you have control over, contact a local landscaper and go over a 10-year plan to turn your already nice property into a magnificent example of local landscaping. It need not be expensive, and as you only visit the home during vacation time, your own enjoyment will be increased because the plants will grow and surprise you between visits. Keep in mind the reason you wanted to live in the area, and use your landscaping to reinforce those attributes you like. Local fruits, nut trees, flowers, and pines all add to the natural magnificence of the region. This carefully planned beautification will reap profits when it is time to sell.

Enhance "Fun Areas."   Add to your property as you go, and one of the best returns to your investment will be enhanced recreational or enjoyment areas of the property. Build new decks or expand existing ones to watch the mountain or beach sunsets. Recreation rooms, improved family room facilities, and the like are important because this is a vacation home, and should be enjoyed.

Start with or Convert to Maintenance-Free Living.   Remove carpets, or if building, do not install carpets; instead, put down tile or hardwood floors or other kinds of flooring that fit the area and will last as long as the home, with little maintenance. Think of long-term upkeep because it will pay off with big dividends when you sell, or while you own the home, it give you added time to enjoy the area.

Provide Quality in Relaxation Zones.   Start with the master bedroom. Does it have a great view? Is it soundproofed from the rest of the house? Does it have a large, very comfortable bed? Is there much closet space? The kitchen should be a relaxation zone too. Many vacation properties skimp on space in the kitchen with the rationalization that because this is a vacation home, no one is going to spend much time in the kitchen. That may or not be the case for you (not in mine) but a well-planned kitchen is a selling tool. It can be compact and may not need all the conveniences of home, but it is best to plan space for those appliances you may find you miss the most.

   Planning for a new property or remodeling an old one is fun, if you let it be, but it is critical to think of these relaxation zones.

Do Preventative Maintenance—and Keep It Up.   Preventative maintenance that is performed on a regular basis will save you a lot of money over the years and will show to any prospective buyer that you are an owner who takes pride in real estate ownership.

Plan for an Eventual Sale.   Even before you purchase the property you should take into consideration the possibility of a future sale. Talk to your lawyer and accountant to make sure that your timing on the purchase and the method of taking title are best for you now and at the time of a future sale. Do this even though you may not have a sale in mind.

66. How Can I *Syndicate* My Own Vacation Property?

Begin with the idea that you will find a property that *you* would like to own and spend time at for a long time to come. Add to that the concept that you can sell rights of time to other investors or friends so that together you all get the benefits of having a second home, and the cost is shared over several owners. The end result is a type of time-share property but with many advantages and some disadvantages. We will look at both situations once you see how to syndicate your own vacation property.

Nine Steps to Syndicating Your Own Vacation Property

Obtain an option on the property

Show a solid management program

Have strict rules and regulations

Show how the rules will be enforced

Have a method of flexible use

Demonstrate the solid value of the deal

Have the answers to all possible questions

Give the "buyer" a short option to accept or reject

Have "buy out" provisions

Obtain an Option on The Property.   Never attempt to syndicate any real estate until you have gone to contract on it. This does not mean you have to buy it, only make sure you have a good option for a long enough time to ensure you can put your syndicate together.

Show a Solid Management Program.   Local management should be found to look after the property because you and the other owners will be absentee owners. Know the cost for that service, and what the management expects you to commit to for a long-term agreement. Be sure to have copies of the management agreement already signed and executed by the company. This will ensure that there are no last minute changes in the fee structure.

Have Strict Rules and Regulations.   If you want only nonsmokers, then make sure this is in the rules you write. I have found that if the rules are strict you will actually appeal to more people than not. But make sure you can back up the rules with enforcement.

Show How the Rules Will Be Enforced.   You have a right to take away the use of time if payments are not made as each member is obligated. If the payments are not met within a specific period of time, then the time-share will be revoked. Again, the stronger you make enforcement of nonpayment, the better reliable members will like it.

Have a Method of Flexible Use.   If you sell only the off season and want to keep the best time for yourself, you may have some real difficulty in selling. It is better to have a flexible system that guarantees certain time on a rotational basis and then allows the members to reserve in advance, on a first-come basis for future weeks. This could be done a year or two ahead, and each member could then trade among themselves or rent out their time if they wanted (and if the rules allowed rentals).

Demonstrate the Solid Value of the Deal. This means you should know what a commercial vacation time (time-share) resort is selling for and what their annual charges are. If you can offer twice the space for one-quarter the price (you should be able to do that easily), then you can offer a friend a real bargain you would not be embarrassed to sell them.

Have the Answers to All Possible Questions. Sit at both sides of the table and ask the hardest questions you can, then get the answers to them. Become well informed about the location, too, e.g., where Puerta Vallarta is, what you can do there, what makes that part of Mexico so interesting, etc.

Give the "Buyer" a Short Option to Accept or Reject. Because you now have absolute control over the property, you can go to a prospective buyer and say, "I've acquired this beachfront villa in Puerta Vallarta. Not only did I get a good buy, but everything indicates that the value is going to go up tremendously. I have structured a package that will allow 10 additional owners to join me in ownership of this four-bedroom villa, for a total investment of $30,000 each and an annual fee of $1,000. This would give you the rights to four weeks holiday at the villa for you and your family and friends. I've checked the area very carefully and a villa like this rents for over $2,500 per week in the season, and everyone is guaranteed to have two weeks in the high season. There are only 10 slots open. Take this videotape I made a few weeks ago when I was there last and feel free to ask me any questions not answered in the information in this folder. Please let me know if you want one or two of the shares by this time next week, okay?"

Have "Buy Out" Provisions. This is all part of the control you want to have. Build in a price at which you can "take out" any of the investors. It should be a price that would allow them to make a profit but let you stay in control over the situation. All buy–sell provisions should also contain a clause that would require anyone who wants to sell their interest in the facility to first offer that share to the remaining members on a prorated basis. For example, if there were 10 owners and each had an equal share, and one of them wanted to sell, each of the remaining 9 could pick up $1/9$: of the seller's interest or more, providing that collectively the remaining 9 acquired 100 percent of the seller's interest. You might bid, for example, for $4/9$ of the interest, and everyone else might make similar bids; an obvious overbid would require the divisions of the share being sold to be split up in an equal ratio between the remaining members who want to buy more.

67. How Can I Get the Most for My Money When I Sell My Vacation Property?

In addition to rereading this entire chapter, especially the answers to question number 60, there seven great tips that can help put you on the road to success in selling your vacation home.

Seven Tips to Help You Sell Your Vacation Home

Tip 1. *Be ready to sell during the prime season.*   Many sellers overlook the fact that the prime holiday time for that area is when emotions are highest and it is easier to sell the benefits of your property to prospective buyers.

Tip 2. *Make sure the agents sell the "sizzle."*   Selling a vacation property is easier when all the sizzle is stressed. One of the problems that occurs is that the local real estate agent is apt to be a year-round resident of the community and may take many of the qualities that bring the vacationer to the area for granted. As owner of the property be sure your agent has not forgotten what it was that made you fall in love with the property.

Tip 3. *Leave a "fun time" photo album open for buyers to see.*   This is a simple but very effective tool—photos of you and your family having the time of your life in the home and enjoying the area.

Tip 4. *Clean, clean, clean.*   Because dust can accumulate quickly when a property is not occupied, make sure that the place is kept spotless even when you are not around. As long as there is a chance a prospective buyer will want to inspect the property, have someone keep up with regular cleaning. You do not want to leave the furniture covered with sheets.

Tip 5. *"Good memory" smells entice buyers.*   Be sure the agent brews coffee, or even puts some apple popovers in the oven just before the prospective buyer arrives.

Tip 6. *Have absentee management lined up.*   Even though you did not need management, keep in mind that prospective buyers might. Make sure your agent has several management firms (in addition to his or her own, if appropriate) take a look at the property, give an opinion of what the accommodations would rent for, and specify the management fee agreement they would require.

Tip 7. *Be creative in helping a buyer finance your property.* If you are following a sound plan, the sale of this property should be moving you closer to your goal. Have you reviewed all your options to get you to your goal? Could you lease with an option? Would you be in a position to hold a first or second mortgage for a long period of time? Would you consider an exchange for all or part of your equity? A positive answer to these questions will start you on the way to being creative in financing the sale.

8

Questions That
Every Senior Citizen
Needs Answered

68. Why Should a Senior Citizen Look at Real Estate Ownership Differently than a Younger Person?

Real estate ownership should be goal oriented. In other words, real estate should be acquired and kept only to attain or advance the investor toward a desired goal. As goals should be constantly reviewed and adjusted, it is logical that as a person matures, lifetime goals for many people will eventually level off or at least take a different direction than when growth of assets and wealth may have been more important.

In the youthful years of real estate investment, elements such as risk and sweat equity apply at completely different levels of importance to the senior real estate investor, whose thoughts dwell more on good health and the maintenance and enjoyment of assets attained rather than expansion of wealth and holdings. Naturally there are senior citizens who go to their grave with a purchase contract for another shopping center clenched in their hands, and for these people this chapter has yet to apply.

If you are a senior citizen your primary concerns should be focused on the following items and how they apply to your estate.

Tax

Inheritance

Lifetime goals

It is recommended that all investors anticipate the date when they will be honored to be senior real estate owners; they should seek advice early about the right form of ownership to fit their needs and goals.

69. How Much Can Retired Senior Citizens Afford to Pay for Their Housing?

A good rule of thumb that works for anyone would be that your housing cost should not exceed 25 percent of the total income available. There are several elements that would cause a different percentage to apply, such as the following.

Extraordinary expenses that create extra burden on the available income. Often it is possible to insure against this kind of expense, and every person approaching retirement should have supplemental insurance when it can be afforded.

Retirement home living can consume a greater share of available income because it usually includes other costs that would not be associated with living in your own home. A-full care facility can, of course, require the majority of a person's income.

Debt service on existing property can continue to drain income until the property is paid off. One good retirement plan is to schedule your mortgages to be paid off prior to your retirement. Having a free and clear home can be a good nest egg and hedge against future extraordinary expenses. There is a mortgage program that allows seniors to borrow against their equity and receive a monthly payment over a period of time. This reverse mortgage allows the total loan to build up to a fixed or adjusted (upward as values rise) amount and in reality to be paid off after the death of the owner from the sale of the property. Personally I do not recommend this kind of loan as a planning tool because loan policy can change overnight and that kind of loan may not always be around. However, if you need to use it, and it exists, shop around because it is likely that a wide range of terms is offered by different lenders.

70. What Are Some of the *Options* of Ownership That Senior Citizens Should Be Aware of for Their Housing?

The first option to consider would be *not* to own at all. This concept has been discussed in the answer to question number 13, and a review of all of Chapter 3 may be a good idea if there is a chance that your option may lean toward renting rather than owning. The other primary options of ownership are the following.

Gift title to others (heirs) and retain a life estate

Gift title to your spouse

Put title in the name of a corporation (with or without a lease back)

Hold title jointly with spouse

Hold title in your own name only

Exchange title for a life residency in a retirement living facility

Before you do any of the above make sure you have discussed your plans with both your lawyer and your accountant. Each decision can have a different consequence depending on your present or future estate and the goals you want to accomplish. Because this matter is absolutely unique to your own situation, to provide every answer for every scenario is subject matter for a separate book that would be larger than this one.

71. How Can Senior Citizens Reduce Their Annual Housing Cost?

The first step to any plan is to review the current situation and options that are available. This means that a total picture has to be looked at before any decision should be contemplated. There are five major areas to review:

Fixed income that will not change

Income subject to change

Fixed expenses

Expenses subject to change

Benefits available

The first four are self-explanatory. Income and expenses are the critical factor, because if the expenses exceed the income, then you are already in trouble. If that were to be the case, something must be done to produce income, reduce expenses, or devise a combination of both to attain a positive end result.

Possible available benefits are usually overlooked as an avenue toward other options, and these need to be studied on a case-by-case basis as applied to your unique situation.

For example, if you have not used the one-time $125,000 capital gains exclusion allowed by the IRS, then at your retirement you may want to take advantage of moving your equity into a smaller and less expensive property. This provision allows you to keep a total of $125,000 of any gain on the one-time sale of a residence. The funds you have left over after acquiring another property can then be invested in some other property or put into savings. Or you may take this opportunity to achieve a lifelong goal to buy a country inn in Vermont and retire to a new career.

The basic rules of this IRS provision are as follows: Any taxpayer who is 55 or older and has lived in a residence for a minimum of three years out of the last five years can qualify. At the age of 65 or older, the residence test is any five years out of the past eight. In either case, the number of years of residency do not have to be consecutive.

Other benefits that may be available can include a Veterans Administration

(VA) loan entitlement that you may have forgotten you had coming to you or that you never knew you had. You might sell your present property and buy another property with this low interest rate loan available through the VA.

Homestead exemption provisions, when they apply to your state, may reduce the annual taxes of property you own substantially so that the savings can make a difference in the standard of your life-style. This benefit is lost by many people because either they do not know about the laws or they have not properly filed to take advantage of them. This is a factor that may change your thoughts about giving actual ownership of a property to another person, because to qualify for a homestead exemption to tax you must be the owner and have occupancy as of the first of the taxable year.

72. What Is the Single Most Important *Estate* Factor a Senior Citizen Should Take into Consideration?

In seeking council from lawyers and accountants for my own estate, I have heard everything from planning for future tax consequences to making sure that my heirs have the least problems possible. My lawyers argue that my will needs to be letter perfect, my insurance just the right amount or more, and that every "i" be dotted and every "t" be crossed. My accountant insists that dealing with the IRS should be considered in every possible detail and that state laws are critical as well. The location of my residence is information both my lawyer and accountant want to know in case a state where I own a time-share suddenly decides that my multibillion dollar estate (who knows what it will be in the future) belongs to North Carolina instead of Florida, where I live.

All of this is important, but the most important item has not been discussed yet.

The single most important *estate* factor a senior citizen should take into consideration is *whether or not their estate will take care of their own and their spouse's expenses in their retirement years*.

Once that question has been answered properly and planned for, then the other important needs can be dealt with (such as a continuing income for family members dependent on the estate, as would be the case of children or relatives who are handicapped or cannot provide for themselves for whatever reason). All those things the lawyers, accountants, and insurance agents harp on are also important, but come next in line.

73. What Is the Best Way for a Senior to Transfer Ownership of Real Estate to Reduce or Eliminate Estate Taxes?

The two best ways in which property can be transferred to reduce or eliminate future estate tax are as follows:

Transfers by gift

Transfers by exchange

You should keep in mind that state laws may vary, so if you live in one state and your gift or exchange property is in another, make sure you know the specific laws and how they may affect your intended plan. A long-range plan is helpful in establishing a pattern that will be easier to follow and easier to enable your advisors to best assist you to maximize your future benefits in balance to present counterbalances.

Transfers by Gift.   The IRS allows you to make an annual year-end gift tax exclusion of $10,000 per person you gift to. This means that a husband and wife can make a combined gift of $20,000 to any individual without incurring any federal gift tax. This gift does not have to be cash; it can be an interest of ownership worth that sum.

Estate planning requires accurate up-to-date information on the tax laws, and it is important to know that estate taxes are one of the areas that frequently come under attack. In 1992 the Democratic-controlled Congress floated a bill to reduce the gift and estate tax exemption from $600,000 to $200,000, and while it was not passed, this kind of legislation could appear in the future as Congress searches for more tax revenue.

If you make a gift of a property you "need" to live in, then make sure that you retain a life estate or long-term lease to accomplish that need.

Transfers by Exchange.   IRS Section 1034 allows a property owner to "sell" or "exchange" their home, and if they acquire another within a prescribed time limit and meet the IRS rules, there may be no capital gains tax to pay. The use of Section 1034 and the one-time gains exclusion of $125,000 can be combined to shelter possible gain.

Section 1034 enables a property owner to exchange (or sell and then purchase) one residence for another and in so doing avoid or reduce a capital gains tax on the first property. To understand how this works there are several terms that need to be explained.

New residence: This is the new property that you claim to be your replacement residence. It is possible to own this property prior to the sale of your old residence, as you will see.

Old residence: This is the property that you plan to (or have already) sell, exchange, or otherwise dispose of, which was used by you as your primary residence at the time you made the election to establish a new residence (either into a property you already own or one you plan to buy or exchange into). Both the new and old residences can be any type of legal residence—including a houseboat, house trailer, manufactured home, a home, apartment, condominium, or stock in a cooperative apartment that contains living quarters.

Adjusted sales price: To calculate a gain, should any exist, the sales price should be adjusted to reflect certain expenses incurred that were to aid in the sale of that property. These "fix-up" expenses must meet the following conditions to qualify:

1. They cannot be otherwise deductible in computing taxable income. In essence, repairs, painting, decorating, cleaning, etc., that are not usual deductions from income can be deducted.

2. They cannot be *selling expenses,* such as lawyer's fees to handle the closing.

3. The expenses must have been done during a 90-day period that ended with the date you executed a contract to sell the property (not the date you actually close on the sale and pass title to the buyer).

4. In addition to the above, you can also deduct normal selling expenses as would apply to any real estate transaction.

Sale date: The actual date you deed your old property to the other party. This is not the contract date on which the fix-up expenses are based. The sale date establishes the exact day and year from which you can count a 24-month period before and 24-month period after said date to acquire or shift your residency to another property and still qualify for the Section 1034 exchange.

Time period: With very few exceptions your time period is 24 months before and 24 months after the sale date. Exceptions may apply if you resided outside the United States or are in the U.S. military during any part of this time. To get an accurate explanation of those and other possible exceptions, see your accountant or tax lawyer.

Time and manner of making the election: You make the decision to abide by the Section 1034 ruling in the taxable year you dispose of your old residence.

A detailed form has been provided as a part of the answer to question number 51.

74. How Can Senior Citizens Use the *Installment Sale* to Their Best Benefit?

The installment sale is a provision that allows the seller to postpone tax on a capital gain. The rules to qualify for an installment sale have been greatly simplified over past years, and now all that is required is that the seller receive a portion of the proceeds of the sale in one or more tax years other than the year of the sale.

For example, June and her husband own a strip store that they originally purchased 40 years earlier. At the time of the purchase they divided the asset into land and buildings, giving the land a value at that time of $10,000 with buildings worth $140,000.

Over the past 40 years the buildings have been depreciated to a book value of $0, giving the owners a basis of $5,000 in the property. Along comes a buyer who offers them a fair price of $350,000 net of all sales and closing costs. They want to sell the property because they no longer feel they can manage it and want to reinvest the proceeds into an interest-bearing account or a bond to give them worry-free income.

Problem one: A large capital gains tax to pay. As their basis is only $5,000 (the original land value), they will have a taxable gain of $345,000 and a likely tax of $106,950 (31 percent of the gain). If they sold for all cash they would be left with $243,050 to reinvest.

Problem two: Reinvestment return drops due to tax paid. If they were able to invest in a bond or other moderately secure investment of their gross asset value of $350,000 after costs, an 8 percent return would give them an annual return of $28,000. However, after they pay their tax, they have only $243,050 left, and at 8 percent they now only get $19,684. This is a substantial reduction in their possible retirement income.

Problem solved: Use the installment sale. One method of tax deferment they could use would be the installment sale. Assume that they entered into a deal with a zero down payment and held a first mortgage on their own property that paid them interest only at 9 percent for a period of years, then ballooned (all principal became due and payable) at the end of 15 years. Normally they would not be advised to take a zero down payment deal, but a strong buyer could offer them additional collateral to secure the mortgage.

Using the installment sale here allows the sellers to report capital only when they get it. As the mortgage is interest only, there is *no gain* to be reported until the mortgage is finally paid off.

The interest rate of 9 percent would be reasonable; in fact, it might even be a bargain for the buyer, so the annual payment of $31,500 would be an increase of revenue to the sellers rather than a reduction. If the sellers had followed the advice of a tax planner prior to making the sale, they may have already gifted some of the ownership interest of the property to children or a retirement trust fund, whereby the income might be partially sheltered from income tax.

Keep in mind that there is a great deal of flexibility in mortgage terms and payback dates. This transaction could have taken any of a dozen different paths to solve a dozen slightly different ownership problems.

75. How Can Seniors *Save Money* When They Own or Rent Real Estate?

Maximize deductions allowed to senior citizens by taking advantage of the following seven tips.

Money-Saving Tips for Seniors

Apply for maximum homestead exemptions

Change to free checking

Pay off high constant-payment mortgages

Check for special "senior's only" insurance rates

Get tax advice on *active*, *portfolio*, and *passive* incomes

Shift to income property in a "down" market

Form a management company to manage your own property

Apply for Maximum Homestead Exemptions.   When your state has a homestead exemption law, this allows you to reduce the tax assessment by an amount to determine the final *taxable value*. Most states with homestead exemption allow different amounts to be deducted from the value based on tenure of residency, with extra exemptions for widows and widowers, as well as for certain disabilities.

Change to Free Checking.   Many banks provide seniors with free checking accounts. If you have more than one account, for example, one for each rental property you own, and your bank will give you only one free account, then open an account at another bank or sit down with the president of the bank and get them to approve additional free accounts. Other services the bank offers may also be free, such as money orders, cashier's checks, traveler's checks, and so on. If you are a good client, ask for a free safety box too—even if you do not use one at present. If they give it to you, you will find use for it.

Pay Off High Constant-Payment Mortgages.   Many people overlook the actual cash drain a mortgage causes and look to the contract rate for the interest they pay. Take a 30-year mortgage that is in its final 3-year term. At the time you took out that mortgage the interest rate may have been 7 percent. If the original principal balance was $100,000 and your mortgage payment was based on a full amortization of principal by way of 360 equal monthly payments of principal and interest, the mortgage history would look like this:

Original mortgage loan:	$100,000.00
Interest rate:	7 percent
Monthly payment of principal and interest:	$665.30
Constant annual rate 1st year:	7.984 percent
Owed at the end of the 17th year:	$21,546.80
Constant rate for 18th year:	37 percent

Because the monthly payments for this mortgage will remain the same, $665.30 per month for the entire 30 years, the usual method of principal reduction in most mortgages is weighted to heavy interest payments in the early years, and the principal slowly is paid off. As you can see, with only three years left there is still $21,546.80 outstanding (caution—most calculators will differ slightly in this amount, depending on how many decimals the calculation is carried out; even amortization tables will vary slightly and should not be a concern unless the amounts are more than a few dollars).

The debt payment on the $21,546.80 is $7,983.60 per year. If you had $21,546.80 in savings earning you 6 percent interest (only $1,292.80) and you paid off the mortgage, you would add $6,690.80 in cash flow to your annual income (money you do not have to pay after retiring the mortgage $7,983.60 less the 6 percent income you were getting of $1,292.80 equals $6,690.80).

Check for Special "Senior's Only" Insurance Rates.   Some insurance companies have rates that are good for senior citizens. The only way you can find out about them is to ask your insurance agent, or to become a member of one of the national associations that cater to senior members of the community.

Get Tax Advice on *Active*, Portfolio, and *Passive* Incomes. The IRS has different rules and regulations that govern what and how much you can deduct from these different categories of income. By proper planning you may discover you can shift income into a better category to suit your individual tax needs or obligations. Seek professional advice on all tax matters.

Shift to Income Property in a "Down" Market. Use a "down" real estate market to shift to income property. If you want to sell your residence, for example, but the market is down, then try converting it to an income-producing property. Either rent it out as it is, convert it to something else, such as a professional office complex, or add more units. Later on, when the market improves, you can sell it, or, if you have established another residence in the meantime, and do not need or do not qualify for or have already used the $125,000 gains exemption, ask your accountant if you could qualify for a tax-free exchange under the provision of the IRS Section 1031 exchange.

Form a Management Company to Manage Your Own Property. Having your own corporation can provide you with many advantages. When you legitimately use that company to manage your own properties you can legally use the management fee to cover expenses that you may not get personal deductions for. In addition, your private company may qualify as an S corporation, giving additional benefits to some. It would be a good idea to discuss all of your holdings and income sources with a good tax lawyer to ascertain what kind of corporation you should form, how you should channel income into that company, and how you best can take expenses to maximize your year-end cash flow. One added bonus that may appeal to some taxpayers is that corporations are less likely, I am told by several different certified public accountants (CPAs), to be audited.

76. What Are The Four Best *Insider Tips* That Would Help a Senior Citizen in Ownership of Property?

Know Your Goals and Plan for Them Well in Advance. Everything discussed in this book underscores the importance of goals. The sooner you have them and the quicker you establish a sound plan to attain them, the better off you will be. Remember, it is better late than never, so if you have no discernable goals and no active plan, then start now. A husband and wife team should be able to recite the mutual goals and understand the plan.

Maximize Your Own Lifetime Benefits. Far too many people work all their life building, adding, investing for the future, but never seem to find the time to sit back and enjoy what they have. Do not let life pass you buy without smelling the roses that come before you.

Establish Measures to Maximize Your Surviving Spouse's Benefits. This should be the primary purpose of estate planning, as has been mentioned elsewhere in this chapter. Once that has been taken care of, then other members of the family can be considered as needed. Beyond that, everything else is subject to your own wishes.

Have a Will Drawn by a Tax Lawyer Versed in Estate Planning. Not just any lawyer can advise you properly. There are many very complex matters that go into proper estate planning, and not everything deals with federal tax alone. Each state may have a different application of tax laws that can eat away at your final estate. A final disposition of your assets should be planned well in advance. In many situations your lawyer will want you to set up a trust fund that will administer your estate, and in some circumstances the surviving spouse can be the administrator of that estate. This kind of structure can postpone or save thousands of dollars in tax at the time of the first death. It is essential that you review your will and any trust you have established to implement even the slightest change that may be required to adjust to a new or a changed law.

9

Master Wealth Builder: Buying and Selling Land

77. Why Has *Raw Land* Been the *Millionaire Maker* of the Past, and What Is Its Future?

Many millions of dollars of wealth have been made through the purchase of vacant land. Some of America's most wealthy families have made their fortunes from the thousands of cheap acres they purchased or obtained through land grants. Others have profited by buying farmland that skyrocketed in value as towns grew. While the original purpose of the land might have been to raise cattle or sheep, drill for oil, or grow cotton, it is the land itself that became valuable in the long run.

The natural growth of cities into rural areas, where land that once sold for $100 per acre in the recent past and now goes for $500,000 per acre or more, is not at all uncommon. This kind of growth is well documented and is still possible today.

However, unlike the investment patterns of the past, investing in raw land today can be much more risky. Gone is the "TADAAMABWEIL" method of investing (throw a dart at a map and buy wherever it lands). Today there are more elements of control that govern the use of a property and therefore affect the ultimate value of that property.

However, the fundamentals for the selection of raw land that is destined for growth potential still do apply.

The Key Factors to Value Appreciation of Raw Land

Growing population and demand

Improved infrastructure, making growth easier

Increased spending power building top end buyers

Decline in supply of land available for development

When the above four elements are present, property that is in the path of outward growth from any city will experience an increase in value. The key for an investor to recognize is the proper timing of the investment. The usual mistake made by an investor is to acquire the land too soon, so that growth does not come as soon as the investor anticipated. This factor plus the inability of the investor to generate the needed income from the property itself to carry the property can overwhelm the investor with costs.

It is very possible that the cost to hold onto a future gold mine will be more expensive than the investor can support, which is substantiated by many unfortunate examples.

78. What Are the Key Steps to Buying Raw Land?

The following twelve key steps will aid you in the quest to purchase raw land. All of the information needed to accomplish these twelve steps comes from your local community. You will find that a local real estate broker can be very helpful in providing much if not all of the basic data; however, it is highly recommended that you get involved by attending city and county council meetings and other public meetings that deal with your community and the real estate in it. The idea is to become an insider in the market, and the only way to do that is to meet with other insiders until you become one of them.

The Twelve Key Steps to Buying Raw Land

Plot growth trends

Understand zoning regulations

Recognize use zones

Classify areas demographically

Isolate target areas

Attend planning meetings

Get to know DOT officials

Obtain utility expansion plans

Review historic examples of similar growth

Maintain contacts with lenders

Learn how to rezone property

Prepare your investment team

Review each of these steps and put them into the context of your own situation. You may have already taken care of some of the steps without really knowing it, and once you see the whole picture you will begin to see how everything fits together.

Plot Growth Trends.   Start with a map of the area and go to the county planning office. Ask one of the senior planners to help you plot out the business, industrial, and residential growth of the community over the past 30 years (more or less). The idea is to see how areas have grown and where the upper-income areas of town have established themselves. These are the primary areas where you want to focus your attention.

Understand Zoning Regulations.   Zoning rules and regulations are the most important of all the local restrictions that control use and therefore value. Visit each of the different zoning offices that govern land in the area you are researching. This may require visiting more than one city, and a county office for unincorporated land areas. Get copies of the zoning ordinances and read through them. Make sure you understand each classification of zoning and the differences among the different communities.

   While you are at the zoning department ask if there are any other restrictions that may apply that are unique to the specific area of your interest. It is possible that environmental controls may be even more restrictive than zoning rules, so if the property fronts a lake, river, or ocean, has marshes, endangered plants, or animals, is part of a tidal system, once was a landfill, was or is used for mining minerals or drilling of oil or gas, or has any other such characteristics, then make sure you mark that area with a big red banner: *Warning—Many potential problems exist.*

Recognize Use Zones.   Areas of a community often develop into use zones. Downtown areas, for example, may become mostly office use, with little or no residential activity, even though the zoning may allow it. Suburb areas may be overly heavy in single family homes with little apartment or commercial use even though the zoning may allow it. These patterns may indicate possible profit centers if you can take advantage of an allowable use in an area that is light on that use. The key is to understand why an area was developed for the particular use that exists, even though the zoning of the area was flexible and permitted other uses. You may find that historically the area went through a change, such as a city center area that became so commercialized that residents moved out to the suburbs, and where apartment buildings were slowly torn down and replaced by higher rent office buildings. Sometimes these areas can and should revert back to mixed use to create live-in city centers.

Classify Areas Demographically.   Code your areas to the demographics of the community. Some residential areas will cater to a higher income level property owner than others. When you see growth moving outward from one of these areas you might assume that the demographics of the new area will be equally high or even higher. However, do not assume this without examination of all other factors. The key to good information is to cross-check the data with several different sources. The tax assessor's office can give you information based on property values, whereas the telephone company will have areas broken up into demographics of phone bill charges. The American Express Credit card company segments zip codes into areas as well. By selecting several sources, you end up with a better picture.

Isolate Target Areas.   You need to limit the area of your research as quickly as possible or you will be frustrated in the monumental task of finding the right property to acquire. Try to stick to one set of governmental controls by staying within one city and county rather than several different ones. The key to selection of a target area is to have a general idea of all the possible optional areas first.

Attend Planning Meetings.   Once you know which city and county you plan to invest in, start going to the planning and council meetings. The insiders attend these meetings, and to become one of the insiders you need to attend them too. You will learn more about your own community in two visits than you ever thought possible, both good and bad. Be sure to make notes of all the people you want to meet personally. Start with the mayor and work down. The key to attending public meetings is to obtain an agenda, understand the procedures of the meeting, make notes of the VIPs at the meeting, and take steps to meet them.

Get to Know DOT Officials.   The officials of the local departments of transportation (DOT) are very important because these three departments, state, county, and local, will have the greatest available data on potential property value changes. These departments are found at three levels (state, county, and city); each is critical and each will have a long-range master plan that is available to you. While these master plans are subject to (and frequently do) change, they will provide you with a "reliable" forecasting tool showing areas that will experience improved traffic flow or become open to new traffic. The key to getting to know any official is to maintain contact with that person to ensure that they get to know you. This is a primary step in becoming an insider—the fact that local VIPs recognize you as someone also on the inside.

Obtain Utility Expansion Plans.   The local water, sewer plant, city gas, electric service, cable television, telephone company, and other public works each have a master plan and timetable to ensure that they are ahead of the growth patterns. Because it is difficult to build homes in areas where there is no electricity, the electric company would be the first place to start.

The demand levels of their service that each of the above utilities expect for the future from the different areas of the county or state would be highly useful information for any real estate investor and absolutely indispensable information for the vacant land speculator. The key to obtaining data from utility companies is to request the information in such a way that it appears to have already been offered. For example, contact an official in the company: get the name of one of the top officials, say, the director or the president. Call that person and ask them who would be the best individual to talk to about public relations information and other data that would be helpful for a report you are compiling. Then call the public relations person and tell him or her that the president of the company (or whomever you talked to) asked you to call him or her about the demographic and planning data.

Review Historic Examples of Similar Growth.   Go back to the first step and take a look at the patterns of growth you plotted out. How did the growth occur and what were the results? If you know there is a new airport planned for an area that is nothing but farmland now, then look around and find a community not too far away that had that same event 10 to 20 years ago. Look at how its growth evolved and the change in land values. Be sure to make adjustments for price levels and be aware that some of the mistakes that happened before just might happen again. The key to getting useful historical information is to make every effort to find past events that are as similar as possible to the situation you are studying. This is often very hard to do and may be one of the most difficult of the twelve steps to complete satisfactorily.

Maintain Contacts with Lenders.   It is important for you to know what situations appeal to the lenders and what they will loan money on. Even though you might not be a developer and are only looking at a tract of land as a speculator, you will find that the more you know about the problems a developer goes through, the better you will be at selecting the right property in the first place. Smart developers build what they can finance. The key to dealing with lenders is that they get to know you as an insider who is or may become a prospect for them in the future. This requires you to introduce yourself as a real estate investor looking at the local market to determine if it is a good place for you to invest in. As a potential client, the mortgage broker or banker will supply you with more information than he or she would otherwise.

Learn How to Rezone Property.   The ultimate and maximum profit you get from a vacant tract of land may come only after you change the zoning to a different use. Because value is a function of use, you should begin to become aware of all the steps necessary to effect a zoning change. To accomplish this, you should first make an inquiry at the zoning office about the necessary paperwork. The second step will be to attend several rezoning meetings to get firsthand information about how the professionals do their job. It is both interesting and highly informative. You will meet the people in town that specialize in rezoning and will quickly spot those who are more adept at that task than others. The key to rezoning is to know what "new zoning" is likely to produce an economic conversion of the property to your benefit.

Prepare Your Investment Team.   Your team should include all your partners (your spouse being the most important), a real estate lawyer, a good tax advisor (lawyer or CPA), and one or more real estate agents. All the members should know your goals and be committed to helping you attain them. The key to forming an investment team is to shop around. Find and use people who are compatible with your needs and who understand that you expect them to assist you in the attainment of your goals.

79. When Buying a Vacant Lot, Is It True That *Location, Location, Location* Is the Single Most Important Factor to Consider?

There is a cliché that the single most important aspect of real estate is "location, location, location." The point of the triple play on the word is to stress that real estate is a function of location.

Broadly speaking, this is a definite fact. What happens in Chicago may have absolutely nothing to do with a New York property that has the same exact size, shape, and similar location (the corner of two very busy commercial streets, for example). The final value of each of those two corners will depend on other factors, of which the following four property analysis factors will play a very strong role in an analysis of two or more different properties.

Factors for Analyzing Property

Ultimate use

Ease of access

Desirability of market

Affordable location

These four elements, and others, combine to create a standard that any specific user can follow to determine the value of a site for the user's need. After all, it is logical that one user would have a better use for a particular site than another, and as economics determines the final value, that user would be able to pay more for the site. For the seller of any such site the key to value is often finding that specific user who can pay the most money.

What makes a location an *important location* becomes the real question. To find the answer, look at all the data that determine control over the four property analysis factors. Look at each in detail.

Ultimate Use.   The final use of any property is determined by local zoning rules and regulations and local building restrictions. First, zoning ordinances are laws enacted by the community to control use of land. The purpose of this is to establish a well-distributed community for the development of zones of work, industry, parks and recreation, homes, apartments, and so on. Because this is not an exact science, many communities have made mistakes in their distribution of such zoning, and most cities are undergoing frequent changes in their attitudes about the location and extent of use in city planning.

Every real estate investor should discover the totality of what the zoning rules and regulations are for each of the communities in which they plan to invest. There may be similar sounding zoning names, such as R-2, B-1, I-2, heavy industrial, etc., but each community may assign a different set of rules and regulations to go along with those titles. Never assume that B-1 property in San Francisco is the same zoning as B-1 property in Atlanta.

Building regulations affect use as well, often in a subtler way than specific category of use. For example, you may have narrowed your search for an automobile gasoline and repair station site to two different corner lots, each with a zoning that would allow a gasoline service station to be constructed. However, one of the lots is in a residential area that has a setback requirement for potential fire hazards (and the local laws classify gasoline tanks as such a hazard) from any schools or churches. If one of those corners was within the minimum distance from either a school or church, then even though the zoning allowed the use, the building restriction would prohibit it.

Unless the potential user could obtain a variance to the building rules (by getting the city council or other similar body to grant the use despite the rule against it), one of the two sites would be eliminated automatically from choice.

Other building rules that can affect use are lot line setback rules. Again, two similar corners may have different setback distances that establish the minimum distance a building structure could be erected to a street or lot line. These rules often vary with the street and subdivision and are not uniformly enforced in the same community. Because corners have two or more streets from which buildings must be distanced, even a small difference in setback in the comparison of two different properties can make a big difference in the size of building that is constructed. It is not unusual for corners that are opposite each other to belong to different subdivisions or even different communities. Streets are usually the divisions of communities and subdivisions.

If you were looking for a site to construct your fast food hamburger restaurant, and you found two identically sized lots diagonally across from each other at the intersection of the best two commercial streets in town, you would first want to check the zoning and other building restrictions that may affect your final use. It could be possible that neither of those two will work at all for your need and use.

Ease of Access. Access to a property is more critical for some uses than others. If your business did not depend on actual drive-in or customer access, but you wanted good exposure to advertise your service or product, then a reasonable access for you and your employees may be all that is necessary. However, for more commercial use, such as restaurants, shops, gas stations, and so on, the ease of access for clients becomes one of the most essential factors when establishing value. The best location as far as exposure to traffic may be worthless to a fast food restaurant if traffic cannot turn into the site.

The Department Of Transportation for the local community may consist of three different DOT offices. This is because each of three major levels of government within any state usually has its own Department Of Transportation. The city, the county, and the state DOT offices may all have input on a specific site. When you deal with more than one DOT, usually the higher authority is the governing one. Thus, if you are in a community and your property is on a highway designated as both a county and a state road, the state DOT should govern. However, there are times when, regardless of a higher authority the city DOT will exert the most control over your property. To some degree this is part of political conflict and sometimes all three DOTs will try to obtain different and conflicting concessions from you. Final solutions are often only possible through a work-out between all three DOTs.

Local building regulations and local, county, and state DOT rules may make a corner lot very difficult to use and to access. From streets where there is heavy or high-speed traffic DOT rules may require long right- and left-turn storage lanes to be constructed to allow for ample room to stack traffic that may want to turn into your property from either direction of traffic. These traffic storage lanes can be very expensive, running up the cost of the property you buy, and worse, the land for the lane may come from the very site you just bought. By building a road into your property (the stacking lane) the setbacks have been pushed deeper into the lot, possibly using up the land available for building your fast food restaurant, for example.

Worse yet, the local DOT may not allow you access at all from one or two of the streets the property fronts because of potential danger of accidents or other traffic reasons.

Desirability of Market.   The practical nature of any business will dictate that a location should be found where there are people who will patronize the establishment or use the services offered. This is a factor that is unique to the specific business or use in mind. If you were an investor looking to acquire a property for future appreciation and resale and had no use in mind, you would want to make sure that the market area either supported or had the potential of supporting a wide range of uses such that in the future top dollar could be paid for your future site. Yet, if you are looking for a site for specific business, you want to find the best location that would also meet your other requirements.

Affordable Location.   When the decision comes down to two different locations that in all other ways seem to be equally acceptable, the final decision of which property to acquire could be based on the overall cost and payment terms of one site over the other.

Being affordable may not mean the least expensive. It could well be that the most expensive of the two sites turns out to be the most affordable due to a combination of other factors. For example, you are considering buying one of two sites: A and B. Site A is selling for $100,000 and needs no further work, does not require any zoning changes, has a turn lane that is acceptable to you and your needs, and is, in fact, right across the street from site B. Site B is selling for $70,000 but needs further work, including fill to bring the site to grade and a turn lane that may cost from $10,000 to $20,000. The final cost for site B could still be less than A, say around $90,000. So far B looks cheaper. But what about time? Site A is ready to be used *now*. What is that worth? You would not make a decision until you knew exactly how much B would really cost you, and meanwhile you might lose site A to a competitor who would cause you to lose interest in B anyway.

80. How Do I Compare the Differences among Different Vacant Tracts?

This is one of the most difficult of all investment decisions. Which of the different opportunities available should you take? Most investors get sidetracked from their original purpose, however, making the decision even more difficult and complex than it need be. Therefore, you should begin with the basics and work torward the final decision. The following checklist will help you make that determination.

Checklist for Vacant Land Comparisons

Review your goals. Step back and remember what it was you started out to find, and why.

List the important criteria of those goals. If you want a tract of land that you can use to raise pigs now, with the prospects of building homes on the land later, then that need will have different criteria from a goal for a winter hideaway with future recreational use later.

Get all the important data on current use. Then study that information carefully. Do the present zoning ordinances allow what you want or would you be required to seek a zoning change?

Negotiate to find the seller's bottom line. After all, this might be the final and most important criterion of all. By use of letters of intent, which are not binding contracts, or offers that have contingencies that give you a release from the agreement, you can see just how good a deal you can make with the seller. Sometimes the key factor is time. If you can tie up the site long enough, for example, without being committed to buy it, and can get the present zoning changed, you can ensure a profit without taking much or any real risk.

81. Why Is Zoning So Important When Buying Vacant Land?

Zoning is the primary factor that determines the use of any property. The importance of this fact is that as an investor of vacant land you would want to know the answers to following three questions:

What does the present zoning allow?

What are the optional zoning categories available?

Of the optional zoning available, which is likely to be obtained?

Review each of these questions to see how to deal with them in the context of buying vacant land for profit.

What Does the Present Zoning Allow?   Most vacant land that is outside of town is often zoned into an agricultural type of zoning. This "farmland" category may vary around the country and may not be limited to growing crops or raising animals. Some farm zoning allows limited residential use, mining, oil exploration, certain limited industrial use, and so on. Sometimes this "broad spectrum" use causes problems when developers attempt to build a residential community next to land still zoned "farmland" that can allow elements of undesirable nature, such as a two-thousand acre pig farm or chicken hatchery to be constructed next door (upwind, too).

The goal for a vacant land speculator is to buy land that is presently zoned at the lowest possible tax base and located in an area that is poised for the greatest possible growth of a high demographic use. This ideal sometimes happens, but usually there is a trade-off somewhere along the way. Clearly, not all vacant land in the path of growth will experience the same upward value growth.

What Are the Optional Zoning Categories Available?   A study of all the zoning categories that are used by the local community will be a start. One of the critical aspects of this study is to determine which communities to visit. As towns grow into unincorporated or county governed land, one of the cities may eventually absorb the area and assign its own zoning restrictions that will supersede those of the county. But which city will absorb the area first? This can and frequently makes a very big difference—so much so, in fact, that developers who are looking at the acquisition of a large tract of land (or the sellers of that tract) may approach different cities to see which community can offer the best "development package" if the property is taken into its boundary.

Of all the zoning available, you would look for zoning that seemed to fit the pattern of growth and at the same time fall within the high end of demographics. If the tract of land in question was large enough to have a mixed use, then an overall site plan might be required to establish this mixed use through a rezoning process.

Of the Optional Zoning Available, Which Is Likely to Be Obtained?
Local politics can be the toughest obstacle to overcome for an investor of vacant land or the ultimate developer of that land. Because of this, before the land is purchased, you would want to get a good "feel" for the political attitude in that community about development in general and developers specifically.

You would do this by visiting the local planning and building departments (not always at the same place) to discuss the past, present, and future trends of the city and county. You would also explain why you are asking questions, as your interest is to be a better informed real estate investor and property owner in the community. Be specific about the site or location of the property you are considering. You may find that some controversy is involved, and you will learn more about the property and the area than you could ever think.

From the building and planning departments you would then go up the chain to the city or county leasers—the council and commission members. Make appointments with each of these officials, and get their opinions on what is going on in the area and how they view growth. Are there upcoming changes of which you are unaware, such as new roads, bridges, highways, canals, airports, trash dumps, etc., that can affect the area in a positive and/or negative way?

Ask these officials what their opinion would be if you requested a specific zoning, or ask them what category of zoning would they see as being viable for the area. In asking these questions you should be prepared to get a variety of answers depending on whom you talk to. The end result of this study should, however, give you a trend that can aid you in making a decision on buying the land. Keep in mind, however, that political officials do not always retain their jobs, and there may be an election in between the day you get their opinions and the day you expect to profit from those decisions.

82. What Is a *Master Plan* and How Does It Affect the Future Values of Property?

A master plan is the overall plan for the development of a community. This plan is usually a function of several overall plans that may start at the state level and work down through the county planning office to end at the community or city level for final implementation. Often the least comprehensive of the plans is the one at the state level, as it may govern elements such as total water consumption and funds available for roads, bridges, and so on. When environmentally sensitive or public property such as ocean-, lake-, or river-front properties are involved, additional restrictions may be needed such that each of the underlying levels of authority may need to adjust their plans.

The county government establishes a countywide master plan that each of the cities within that county must totally or substantially conform to. The difference in this conformity may be to allow the city to adjust within its boundaries certain areas to allow for a slightly different balance of commercial areas over residential areas, for example. Generally, however, once the county sets up its master plan, each city has a period of time to make those adjustments in its own plan.

When the city has a master plan that is approved by the city council members, which generally follows a long and often very heated battle between property owners and political leaders, the property owners within that city soon discover that any change contemplated in a use of existing property must conform to the new plan.

If the property in question is currently a motel, it could be that the new master plan has designated the location as low-density residential use only. If that were the case, then conforming to the new plan would require a new use other than motel use. Usually, however, the motel use would be "grandfathered-in." The term *to be grandfathered* means that a change in the building code or zoning ordinances occurred after the present use was established and that the present use will be allowed (sometimes only to the present owner, other times to subsequent owners as well), but any change to the existing structure may require the entire property to revert to the new use according to the codes and ordinances in effect. This can and frequently does cause hardships on property owners who have a fire or other damage that requires a new building permit (for substantial change or building), and discover that the new laws will not allow them to rebuild their business.

Master plans are not etched in stone, and as if to prove that fact, communities frequently undergo changes in their master plan and every so often devise new ones just to show how outdated the thinking was several years earlier.

Knowing the future thinking of those in charge of master plans for your area is very important but should not be viewed as the final word. A long time can elapse from a thought, to a plan, to the implementation of that plan; the final product may not even closely resemble the original thought.

83.   What Are the Major Pitfalls When Buying Vacant Land and How Can They Be Overcome?

The following pitfalls often come in tandem. When one happens, another can soon be on the way.

The Five Major Pitfalls of Buying Vacant Land

Change in zoning

Change in building regulations

Decline in neighborhood

Building moratorium

Change in community infrastructure

Take a look at any of these pitfalls. If one has already occurred, it can be a prelude to another.

Change in Zoning.   When the local officials change the zoning of your property or other property around you, this can signal a shift in the demographics and use zones of that area. This factor does not, by itself, mean the value of the property will go down, but it does indicate that there is going to be a change and that the value of some properties may go up and others go down as a result.

Change in Building Regulations.   Any change in what you can build or how you build it also triggers a change in the status quo. Usually building restrictions become more stringent and costly rather than the reverse, so this added cost may cause values to go down. These regulations can be increased setbacks, reduced density, lower building heights, more comprehensive fire sprinkler systems, etc.

Decline in Neighborhood.   Long-range investing takes into account a steady improvement in the status quo. With a downturn, however, the best-laid plans become worthless. Declines in neighborhoods can come slowly or suddenly. A slow decline can be seen coming, and investors who continue to invest in the area, rather than seek a way out or turn the decline around, do so with ultimate losses. A sudden decline usually occurs because of a major infrastructure change or improvement. A new highway may be viewed as an improvement to the overall traffic situation of a community, but for the formerly attractive residential subdivision that is now sliced into two less desirable areas it can mean a sudden and dramatic drop in values. Foreclosures can result, banks then dump their real estate owned (REO) properties, and the economic demographics of the area plummet.

Building Moratorium.   The building regulation that developers fear the most is the *moratorium on development*. Communities often establish a period of time when no construction permits are granted to enable new rules and regulations to be formulated or for infrastructure to catch up with development demands. These moratoriums can effectively halt development for long periods of time, causing builders to shift their attention to other less restrictive areas of the city, county, state, or area.

Changes in Community Infrastructure.   This factor has been stressed already several times. Whenever a community does something for the betterment of some of its members, there is apt to be a reduction of benefits for others. Every citizen of a community should be wary of improvement for improvement's sake. Also, some time after the completion of any infrastructure improvement and you will find that it is rare for any highway to ever meet the demands put on it (because the demand increases) or for any bridge to solve the problem for which it was designed.

84. How Can I Maximize Income from My Vacant Land?

A creative approach to turning vacant land into income-producing property may be nothing more than putting up a sign on it that reads "For Rent."

One of the first steps for creating income from vacant land is to find out what the current zoning allows, and if that is not productive enough, find the zoning you can likely get that will give you income potential.

Consider some of the following conversions from nonproductive vacant land to an income stream:

Parking lot for local community members, rental car companies, nearby businesses

Storage lot for trucks, boats, etc.

"U-Pick-It" strawberry patch or other crops

Temporary grazing land

Used car sales lot

Equipment sales lot

Landscape sales lot

Fruit stand

The list can go on, but you get the idea. As you drive around your area look at what businesses function with little or no property improvements other than showing the product they sell or a display of the services they render.

A longer-term program for a large tract of land would be the planting of growth timber or other landscape material. The key is not to let the land just sit there without using some effort to increase the value by doing something to the land. Often the effort alone attracts investors who suddenly are interested in a site they had not noticed before.

85. How Do I Entice a Buyer to My Vacant Land?

Every seller can be active in the development of a sound marketing plan. The keys to success are the following strategies.

The Five Proven Strategies to Entice Buyers to Vacant Land

Change zoning

Landscape for value

Target users

Show flexibility

Offer out in exchange

Review each in detail.

Change Zoning.   As zoning is the determination of use, and use is the guide to value, you may find that by petitioning the governing bodies to grant you a new zoning you will broaden the market for your property.

Landscape for Value.   Landscaping can produce long-range benefits regardless of what plants you put into the ground. The best results would be to use landscape material rather than timber, but timber works too in the right situation.

Target Users.   Once you know what your zoning is or has been changed to, you can make a list of all the possible users for the site. Do not worry about your idea of the viability of the site for a user—let them make up their own mind. The key to selling anything for top dollar is to find that buyer out there who is attracted by what you have to offer.

Show Flexibility.   In a buyer's market sellers have to be creative and flexible. By learning of some of the different creative selling techniques, as well as creative buying methods, you will be in a better position to deal with a buyer who may need to be enticed to buy your property.

Offer Out in Exchange.   One of the best ways to sell is to become a buyer. By turning the market into your favor, if it is a buyer's market, you may find you can solve your problem of "selling" your property by using it as a way to acquire another.

86.   What Are the Key Steps to Follow When I Sell My Raw Land?

1. *Have a plan that fits your goals.*   Everything starts from this point, and by keeping your goals clearly in sight you will be less apt to make a mistake.

2. *Gather demographic data.*   As part of your marketing plan this information can help you target the right buyer or deal with that buyer when he or she appears.

3. *Show growth trends.*   This reinforces the reason for growth of value. Steady growth trends should also indicate room for more growth too. The buyer may want to know that there is still value appreciation left in the site.

4. *Plot areas of similar use.*   Show how that similar lot down the street has doubled in value over the past few years.

5. *Estimate future uses.*   This will help you target the right buyer and at the same time show flexibility in use to the investor who has no ready use in mind.

6. *Show how easy it will be for the buyer to acquire your site.*   Offer a purchase package that works for the buyer. You do not have to be the cheapest property

on the block to attract a buyer, only the one that works best economically. Use some creative techniques that can let the buyer use the IRS to the best advantage and save while paying you more.

7. *Develop a marketing brochure.*   Give all the facts and then more. A picture can be worth a thousand words, and advertising pays off. Any up-to-date print shop can take your data, such as an aerial photograph you order from a company found in the Yellow Pages, and produce an inexpensive brochure that looks very professional. Sometimes all you need to do is give that buyer something to think about at the end of the week when he or she has inspected a dozen properties and now must select the one for his or her company to buy.

8. *Insulate yourself from buyer.*   List the property with a qualified real estate agent. Pick one that handles the kind of property you are offering, and make sure the agent understands your goals and is committed to help you reach them.

9. *Help the prospect mentally become an "owner."*   Give a lot of "sold" signals as he or she is negotiating for your property. Until a buyer is mentally an "owner" there is always risk of losing the deal.

10

Income Property for the 1990s: Buying and Selling Residential Rental Properties

87. How Can I Successfully Buy Residential Rental Property?

The following key elements are the essential steps that you should follow to ensure that you are not overlooking something important about a specific property you may be interested in, or that an "opportunity" slips past because you did not recognize it as such.

The Six Steps to Buying Residential Rental Property

Know the local market conditions

Know the local income and expense ratios

Inspect the property thoroughly

Watch out for hidden "time bombs"

Review existing leases and tenant records with a fine-tooth comb

Be ready to negotiate for *time* and *terms*

Know the Local Market Conditions.   This step is never finished because the local market is constantly going through changes. If you anticipate being able to find properties for sale that represent an opportunity for you, then the most critical element for you to master is your own local market conditions.

Each community and each area within that community will have something about it that makes it unique and different from any other area or part of town. The factors that cause this difference may be very subtle, such as a slightly lower tax millage, a better water system, or a highly sought after school district. Even the obvious, an area close to high-paying jobs, will create different layers of economic levels within a small area, and those layers will be translated into different rent zones. These rent zones will establish the likely maximum rent that can be charged. This is very important because if your total experience is within the top demographic zone and you are used to charging top rents, a rental property that is several blocks away may look very attractive and you may make the decision to acquire it simply because you have applied your thinking and knowledge to that property; your conclusions could be very wrong unless you knew the market for that rental zone.

The following are some questions that you would need to discover the answers to.

- What will lenders offer loans for with favorable terms?
- What does the average investor expect to get as a return for his or her invested capital?
- What is the trend for the neighborhood?
- Is employment up or down and which way is it headed for the future?
- Is this a buyer's market? Are there special factors that give buyers the edge?
- Which lenders in the community like to make loans on residential rentals?

The key to getting to know your local market conditions is to begin to observe what is going on. Attend local city council and county government meetings and read the public announcements in the local newspaper—each of these events provide early signals to what may transpire. Get to know several savvy real estate brokers who have been working in the area for a long time. Get them to reveal what they feel may happen. Check with the city and county planning officials and find out what they have planned for the community.

Walk the neighborhoods where you plan to invest. This gives you a slow and easy way to observe everything. Sometimes you spot things that disenchant you about the area, which can be the most important thing that could happen. It is better to know the "bad things" before you buy. Best of all, walking the streets of the neighborhood can reveal a lot about the owners in the area and give you the opportunity to meet many of them personally. In a few months you can become an expert on what has been happening and what is about to occur within your community.

Know the Local Income and Expense Ratios.   The income that you can expect to collect from a rental property can be estimated very accurately once you know the local market conditions and the vacancy level you will encounter. The actual rent you can collect will be a function of the rent zone where the property is located. However, it is possible to raise a property from a lower rental category to a higher one when the geographic situation warrants it. For example, if you find a property that can be cosmetically improved and the standards of the units enhanced to match or exceed those units in a higher rent zone, you can increase the income level of a property considerably. This factor then becomes one of the important elements that you should look for.

While property management is approaching an exact science, there are many local factors that affect the overall cost of the operation of any specific category of property. You should make an effort to learn what the local expenses should be for any rental property you may be interested in owning. This is most critical for residential properties because this kind of property is usually more management intensive, and there are fewer expenses that can be passed on to the tenant. A shopping center owner is used to having "add on" charges for common area maintenance (CAM), real estate tax, sales tax, advertising, security, and so on. The residential tenant customarily pays one payment that includes everything (except, in most cases, electricity) and if any part of the fixed cost to operate a property increases, the owner has to absorb that cost out of the rent collected.

Where Can You Get Local Income and Expense Figures?   Try your local tax assessor's office. Often this department conducts a detailed study on many different aspects of the local market. They are looking for backup information to use when they appraise the real estate within their jurisdiction. This information may contain some or all of the following data.

- Income levels by geographic zones
- Property values by geographic zones
- Rent zones
- Numbers of rental units available by geographic areas
- Employment by geographic areas
- Vacancy factors for all rentals by zone
- Vacancy factors by percentage of gross revenue
- Growth trends
- Expenses for rentals by percentage of gross revenue
- Real estate taxes by percentage of gross revenue
- Utility cost by percentage of gross revenue

All of the above information is helpful to any real estate investor.

Inspect the Property Thoroughly.   It is very important that a property inspection be completed by a team of professionals prior to your being fully bound by the purchase agreement. This is important for the following reasons.

1. You do not want to spend the time, effort, and cost to make a detailed inspection of the property and the review of that study unless you have the property tied up. Too many would-be owners have spent all that time and money only to have another investor snatch the property away from them.

2. You do not want to be bound to the contract in the event you discover something wrong that exceeds your level of interest in that property.

Some real estate agents and most real estate "standard form" contracts provide for property inspections and have a provision that requires the seller to "fix or repair" any item found to be in need of repair. Often there is a blank space that the buyer or seller can fill in setting the maximum exposure for such risk to "fix or repair," and some contracts continue to say that if the blank is not filled in there is an automatic limit of 2 or 3 percent. This inspection provision may work for you, but in most situations it will not be adequate to take care of all the possible problems that can come up. First, 2 or 3 percent off the gross price may be an amount the seller is already anticipating is going to be returned to you because the seller knows something you do not but might find out during the inspections.

It is more prudent to add to this "standard inspection provision" a paragraph that takes into consideration your need to be absolutely sure that you agree and accept any potential problem that the property inspection may uncover. An example of wording I would use is shown here. Before adding anything to a standard form (or for that matter, before using a standard form), make sure you get good real estate legal advice.

> "...and in addition to the terms of the inspection provision, paragraph ____ of this agreement, it is herein agreed between the parties that if for any reason the Buyer is not fully and completely satisfied with the findings of the property inspection report(s) that have been completed within the deadline for said inspections as provided, then the Buyer retains the right to withdraw from this agreement by giving written notice to the Seller that this agreement is no longer in effect, and in that event the Buyer shall have promptly returned any and all deposits that the Buyer has placed in escrow pending the closing of this transaction."

Watch Out for Hidden "Time Bombs."   There are many time bombs that await the lax real estate investor; do not let any ruin your investment dreams. Fortunately, if you follow simple guidelines the chance of your being affected by a hidden time bomb will be rare. The key is to know the most damaging time bombs that might exist and how to avoid them. The following are some of the worst and most expensive problems to fix or avoid if they are present when you buy a property.

- *Hidden legal action* can exist due to problems that occurred months before you even looked at the property.
- You have been given *bad title* and now have legal problems as a result.
- There are *existing code violations* and the local building department wants you to tear down a building because of them.

- *Termites* are having a feast on your property and you are faced with having to rebuild a major portion of the building.

- The *lot size is much smaller* than you thought it was, even though you have been given all the information that would have indicated the exact size long before you made an offer—only you did not know what to look for.

- There is *another mortgage on the property* that no one told you about, and the lender wants payment in full *now*.

- *Existing contracts* you may be bound to pay for leased equipment, telephone service, advertisements in the *Yellow Pages*, employment contracts, future advertising commitments, etc. This can add up to a lot of money.

Fortunately, all these problems can be dealt with before you close on the property, at least to the extent that if one of them occurs you will have some recourse against the seller. This list of time bombs by no means contains all the things that can go wrong.

Review Existing Leases and Tenant Records with a Fine-Tooth Comb.
The ambiance of any rental project will be determined by its makeup of tenants. However, to maintain a quality tenant list takes hard work and the willingness to incur expense to run credit reports and to follow up with reference checks. When management gets sloppy anyone with some cash as a deposit ends up with an apartment. When the wrong kind of tenant moves in, the right kind frequently moves out, hastening the decline of the property. Lax management also generates sloppy rental contracts with provisions that do not meet your criteria. Options to renew for several years, the right to paint the interior of the apartment without your approval, approval for pets, an okay to have five children and three adults in a two-bedroom apartment, etc., are all conditions that you may not want to live with. When you find leases like this, you can put in your purchase contract a provision that the seller must "buy out" those leases and deliver those apartments to you free of any tenants you want to exclude. The seller may not want to do this or the tenants may refuse to move, but at least you have made an attempt to rectify the situation.

Be Ready to Negotiate for *Time* and *Terms*.   In real estate the single most important factor is *time*. In contract negotiations the most important element is the *term* of payment. By combining these two factors you have the basis to make any transaction work.

For example, you want to buy a 25-unit apartment complex and the sellers are asking $1 million for the property. It is free and clear of debt and the sellers indicate they will hold up to 80 percent of the price in the form of a first mortgage. There is a balance due at a closing of $200,000 if you buy the property at the asking price. You take a hard look at the tenant situation and decide that if you could increase the rents by 15 percent the property will be worth more than the asking price.

You make an offer as follows: You agree to give them $200,000 at closing, and they hold a first mortgage of $800,000. On the surface this looks like you have offered them the full price of $1,000,000. However, you structure this offer so that $120,000 of the down payment is two years of prepaid interest on the mortgage. The mortgage is at 7.5 percent per annum ($800,000 multiplied by 7.5 percent equals $60,000 per year). Your real purchase price then is closer to $880,000 ($800,000 mortgage plus $80,000 principal paid at closing). Notice I said closer to $880,000 rather than exactly $880,000. This is because you have prepaid $120,000 in interest and that has a discountable value for the buyer. For the seller prepaid interest is worth more because of *time*. If you paid the interest as it actually came due, say in monthly installments of $5,000 per month for two years, that total would still only be $120,000. Now the seller has the full amount of interest, which can be reinvested and will earn additional money during that same period.

In the above example you have used both *time* and *terms* to structure a deal that pays the seller's price, but allows you to use time and terms to your benefit. You could play with this concept and come up with several other possible combinations that may work better to help you achieve your goals and that would be acceptable to the seller.

88. What Are the Most Important *Risk Enhancers* I Should Avoid When Buying Residential Rental Properties?

The last thing you need is to increase your risk when it comes to buying anything. When it comes to residential rentals there are sufficient risks in normal situations, so the following list will give you the nine most important factors that will increase your risk. The key is to avoid them by knowing what they mean, and then discount the price of the property accordingly. If you cannot buy the property with these risk factors already discounted, then avoid purchasing the property.

The Nine Factors That Increase Your Risk When Buying Residential Properties

Deferred maintenance

Nice cosmetics but obsolete equipment

Hidden lease terms

Hidden debt terms

Environmental problems

Poorly paying tenants

False income and expense statements

An appeal to your greed

A scheduled decline in income

Deferred Maintenance.   Sloppy management or, worse still, absentee management usually allows a property to slip into disrepair. At first it may be small items that begin to suffer from preventative maintenance, such as air conditioning equipment, pool pumps, plumbing, unpainted wood, cracked walls, and missing tiles or shingles on the roof. Also, landscaping may start to die because the lawn sprinklers no longer function, door jams start to rot due to leaks, plaster crumbles, and wallpaper falls off the wall.

Some sellers recognize too late that their property has gone downhill, and in an attempt to sell they paint and patch but do not really fix the problem.

When purchasing a property that has not been maintained for a long time the word *caution* should flash bright red in your mind. The fact that the property is run down is not a reason to avoid it, indeed, it could be that the very reason the property is for sale is because it is a management nightmare for the owner. If you can turn the property around you may find one of those gems you have been looking for. However, know what you are getting into. Repairs can be expensive and should never be taken lightly.

Nice Cosmetics but Obsolete Equipment.   Some properties look great, and are except that too much money has been going to maintain obsolescence. Even the best looking property may have a lot of old equipment that is at or near failure point. This is another reason why a detailed inspection of a property is essential. The key to avoiding this problem is to check the age of everything that will eventually need to be replaced. Start with the roof (you can count on a maximum of 20 years unless it is copper or lead sheeting) and work down. Everything electrical, mechanical, or that will rust, rot, or be worn away should be listed, along with the maximum life expectancy of these items for your area of the country. You can find out the life expectancy by checking with other property owners, lenders, and savvy realtors in your area. When you find a 25-unit building that has 25 water heaters that are all 20 years old and look to be in good condition, you should anticipate that within a few years you will have to replace all of them. While the life years will vary, the same can be said for kitchen appliances, air conditioning equipment, asphalt paving, patio decking, wood decks, and so on. Add the costs that you would have to spend to bring everything up to present-day standards and take that sum into account when you buy the property. If the asking price is already low enough to take obsolescence into consideration, then move forward.

Hidden Lease Terms.   Sometimes a lease is modified by a letter or other communication that may not show up in the file the seller hands to you when you review the leases. Because of this it is essential prior to closing that you obtain *estoppel letters* from each of the tenants that verify that the copy of the lease attached to the estoppel letter is the full and complete lease. This letter simply states that the document attached to it (also described in the letter) represents the total of that contract as of the date of the letter.

Hidden Debt Terms. Just as a lease can be modified, so can a mortgage or other debt. This may be something as simple as an extension of the payment terms to include two or more years payout, an increase of interest, or the agreement to balloon the payment next year.

The same type of *estoppel letter* used to verify lease terms will work for mortgages.

Environmental Problems. We live in the age of the Love Canal, old dump sites, junkyards, and other possible pollution sources are rampant. Old farmland might contain underground fuel tanks that have been leaking their oil into the ground for the past 40 years. Residential sites can be built on top of landfill that is leaking methane into the buildings. Former phosphate mines have been leveled and office buildings constructed over them only to have dangerous levels of radon gas accumulating in the basement and subsequently circulated through the building by the heating system.

The only way you can be absolutely sure there are no problems is to test the entire property environmentally, which can be very expensive. The alternative method is to do spot checks and obtain indemnification from the seller against problems that may occur later.

When it comes to environmental problems, it is best to avoid a property where there is any potential problem.

Poorly Paying Tenants. There is nothing more frustrating than to have a building filled with tenants that are constantly late with their rent. You may want to remove these tenants from the building. The lease will not show the prompt or late-payment schedule of the tenants, so insist on seeing a rent collection log. If the management does not have such a log, then ask to see the bank deposits, which should indicate which tenants have made their payments and when.

False Income and Expense Statements. Many property owners are very sloppy about the records they keep, and when it comes time to give a prospective buyer a summary of the income and expenses for their rental property it becomes "fairy tale" time.

There are several ways you can get close to finding the actual truth, but it is unlikely that you will ever learn the whole story of income and expenses. The following list of records and what to look for will help.

- *Sales tax reports* may give you a way to figure out the actual rents collected. For example, if the owner has made a report to the state sales tax department and the monthly reported average is $300.00, based on a sales tax of 6 percent you can ascertain that the monthly rent on which tax was paid would be $5,000 ($300.00 divided by 0.06 equals $5,000). This works only when there is a state sales tax applicable to that kind of rental. Remember that sales tax may vary among states and communities within the state.

- *Income tax reports* to the IRS may show the actual amount of rents collected. Some owners do not want to show you their year-end income tax report because they have combined other income and expenses into one report.

- *Bank deposits* can be helpful to backtrack the rent collections. To be accurate, however, you would need to see both the bank statements and the deposit log.

- *Cancelled checks* are what the IRS would ask for in an audit, so why not ask to see them too, but make sure you have the checkbook stubs as well. Often the stub has one thing written on it that differs from what the check may indicate. The idea is not just to know how much was paid out, but what it was for.

- *Copies of bills and invoices* that have been paid can give you a trail to follow that may lead to the truth. Sometimes you find a check that corresponds to a stub in the checkbook, say, for $5,000 indicating the payment was for work to repair a roof. However, the invoice shows that the payment was for a cruise to Hawaii.

An Appeal to Your Greed.   Sometimes a seller will look you in the eye and tell you that the property is really a gold mine because so many of the tenants pay in cash, the laundry room is awash in quarters every week, and the money from your soda machines has to be collected twice daily.

Many owners of rental properties (as well as other types of income property) do not report every dime that is collected or earned. However, when the seller cannot verify what is collected and simply winks at you and pats his or her pocket, then watch out.

An appeal to your greed is the oldest game in town, and if you play it you may end up losing.

A Scheduled Decline in Income.   At times an event is scheduled to occur that will guarantee a drop of income. This drop usually comes from a greater than usual vacancy factor and comes as a result of a decrease of potential renters or renters who shy away from the property.

A plant closing, a long-term strike, or some other labor problem can turn a small community into an economic disaster. A new highway, bridge, or other major construction can make the rental project undesirable for a while or even permanently. However, none of those "future" events may be evident right now. Make sure you know what is going to happen in the community that might affect the property you wish to buy.

89. Which Is Better to Own— Seasonal Rentals or Annual Rentals?

This is an interesting problem for many vacation areas of the country, or for properties that are located near sources of temporary renters. The first step would be to get a twelve-month calendar that shows all the months on one large page. Mark on the calendar, using a red felt pen, the number of days from each month that your property would rent, and how much rent you could get were you able to offer fully furnished units on a short-term basis. The actual term you chose can be limited to a one-week minimum or any other period you might select for the kind of units you have.

To fill in the calendar correctly you will need to do some homework. One of the best ways to discover this information is to look at properties similar to yours or properties you are contemplating purchasing that rent to temporary or seasonal tenants. Through a review of the year-round occupancy on a week-by-week basis, you will quickly spot the trends for your local area. The more such properties you review, the more accurate the information you will obtain.

While "inspecting" properties for sale, you can find an enormous amount of information that will be useful to you. The amount of rents that can be charged, the usual expenses a property will incur, etc., begin to crystallize as you make comparisons. Of all the data you find, one of the most important will be what is called the average daily rate (ADR), or in the event of weekly minimums the average weekly rate (AWR). This is usually compiled on a monthly basis and is found by taking the actual income collected for any given month and dividing it by the number of nights (or weeks) of actual occupancy. For example, if a property has a weekly minimum and has 25 units, a gross rental collection for the past four weeks during which time all 25 units were rented for $50,000 would indicate an AWR of $500 per week.

90.   What Are the Key Steps to Follow When I Want to Sell My Residential Rental Property?

Keep good rent collection records

Maintain a property maintenance log

Keep income and expenses separate for each property

Establish a programmed upgrade policy

Keep expenses within local margins

Create strict tenant standards and enforce them

Set the rental price 15 percent above the market

Keep Good Rent Collection Records.   This works to your own benefit. Have a log or chart with each tenant's name and apartment number at the top. Indicate the monthly rent and the date due each month. When the payment is made, record the date and indicate if a late charge was also collected should the payment be late.

Maintain a Property Maintenance Log.   This is a very helpful log or diary to keep. Some of the important facts about the building should be recorded in this log in addition to maintenance records. For example, the brand name and color of paint used in the building will make it easier to touch up needed areas rather than try to match colors.

When repairs or replacements are made, the log should indicate the following information:

- Description of work done
- Date the work was done
- Apartment or building area where the work was done
- Name of repair or service company
- Quality of the work
- Date payment was made
- Check number and amount of payment

Keep Income and Expenses Separate for Each Property. It is a good idea to keep a separate checking account for each rental property you own. This will allow you to account properly to the IRS and will make a review of the records by you or a prospective investor when you want to sell much easier.

Establish a Programmed Upgrade Policy. There should be some automatic upgrades that you effect when a tenant moves out of an apartment. Also, certain repairs or preventative maintenance should be put on a timetable so that you keep ahead of the problems rather than constantly react to them.

Keep Expenses within Local Margins. If you find that your expenses are greater than the local standards, then find out why. Utility bills that skyrocket may indicate there is a problem somewhere. A leak in a water line can increase your water bill to many times what it should be. A faulty electrical meter can give readings that are several times greater than the actual usage. A tenant may have a faucet that leaks but is afraid to tell you about it in fear that you will raise the rent. Track down expenses that are greater than the norm and deal with them.

Create Strict Tenant Standards and Enforce Them. If you do not allow pets and find them in the apartment when you meet a repairperson, then you need to act quickly to make a change either in the policy or to enforce your rules.

Strong tenant rules generally do not scare away tenants, rather they help establish a certain quality of tenant. Whatever rules you establish should have some muscle behind them to make sure they are enforced.

Set the Rental Price 15 Percent above the Market. When you attempt to sell your rental property you should make an effort to ascertain what the market conditions are. Have several realtors who deal with apartment rentals similar to yours in the same area give you their opinion of what the market price should be. Then increase that price by 15 percent and price the property at that level.

91.   How Do I Set My Rental Prices to Ensure Low Vacancy and Top Rental Income?

One of the keys to successful management of a rental property is to keep the vacancy factor at a low level. Some property owners follow the practice of keeping their rents slightly below the market in the hopes and belief that this strategy will ensure them of tenants who will stay put. While this can work, there is a management practice that should accompany the policy of charging lower than market rent: strong tenant control and selection. To establish an effective management procedure that can deal with both the rent level and tenant control, begin with the task of finding the right level of rent to charge.

Finding the Right Level of Rent to Charge

As mentioned earlier it will be impossible for you to ascertain how much rent your property can bring unless you know the market, what the competition has to offer, how much they charge, and how your property compares to what is available on the market.

Rental property comparisons should be made in two direct methods: first a categorical comparison such as a two-bedroom, two-bath garden apartment in your area rents from $500 to $700 per month; second, a per-square-foot comparison such as a two-bedroom, two-bath garden apartment in your area rents from $0.50 to $0.70 per square foot per month.

The square-foot comparison enables you to fine-tune your market analysis once you have isolated the most directly comparable properties to your own. Prior to those detailed comparisons, make the overall categorical comparisons.

If your final analysis indicates that apartments similar to what you have are on the market for $600 per month in an annual lease, then this would set your maximum rent to ask at that level. Naturally, if you have apartments that are larger or have special features, then your asking rent can be adjusted upward. Note the words *asking rent*. It would be reasonable that you could modify rental terms for the ideal tenant who might appear as well as to give you some negotiation leverage. The savvy tenant knows that they can ask for lease concessions, and they frequently do and expect them.

The Tenant Selection Process

Many apartment buildings keep a "For Rent" sign on their property even when they have no vacancy. When there is on-site management or the owner does not mind getting frequent calls about such a sign, this is a good idea. It enables the property owner to establish a "waiting list" for the possible apartments. Naturally, many people on the so-called waiting list may not be around or still looking for an apartment when a vacancy comes up, but it does give the owners a backlog of possible tenants to call when they know an apartment is soon to be vacant.

Having a waiting list also gives the owner of the units the chance to take an application from prospective tenants in advance of the actual date an apartment is vacated. Unfortunately many property owners do not put up a vacant sign until the previous tenant has already left and the apartment has been made ready (new paint, carpets cleaned, etc.). This method of looking for new tenants increases the potential vacancy factor.

It is a good idea to charge the tenant a fee for the application, and some management companies recommend that the fee be applied to the last month's rent if the tenant is accepted. This application fee can be used to cover the cost to order a professional business check of the tenant. You will find a list of such companies in the Yellow Pages of your local phone book under *Credit Checks*.

The review of information given by a prospective tenant is very important. The makeup of tenants in any building can determine the future of that property. Because the person who lives in a building contributes to the ambiance and social nature of the facility, property owners should strive to be as selective as possible within the laws that govern tenant–landlord relationships.

While the U.S. Civil Rights Act of 1968 (42 USC 3601-17) establishes that a landlord cannot discriminate against a person on the basis of race, religion, sex, or national origin, many states have gone beyond the parameters of this act, and it is essential that you be aware of all the rights you have within your state as either a landlord or a tenant. Contact your local tax assessor's office as the first source for such information, and if not available there, call the closest Board of Realtors to see if they have a booklet that covers those rights. If that proves unsuccessful, call your state senator's office and ask the administrative assistant to help you find the information you are looking for.

11
Buying and Selling Income-Producing Properties

92. How Can I Determine the Best Kind of Income-Producing Real Estate to Invest in?

The selection of any type of investment you want to make should follow a detailed study of all the advantages and disadvantages of each kind of property. You should also carefully review your own goals in an attempt to discover which kind of property is suitable for you while helping you reach your goals. The ultimate answer to the question stated will depend on your own assessment of the following:

- What are your own attributes and talents that will aid you in achieving a success in a specific investment property?

- Will acquisition of any specific property help move you closer to your goals quicker and safer than some other type of investment?

- Do you have the capital available to make the investment safely?

- Do you have the time to meet the obligations of the investment?

A careful analysis of these four items is essential. If you have not already done so, you should make a written list of all the talents you have that will aid you in achieving success through real estate ownership. Some of those talents may not be limited to any specific kind of real estate, for example, you might be a great carpenter, able to paint or landscape, etc. The idea of being a good handy person, able to fix anything and build anything, may direct you to properties that are more in need of being fixed up. If you are a whiz at bookkeeping, then record keeping will not bother you. Management is often the area that is lacking, and usually only because of lack of experience in dealing with tenants.

Your goals are the key to your ultimate success, so you need to keep them firmly in mind. I know investors who stick to one kind of property until they seem to master it. It does not matter what the property is just as long as owning it fits your goal.

Having sufficient capital to handle the investment is important. The single most critical reason that people fail in a business or with an investment is because they are undercapitalized. This factor should not frighten you away from a challenge, as many investors have made it on nothing more than sweat equity. Sufficient capital does not mean you must have a bundle of cash in the bank, only that you should have enough so that you can weather a storm of vacancies.

For many first-time investors the hardest part of a selection of any specific kind of property to buy is the inability to ascertain how much time will be needed to make the investment work. Time can work for or against you. Time should always be set aside, and, like a demanding child, it will require more time than you may have thought necessary.

93. How Do I Analyze an Income and Expense Statement?

When buying or selling an income property one of the key pieces of information for the buyer is the income and expense statement the seller presents as an accounting of the economic benefits of the property. Another name for similar information would be a *profit and loss statement*.

The essence of these statements or reports is to show the total income less the total operating expenses and in so doing provide a detailed accounting of debt service and depreciation. Take a look at the following example.

Income and Expense Statement

Income		
Gross Income Collected		$125,000.00
Expenses		
Advertising	$ 750.00	
Contract services	4,800.00	
Insurance	1,550.00	
Miscellaneous expenses	850.00	
Professional fees	550.00	
Repairs	4,500.00	
Supplies	1,775.00	
Taxes (real estate)	14,000.00	
Utilities	2,900.00	
Total expenses		$31,675.00
Net operating income		$93,325.00

The above statement shows the total income collected without any accounting for total possible income less vacancy (as might be shown in a *pro forma* or estimated income and expense statement). The expenses shown above are a typical list of bills paid and include real estate taxes.

Before looking at a more complex income and expense statement you should be aware of what is missing, as well as what is apt to change once you become the owner of this property.

Items Missing in Income and Expense Statements

The owner's time is usually the most critical missing element. You will notice that there is no expense labeled *management*. Small businesses, small rental properties, and so on, that are managed by the owner usually do not have a management expense included, or if one is included, it is for a resident manager and not for the actual time and work done by the owner. If your ownership plan includes outside management rather than your own efforts, then the expense of management becomes a real out-of-pocket cost that must be taken into consideration when you analyze the property or make comparison of different properties. At best you should take into consideration the time you must spend as manager of your own property and be compensated for that time and effort over and above the investment return. In essence, pay yourself a salary to keep your property honest.

Adequate repairs and maintenance would be the next item that is usually understated or missing altogether. Several years of poor maintenance can be glossed over with a coat of paint just before the property goes on the market, yet potential problems can surface in a short time when the paint flakes off the wall, termites swarm, or a heavy rain shows off leaks at their best. However, by looking at several past years' income and expense statements, it is easy to get a picture of what has been done to keep the building in good repair. If you see little amounts spent on repairs or big lump payment repairs, you should question these amounts and ask for copies of bills. It is possible that what appears to be a major repair was really a cruise to Hawaii.

What Will Change Once You Own the Property

Real estate taxes are likely to go up the year following your purchase. The reason for this is the local tax assessor's office will see a record of the sale, compute the purchase price (or know it exactly from recorded documents), and assess the property taking into consideration new information of the market values of your property along with other possible similar sales in the area. If there has been a big change for the greater in the price of the property or other properties in the community, then the real estate tax for that property can jump up quite a bit. The amount of possible increase will vary a great deal among communities so it would be a good idea to sit down with an official at the county tax assessor's office and discuss this situation in general before you enter into a contract to buy any property. A 50 percent increase in real estate tax can eliminate the profit you were counting on.

Debt service may increase simply because you increase the total debt on the property when you acquire it. It is critical for every investor to make an estimated income and expense analysis showing all the possible expenses that would be likely after the sale.

Depreciation is an allowable deduction from income for tax purposes and is a very important calculation. The amount of depreciation that the existing owner shows as his or her own deduction will not (in most situations) be the amount of your deduction. This is because your tax basis, or book value of the property, should be much greater than the present owner's, unless you acquire the ownership corporation or exchange another property with a lower basis for the new one. In any event, depreciation is variable so you should seek the advice of your own accountant who knows your personal tax situation so that a depreciation schedule will be established to obtain the maximum benefits allowed under the IRS rules. See the following example of depreciation.

Detailed Profit and Loss Statement

Income by Departments	
Rooms	$ 500,000.00
Food	85,000.00
Beverage	300,000.00
Telephone	45,000.00
Miscellaneous	70,550.00
Total revenue collected	$1,000,550.00
Expenses by departments	
Rooms	$245,200.00
Food	80,150.00
Beverage	195,000.00
Telephone	30,000.00
Miscellaneous	60,255.00
Total expenses paid	$ 610,605.00
Cash flow before debt service	$ 389,945.00
Financial and other expenses	
Interest	$ 250,000.00
Depreciation	200,000.00
Total financial and other expenses	$ 450,000.00
Net profit <loss> from operation	<60,055.00> LOSS

In the above profit and loss statement the final result shows a loss; this is partially due to the introduction of depreciation into the picture. Depreciation is a "paper deduction" that accounts for the reduced life (and therefore reduced value) of the assets owned. Many investors consider this deduction the real value to many real estate investments because it allows the investor to "shelter" income from income tax. In investment days prior to the IRS revisions of 1986 this "shelter" meant much more than in 1993 as the investor converted this income, which would have been taxed at earned income, to a capital gains tax when the property was eventually sold.

Depreciation is an expense that needs to be taken into consideration at least partially as an eventual expense. Every item that is depreciated will someday need to be repaired or replaced to some degree. Over a period of time the cost to repair and then eventually replace an item can far exceed the original cost. These are items that investors need to pay very close attention to when reviewing any income property.

Departmentalized income and expenses show up in the profit and loss statement as total numbers, but there would be a separate accounting for the income and expenses in detail. If you are given only the summary page that shows totals and not the makeup of those totals, you do not have sufficient data to establish a clear picture of the property.

94. What Are the Advantages When I Own an Income- Producing Property?

In general, ownership of income-producing real estate has several distinct advantages for owners. Seven of the most important are the following.

Tax shelter has been described above through depreciation. For many investors this is the prime reason to own income-producing real estate.

Added income to supplement your other income sources is the most widespread reason for owning income property. For some investors this income may be the rent from one or more units in the small apartment building where they also live, that income paying the expenses to maintain the property and pay off the mortgage. This is an example of using other people's money (OPM) to build wealth.

Long-term appreciation has been a major source of wealth for many of the wealthiest of people in the world. Well-located and -maintained real estate can greatly appreciate in value over even a short period of time.

Benefits and allowable business expenses can be paid that otherwise may not be deductible from your own personal income. For example, if you own a property and use your car for some of the activities of that property, have your accountant show you how to pay the expenses of the car from the rent you collect. Your personal insurance, travel, and other expenses can often become legal business expenses when you follow your accountant's advice.

Solve your basic need for housing by providing an apartment or home for you as well as income.

You can become your own boss if the property becomes your major or sole source of income. Financial independence is, after all, one of the elements of life that most people dream of obtaining. Real estate can be a source of that goal.

Employment for family members can be created and is often the main reason some investors acquire labor intensive real estate. Farms, hotels, restaurants, etc., are often owned and operated by whole families, each member working toward their own economic goals.

95. Why Does Ownership of the Same Property Affect Different Buyers Differently?

Consider that a property is much like a boat—it might look the same to everyone that sees it, but each person may chose a different destination to travel to or derive a different recreational sport from it. Such is real estate. A vacant lot can become anything that is allowable under the existing or altered zoning, a building can be converted into something else or removed so that cars can be parked on the empty lot created. Even the same use of a property can produce different end results depending on the method of operation and the kinds of goals the owner desires to obtain.

The multiple use and varied results that any property can give is one of the most important aspects that causes one buyer to be willing to pay more for a property than another. Investors who anticipate that one day they will want to sell their property should learn as much as they can about the different benefits their own property can provide to different owners.

96. What Are the Steps to *Successful Acquisition* of Income-Producing Properties?

Every income property owner experiences first hand the problems that come with property. Smart owners learn from these problems and discover how to avoid problems with future properties by following steps designed to help them find the right kinds of properties to fit the investor's goal-oriented plan. The best of these steps are shown below.

The Seven Key Steps to Successful Acquisition of Income-Producing Property

1. Know your goals and abilities.
2. Know the local real estate market well.
3. Choose the right kind of property to buy.
4. Do not bite off more than you can chew.
5. Negotiate terms that will help you sell.
6. Avoid short-term payback financing.
7. Avoid pitfalls.

Know Your Goals and Abilities. By the time you finish this book you will have repeatedly read of the importance of maintaining your goals just a step above your abilities. You do this because you should continually strive to improve your abilities. This creates a constant positive thrust, and as you enhance your abilities you can move your goals up another notch or two.

The key to personal improvement is to increase your knowledge of the subjects that are needed so that your self-confidence is reinforced. The local adult education division of the junior college in your area may have a wide selection of beneficial courses from bookkeeping to vocational classes in electrical installations to plumbing. Property management courses will prove to be highly effective and worth the time.

Know The Local Real Estate Market Well. Everything you do in your community can have direct input to your knowledge of the local real estate market. One good way to keep on top of local events is to vary the way you drive to work each day so that you get to see what is going on, spot new "For Sale" signs, or locate the site mentioned at a planning and zoning hearing the night before. A few times each month plan spending a few minutes at an open house or talking to an owner of a building that is for rent or for sale.

Every investor can become an expert in their own local community. It is easy—all it takes is proper guidance to the steps you need to take, and the time to do it.

Choose the Right Kind of Property to Buy. Take a look at question number 92. Your success in real estate is tied to many things, and it is possible to overcome a bad investment. However, with care and the proper implementation of the comfort zone method of investing you will gravitate toward the right kind of investment.

My own personal experience in real estate investing has been oriented toward vacant land. Other investors I know do nothing but buy restaurants that have gone out of business and convert them into a theme restaurant that works. Still other investors look for single-family homes in areas where the zoning will permit more than one residential unit. They then use their carpentry skills to add, change, and convert the building to several apartments.

Your first investment may be targeted to attain the basic of goals, your own housing, or a place for your business or income to supplement your salary. Why not combine all these into one acquisition?

Do Not Bite off More Than You Can Chew. This answer covers the total gamut of the situation: money, ability, and time. It is okay to push one or even two of the trio, but to tax all three to the limit may be stretching yourself a bit thin. Once you know how the game is played and have the rules down pat, then you can take a few risks, but in the beginning, do more homework and take less risks.

Negotiate Terms That Will Help You Sell. When you make an offer to buy a property and as you negotiate the counter offers, keep firmly in mind that the terms you negotiate now may be critical to your selling the property later on. Because of this you should learn as much as you can about different forms of mortgages, techniques such as land leases, options to buy, real estate exchanges, release provisions to mortgages, subordination to other financing, and so on. Check the index of this book to find out where these items are discussed in more detail.

An example is as follows: You are trying to buy a 10-unit apartment house. The seller is asking $400,000 for the property and has a first mortgage of $150,000. He has indicated he would hold some financing if he can get at least $80,000 cash down.

You offer the full price of $400,000 and agree to give the seller $80,000 cash, providing he will hold a first mortgage of $170,000 on another property you own. Because the mortgage he is asked to hold is a first mortgage you should negotiate for a lower interest rate than the seller might demand for a second mortgage. Where are you going to get the $80,000 cash? You make the offer subject to your obtaining a new first mortgage on the property you are trying to acquire at terms of your liking, and tie up the property for a period of 45 days in order to shop around with some of the local lenders.

Because all you really need to borrow is the payoff of the first mortgage, the cash to the seller, and the closing costs of the loan and the real estate purchase, your total loan need not exceed $250,000.

Payoff of the existing loan	$150,000
Cash to the seller	80,000
Closing cost estimate	20,000
Minimum loan request	$250,000

If you close on this basis, you will have acquired this property without spending any of your own money. The seller would get the $80,000 in cash he wanted and the balance of his equity of $170,000 in a first mortgage on another property. Your position in this apartment house is established so that you have $150,000 of solid equity. If you want to sell this property in a few years, after you have built up the value to $500,000 you would have many different options open to you: exchange your $250,000 of new equity for a larger property, sell and hold back a high-interest-rate mortgage, or do a combination of the two.

One interesting result of the above example is the property on which you have moved the seller's $170,000 equity to the form of a mortgage now has excellent financing on it should you want to sell it to an investor.

Avoid Short-Term Payback Financing.   The above example would not be very attractive if the seller insisted on a three-year term on the $170,000 mortgage you gave to him. It surprises me how many smart investors end up buying property that has short-term mortgages on them. Such short-term mortgages with big balloon payments can give you many sleepless nights and sometimes a bad day on the courthouse steps as your property is auctioned off. Do not let that happen to you.

Avoid Pitfalls.   The best way to learn about pitfalls is to learn from the mistakes made by others. Contrary to what many people will tell you, the best way to learn is not to make the mistake yourself. But if you do make a mistake, the key to learning anything is to acknowledge that you made a mistake, review the steps that lead you to the resulting problem, and see if you can pinpoint the moment when you could have avoided the mistake by choosing a different path or by making a different decision.

Fortunately, when it comes to real estate, few mistakes can be made that have not been made by others, and virtually no pitfall can trap you that has not already trapped someone else. This book gives you many different lists and examples of such pitfalls, and as you deal in property and become an insider you will hear and witness other such problems and pitfalls.

The next question gives you a good insight into some of the most critical pitfalls that await unsuspecting buyers of income-producing property.

97. What Are the Most Dangerous Pitfalls to Avoid When Buying Income-Producing Property?

It is easy to say "avoid pitfalls" when in reality the difficulty is to know what you are to avoid. For most successful investors getting out of trouble has evolved into the art of staying out of trouble. This requires experience, but fortunately it does not have to be your own experience that formulates the learning process. The following examples will give you a head start.

The Seven Most Dangerous Pitfalls

1. Having out-of-focus goals
2. Exceeding your management abilities
3. Being undercapitalized for the investment demands
4. Having excessive and onerous debt
5. Operation cost exceeding your estimate
6. Income falling short of your estimate
7. Using improper timing for your investment

Having Out-of-Focus Goals.   Good clear goals are the key to any kind of success. When you do not have those goals firmly in sight, or you stray from the intended plan by letting another goal slip in front of your primary goal, then you are headed for trouble. Of all the pitfalls that await you, the most damaging is to start off without your goal firmly in focus. There are many distractions that cause people to stray from the chosen path, and while an occasional diversion may not put your desired goal out of reach, the trip can be longer and rougher than expected.

One way to help keep your goals firmly in focus is to have goals that are attainable, measurable, and staged as intermediate stepping stones that constantly move you forward. One other aspect is very important: the goals should be written down, and 100 percent approved by any other family member who is a party to the attainment of the goal. By having the goals put in writing, there is no misunderstanding about what it was that you set out to attain. By having attainable desires, you should set goals that you can reach, even though you might have to stretch from time to time to get there. Unreasonable goals that sound good, such as becoming a millionaire by the end of the year, may not be realistic for you. Nothing can damage your self-confidence more than to strive constantly to attain something that is impossible. Start small, take short steps, and plan goals that can be attained simply by your own actions—such as "I will meet three city officials this week." Taking small steps is easy to do and if connected to a plan will have a positive result. Small goals are also measurable; using the previous example, you know when you have met all three officials, and if it was easy, plan on four next week. But remember where all the steps are leading, and see the final result as the long-range goal that is firmly in your sight.

Exceeding Your Management Abilities. There are people who find it absolutely impossible to delegate any task to another. These people pride themselves in never asking anyone to do anything they would not do themselves, and because they think they do it better than anyone, they do it themselves. These people make poor managers of others and will have difficulties in owning property that requires management of other people.

The technical aspects of management of real estate can be learned by most people. Record keeping, dealing with prospective tenants, setting up leases, and dealing with lawyers, accountants, and other professional advisors are relatively easy, once you have taken the time to acknowledge that you do not have a skill and set about to learn it or hire someone else who can do it for you.

Know your own limitations and do not exceed your abilities—but do take steps to increase your skills so that you can expand with confidence and with a good chance for success.

Being Undercapitalized for the Investment Demands. This is not a question of inexperience. Some of the most experienced people in the hotel business, for example, get a few friends together and buy a hotel to run on their own, only to have miscalculated the need for deep pockets. When the money runs out, it might be possible to borrow some more but that may just feed the fire, and the added expense of the increased debt hastens the foreclosure sale.

Undercapitalization means there is no reserve funds to cover normal expenses if income drops for an unexplained or unanticipated reason or to pay off expenses that were not expected, despite how well the income flow is maintained. Acquiring a property with the hope that income goes up and expenses can be held at the status quo or even reduced is very risky. Some people manage to succeed and make a lot of money from a very meager start.

But far more people lose their savings and their dream by not having sufficient capital to cover expenses.

Having Excessive and Onerous Debt. Overleverage, that is, a greater cost to pay the debt than the property produces in income, is not by itself a wrong business decision if there are other benefits to offset the negative cash flow and if you have the capital to carry the debt. When you buy a vacant lot, for example, or another property that has little income but you plan to add more buildings or construct something new that will have a solidly positive income stream, the initial debt can be expensive and more than any income produced. Excessive and onerous debt is another situation. This is when the debt is structured with "doom" written all over it. Short-term debt, for example, looks good because the payments for five years is interest only, or even less than interest only with the principal amount owed growing. This kind of payment schedule maximizes cash flow, or allows you to meet the debt payments from the cash available, and works only when something definite is going to occur that will allow you to bail out of that debt.

When you structure debt on a property you buy you should attempt to obtain mortgage terms that give you room to build the income and increase the value of the property in ample time to meet the demands of a possible refinancing of the property. Real estate cycles up and down, and when people get really hurt it is because they were thinking "up"while the market went down. To refinance in a down period may be impossible, and unless the lender wants to weather the storm with you, you can lose the property to the bank or the previous owner who is sitting on a second mortgage that just came due.

Operation Cost Exceeding Your Estimate. The more properties you look at before you buy, the greater your opportunity to learn about the income and expense for that kind of property. However, to learn you have to do homework, and this means that you should dig into the books and records of the properties you look at and not just take a ten-minute tour through the property with the real estate agent.

A seller should be willing to let a prospective buyer look at the income and expense records of the property. Even if you have no real interest in a specific property, if you ultimately expect to own a similar property, then spend the time to learn what is going on in the market.

See if your local tax assessor's office publishes a standard of income and expenses for the type of real estate you are interested in. If it does not, sit down with one of the appraisers and ask a lot of questions about standard expenses for the area.

The key to expenses is to know what they should be, and then to take the expenses that the seller represents to you as "100 percent real" and see what might be understated or missing altogether. Make your own *pro forma* estimate and be very sure that the criteria you use is not below the standards for the area.

Income Falling Short of Your Estimate. Unless something happens to cause a high level of vacancy, the income picture is the easiest to estimate if you stuck to the market rents for an area. A buyer gets into trouble when a property is being upgraded from the top rent for the zone to a higher rent that the area may not immediately support. Old habits are hard to break and if there are other buildings in the same area asking 30 percent or greater less per square foot, your nicer property may stay vacant a bit longer than you would like it to.

Other events can make a dramatic shift downward to your rental income when the city leaders approve a new roadway in front of your property—a great long-range benefit perhaps, but for the next two years your property may become a vacant building while the roadway is under construction and no one can get to your property. Bridges, overpasses, tunnels, and other improvements in local infrastructure can bring similar results.

Using Improper Timing for Your Investment. Timing is very important. You get the seller at the right moment and she says yes, so you think; you read about the new hospital that is going to be built across the street and you plan to expand…but too soon, as a homeowner association around the corner interfers with the hospital plans through ten years of legal hassle. Many different things can happen that will bring a sudden change in plans. Some of these changes may be to your immediate benefit, others quite the opposite. However, most of these events do not happen overnight, and when they do, a prudent investor should have anticipated that possibility.

When in doubt wait, or if you do not want to wait, then go to contract for the property you want to buy with an option that gives you the time you need to find out if the timing is right or not.

12

Managing Your Real Estate to Maximize Profits and Minimize Problems

98. What Are the Secrets to Successful Property Management?

I call this the "open eye" system of management. First, you keep your own eyes open, and second, you make sure your tenants know exactly what is expected of them and the penalties if they do not live up to those expectations and lease conditions. All property management can be summarized by three basic factors: Check, recheck, and double-check your tenants and your property. Follow the ten secrets outlined below for a smoother, more profitable venture into rental property.

The Ten Secrets to Successful Property Management

1. Have clear unmistakable rules that are enforceable and strictly enforced.

2. Do a detailed tenant check. This means credit, employment, references, banking history, whereabouts of family members, etc.

3. Be responsive to tenants' needs. Whenever the property is inspected, the tenant should sign a statement verifying existing problems and then later acknowledging that those problems have been corrected.

4. Keep detailed records—payment records, repairs, improvements, outside work done, payment of expenses, etc.

5. Publicize goals for continual property improvement. Let your tenants know what you plan for the building *only* if you are then going to follow through. When the planned improvements are done, let them know you have attained your goal.

6. Know your market and seek to increase your rental category. By a slow but continual upgrade of the property, you can increase your rental base.

7. Practice problem prevention management. Act before a small problem becomes a big one. As you learn to anticipate problems you will stop them from occurring.

8. Make periodic property inspections. Record the date of the inspection and exactly what is discovered, both good and bad.

9. Make needed damage repairs immediately. When you set a pattern of immediate response, you can also expect the tenants to respond to you equally.

10. Promptly impose penalties to tenants when allowed by the lease. A rental complex is a closed system, and when one tenant breaks the rules it will not be long before others will attempt to try the same.

99. What Can I Do If My Tenants Are Constantly Late Making Rent Payments?

Dealing with tenants who constantly make late payments can be a problem, and the larger the rental complex, the greater the problem can become unless you are aggressive in dealing with this situation. Follow these five steps.

The Five Steps to Effectively Deal with Late Rent Payments

1. *Document the payment records* so that you have a detailed record of that tenant's payment schedule. This will give you proof of a tenant's rental record and allow you to act quickly if the delay in payment starts to grow.

2. *Make a detailed property inspection* to ensure that there are no other problems building. Following the inspection ask the tenant to sign the inspection report that it is correct. If you discover there are no problems in the apartment, everything is working properly, and there is no evident damage, then indicate that. If there is damage, then address that immediately according to the remedy under the terms of the lease.

3. *Give notice of pending default* to give the tenant every benefit of doubt about the situation. Let your tenants know that your computer will send out past-due notices automatically if their rent is not received during the grace

period. Tell them you treat everyone the same and not to think they are being singled out.

4. *Renegotiate the lease* to a month-by-month basis if the tenant has a long-term lease and you want to work with that tenant to see if you can convert him or her into a better paying and more responsive tenant.

5. *Start legal proceedings* according to the laws of your state to evict the tenant. You can stop the procedure anytime the tenant convinces you they are worth keeping.

100. What Can I Do If I Get Stuck with a Bad Check?

Get to know your state laws governing bad checks. You may discover that if you have taken a check that was postdated, that is, with a date later than the date the check was given to you, then you have no recourse on the bad check. This rule may vary among states so make sure you do not accept a post-dated check. It is better to tell the tenant you will hold the check for a few days, let them trust you, rather than your having to trust them.

When the check comes back marked *NSF* (nonsufficient funds), you can legally collect a redeposit fee, plus a service charge to handle the check a second time. If your lease has a late charge penalty you may also collect that by following your legal rights. One step would be to send notice to the tenant that they are in default and that you are applying their security against the bad check and that they must either make up the security deposit immediately or move out.

If that does not produce results, then check with the circuit court or other court that has jurisdiction over small claims in your area, and get the forms and data necessary to use the legal system to collect what is due you.

One word of warning: When you follow legal proceedings you should be aware that the tenant will have more rights than you might have suspected. It is possible for you to be 100 percent in the right and the tenant to be several months behind in rent, and you still can have a long drawn-out battle to evict. If the tenant has any reason to counterclaim against you, the process can go on for quite a while.

The key is to make sure that you, as landlord, have documented your position correctly and have not tried to sidestep the law in any way. The very moment that you feel the tenant is going to be difficult you should get the advice of a good real estate lawyer.

101. How Can I Reduce or Eliminate Tenant Complaints?

This is a very good question, but in reality you do not want to have a situation where there are no tenant complaints. The key is to have the right kind of complaints so that you can continue to move the property in the right direction for potential increases in rental income. Your tenants are your "on-site watchdogs" and should be encouraged to bring any complaint to your attention.

You will reduce or nearly eliminate tenant complaints by removing the reason for such complaints. When you have a chronic complainer who is constantly complaining about everything, you need to take steps to distinguish what is genuine and what is not; then have a meeting with the tenant in your office or some place other than the rented premises and explain that you have made every effort to keep the tenant happy, and if the tenant is unhappy the tenant is free to vacate the property. Let the tenant know that unless the frivolous complaints are stopped, the tenant cannot expect to have his or her lease renewed.

102.   How Can I Avoid a Tenant's "Midnight Move"?

The only sure way to avoid this is to ensure that it will not be worth the effort for the tenant to make such a move. Most "midnight moves" are a tenant's response to getting into you for more rent owned and/or damage incurred than the combined security deposits will cover. If you have not responded to a tenant being late in rent or damage incurred, then you have allowed the midnight move to happen. To reduce the likelihood of midnight moves keep your eyes open, make periodic inspections, and act quickly when rent is past due.

103.   How Do I Evict A Tenant with the Lowest Cost and the Fewest Problems?

The cost to evict a tenant who does not want to leave can be very costly and time consuming. Often the biggest cost, however, is not the legal charges but the lost rent and repairs that are needed to return the property to rentable condition.

The key then to keeping the cost down is to make sure that you act quickly when the situation begins to develop. The mistake that most landlords make is to wait until the tenant has gotten way behind in the rent and then to act with a pillow rather than a legal proceeding to get the tenant either to comply with the lease or to get out.

Follow these three steps.

Three Steps to Save Money When You Must Evict a Tenant

1. *Act immediately* when a tenant's rent is late. This means to start your procedure that may lead to court action. See the answer to question number 99.

2. *Know your rights* by having your lawyer keep you informed about the current rules and any changes to your local and state law and tenant eviction procedures.

3. *Send proper legal notices* to the tenant the first moment you can. This does not mean you need to follow through with the eviction, but why wait? You can tell the tenant through a phone call to expect a legal notice that you are forced to send, but that you would like to work the matter out as quickly and

as painlessly as possible. But get your legal rights protected and start the time clock running...it can take a long time to evict a tenant who does not want to move.

104. When Can I Use a Small Claims Court to Collect Past-Due Rent?

The answer is when the amount of the claim is within the small claims court jurisdiction. Check with your local circuit court to find out the procedures and limits. Keep in mind that you can sue for each month due separately.

105. What Kind of Lease Should I Use?

As a property owner you should have a lease that is owner-friendly. This means that you should *avoid* a standard store-bought lease. The type of lease that you can find in a business supply store is apt to be a "middle of the road" type of lease. While it may properly address some of the legal aspects that are important for both you and the tenant, it is apt to be slanted toward the tenant and not the property owner.

Do you want to know where you can get a great landlord lease for free? Spend a weekend and visit several of the large rental apartment projects in your area. Ask for a copy of their lease; you can bet they have spent a lot of money with some top-rated law firms in the area to hammer out a lease that protects their rights completely. Read over several of the leases from such projects to make sure you understand everything. If there is something you do not understand, ask the rental agent of that project to explain it to you. In a very short time you will be able to spot the difference between a lease that protects you as a property owner and one that does not.

Take the best lease and let your own attorney look it over. She may want to add something that fits your specific situation better or that brings the document up to date to current laws and or regulations.

106. What Are the Most Common Problems Encountered in Property Management and How Can I Solve Them?

Animal smells

Barking dogs

Bounced checks

Broken windows

Clutter in windows

Clutter and trash around the area

Common-area maintenance

Damaged carpet

Damaged furniture

Derelict cars and other vehicles

Encouraging pests to breed

Fire or fire hazards

Fleas

Hanging things out of windows

Holes in the walls

Illegal use of rented space

Improper number of tenants in the facility

Improper parking

Inoperable appliances

Letting plants die

Loud music and other noise

Missing items

Nails in the walls

Nonpayment of rent

Not keeping yard maintained

Offensive behavior

Parking lot damage

Shoddy "tenant improvements"

Storm damage

Uncleaned appliances

Unreported casualty damage

Unruly or dangerous pets

Unruly children

Use does not conform to lease

Animal Smells.   A strict rules and regulations disclosure in your lease should spell out every detail governing a pet. Be sure to include conditions on disposal of animal waste and a strict penalty for failure to abide by the rules. A periodic inspection of the leased premises should be held whenever pets are allowed, and a "pet cleaning deposit" should be added to the lease to provide cleanup money in the event the animal has soiled or damaged items in or on the property. Be sure that the cleaning deposit requires the tenant to replace a depleted cleaning deposit.

Barking Dogs.   Noise control of all kinds should be a part of the lease rules and regulations. Have strict time periods to eliminate loud music, TV, radio, parties, etc., and to cover barking dogs at all hours. Make the violation of this and any other rule or regulation a default in the lease.

Bounced Checks.   Check your state laws about bounced checks. In most situations it is illegal for a tenant to give you a check from an account that has no funds to cover it. However, from a practical viewpoint this can happen to almost anyone, so you may want to be lenient on the first occasion. Make sure that your lease allows you to charge the tenant for any returned checks. You can add a reasonable service charge to the bank charge, as well as impose a late penalty, but make sure the lease spells out these charges in detail.

Broken Windows.   When your tenant breaks a part of or anything in the property they should be charged for it. If you have a security deposit, then apply the repair against the security deposit and make sure that your lease requires the tenant to bring the security deposit back to its original level.

Clutter in Windows.   Unsightly window clutter can be a problem for residential and commercial property owners. Rules and regulations can limit this problem by addressing the problem directly. Commercial tenants should be allowed to display only approved (by the landlord) signs that also meets the local sign ordinances. Residential tenants should be restricted from having any window clutter visible from the exterior of the property during daylight hours.

Clutter and Trash around the Area.   Strict rules and regulations should either make it a violation to clutter, or provide a common-area maintenance charge to pay for the cleanup.

Common-Area Maintenance Payments.   It is a good idea to have a CAM charge regardless of what kind of rental property you have that exceeds one tenant. This spreads the cost of trash pickup, driveway vacuuming, window cleaning, etc., over all the tenants combined. The CAM provisions in the lease should allow you to pass through increased cost directly to the tenant with a minimal notice (say one month).

Damaged Carpet; Damaged Furniture.   There is a clear and undeniable difference between normal wear and tear, and absolute destruction of a carpet; however, there are many different levels of carpet conditions. Some landlords have found that with the right tenant a carpet can last ten years or more, while other tenants seem to wear out their carpet in 12 months. Keys to any kind of damage control are as follows:

1. Periodic inspection of the premises

2. Prompt application of a security or damage deposit to repair any damage, with the tenant's prompt replacement of the security or damage deposit

3. Good screening of prospective tenants

Derelict Cars and Other Vehicles.   Your lease should have a provision dealing with derelict cars, abandoned cars and other vehicles, boats, trailers, and so on. Make sure your lease has a provision for such situations. Require the tenant to remove any such vehicle that is clearly inoperable or has not been moved at all for the past 30 days (unless they have permission in advance from you for such an event). You can issue parking stickers that have expiration dates shorter than the term of the lease. This will require the tenant to renew the sticker (provided their lease is current, all security and damage deposits up to date, etc.), or risk having their car or other vehicle towed away.

Encouraging Pests to Breed.   Sloppy housekeeping, dumping of trash, feeding of pets and other animals outside the premises, and other unsanitary functions can turn a nice apartment into a roach motel.

Include pest control to the inside and outside of all rental property on a weekly basis. There is an added bonus of this weekly service. It gives you access to make a weekly inspection of the property and whoever does the pest control spraying should have an inspection chart to follow.

To give you some muscle do deal with this problem, make sure your lease provides that the tenant must remove any pest-breeding conditions at their expense or be in default on their lease.

Fire or Fire Hazards.   Any kind of fire is something to be avoided. Perodic inspections will help you spot hazards or dangerous habits that may lead to a serious problem. Burn marks on the edge of furniture may indicate cigarettes left burning; burn holes on carpets or furniture indicate a need for immediate action. Storage of combustible materials, improper overloading of electrical wiring, and other such problems can be averted by the following six steps:

1. Get a fire department inspection of the entire building on a periodic basis.

2. Follow their recommendations.

3. Have more than the minimum fire extinguishers available for tenant use.

4. Post fire evacuation routes and instructions and make sure every tenant has read the material.

5. Provide smoke alarms for every apartment and test them on a regular basis.

6. When making periodic inspections, make fire hazards and entry on the checklist.

Fleas. Most animals are apt to get fleas, and while those fleas may seem to go unnoticed by the pet's owner, as soon as that tenant has moved out and removed the source of food for those pests they will live in the carpet and furniture of the premises waiting for any unsuspecting visitor. Fleas must be dealt with swiftly and on a continuing basis whenever pets are or have been in an apartment.

Some of the chemicals used to kill fleas and their eggs are noxious and hazardous to humans, so use of these chemicals must follow the manufacturer's detailed instructions. Even still, the residue from the chemical may cause reactions days after their use, so a thorough cleaning may be necessary a day or so following their use.

Hanging Things out of Windows. Unless you are living in Naples, Italy where it seems to be fashionable to hang things out the window, apartment buildings of any kind should have strict rules on where clothes and other items are placed to air out or dry.

Holes in the Walls. The lease should require the tenant to repair any hole left in any wall of the property that was caused by that tenant. This should include nail holes, doorknob holes, and so on. Periodic inspections will catch many of these problems before the tenant has moved out, and the repair can be dealt with from the security or damage deposit. As with other deductions from a damage deposit be sure that the tenant brings the amount of the deposit back to its original level.

Illegal Use of Rented Space. The lease should be specific about the use to which the rented space can be put. If you discover that the use is illegal with respect to the zoning or other laws, then the tenant would be in default. To ensure that the tenant has been given proper notice as to the "legality" of use, spell out clearly what use is allowed: for example, "said apartment to be used as a single-family residence only," or "said office space to be used as private offices for an insurance company...."

Improper Number of Tenants in the Facility. There are several elements that need to be addressed in this situation. First and most important is the fire code dealing with the number of maximum occupants in the premises. You cannot exceed this amount under any condition and the tenant needs to know what it is. The second matter deals with the local zoning ordinances that govern the use of the space. These ordinances may have subtle restrictions such as the number of parking places that must be provided for certain use. A medical doctor, as an example, may occupy 1000 square feet of your commercial space, and the code may require you to provide a set number of parking spaces for that tenant. Based on that, you can comply with the city parking code. However, a month later the doctor brings in a partner, and now the city says that with two doctors you need to double the parking for that location. Can you do it? Can you stop the doctor from bringing in a partner? Are you in trouble? You may be.

Other city ordinances set the number of families that can live on any plot of land. If you have a tenant whose family suddenly grows to include several generations and distant relatives you may have a violation caused by this tenant. Does your lease spell out the tenant's obligation to abide by the local ordinance? Or did you forget to even tell the tenant what that ordinance was?

The third aspect, and perhaps the most important, is what kind of limitations do you want to impose on your tenants? If you want to limit your tenants to single people living in your property, then address the issue by having a rental schedule that goes up for every extra occupant living in a rental unit.

Improper Parking.   See the section on derelict cars and other vehicles.

Inoperable Appliances.   It is not unusual for a tenant to move out without ever complaining about anything, and when you do the cleanup to ready the property for a new tenant, you may discover that several burners on the range do not work, that the heater in the bathroom is burned out, and that three electrical switches are inoperable. Why? Because the tenant damaged them and was afraid (rightly so) that you would charge them for the repair. The key is to look for these things in the periodic inspection, and whenever possible do not let the tenant move out until a complete and thorough inspection has taken place.

Letting Plants Die.   This becomes a problem when you lease a home to someone and they have full control over the landscaping. It is not uncommon for a tenant who is paying the water charge to shut off the sprinkler system the day they move into a property. If they also have negotiated a lease where by they agree to cut the lawn, they are apt never cut it at all.

The key is to provide a yard service that is given the responsibility to make periodic inspections of the sprinkler system and to ensure that it is working properly and is in fact being used. Lawn and plant trimming should also be given to this or another yard service company and should be a part of the rent over which you have absolute control.

Periodic inspections will help ensure that your beautiful lawn and plants do not die.

Loud Music and Other Noise.   See the section on barking dogs.

Missing Items.   The "midnight move" that many tenants perform with great finesse may also include them taking with them your refrigerator, sinks, carpet (if in good condition), and even wall switches. This is theft and is punishable if you can prove the items taken were yours to begin with and that they took them.

Step one is to document what items were on the property when they moved in. The lease should spell out in detail what is in the property and what the condition of those items is. It is a good idea to get into the habit of having photographs taken of the interior of a property before the tenant moves in (to be used in court as a contrast to the "after they moved out" photograph).

Step two is to make sure you have information that will help you track down the tenant after they have moved out. This will require you to have had a detailed tenant's information sheet filled out. On that form should be information such as driver's license number, Social Security number, credit card numbers, banking account numbers, references, in case of accident who to notify, employment data, references, auto registration and tag numbers, and a photograph.

Nails in the Walls.   See the section on holes in the wall.

Nonpayment of Rent.   The lease should have strict payment schedules with penalty for nonpayment. If your tenant begins to slip behind and asks you to wait for the rent, and you are willing to do so, have them sign a simple agreement that you will apply the last month's rent (if there has been one paid) against the current rent due, provided they make up the shortage within an agreed to number of days, plus a late charge.

When rent is constantly late, you may want to renegotiate the lease as the first step for the ultimate solution to the problem. For example, if your tenant has a lease that is for a year or longer, the tenant's rights may be such that to remove that tenant by legal means can be long and costly, even when they are several months in default on rent.

When the tenant is constantly late, sit down with them and negotiate a new lease that changes their due date on rent from 10 days after the first of the month (as an example) to 20 days after the first of the month, but puts them on a month-to-month tenancy.

When your tenant is on a month-to-month tenancy, your rights to give notice to evict through legal channels improve in your favor.

Not Keeping Yard Maintained.   See the section on letting plants die.

Offensive Behavior.   It is difficult to build in protection for yourself and your other tenants from a tenant who is offensive and abusive of other people. However, such people usually will violate other more reasonable and easier to govern rules and regulations, such as loud noise codes, etc.

If you have a tenant who is suspected of doing illegal things on the premises you may want to increase the inspections of the premises.

Parking Lot Damage.   See the section on derelict cars and other vehicles.

Shoddy Tenant Improvements.   When a tenant makes "improvements" to a property it is critical that the improvements are made *only* after your specific approval and that the tenant has obtained the required city permits for the construction of the improvements. Often tenants circumvent these steps and undertake improvements that would not be allowed by you and that have not been permitted by the city. When this happens, it can place you in the uncomfortable and expensive situation of having to remove the unpermitted construction.

There are two basic ways to approach tenant improvements. The first is to allow reasonable improvements that in your mind actually improve the property. After all, it is your property and if the tenant wants to make changes to the structure or layout that will later benefit you (at no actual cost to you), then there should be no logical reason to object. Keep in mind that any work done must be by licensed personnel and required permits obtained.

The second situation is that the tenant's improvements are only good for the tenant and that when the tenant moves out (perhaps sooner than either you or they expect), you will have an expense to return the property to its original or useable condition. When this is the case, you should expect a deposit equal to the estimated cost to restore the premises when they vacate the property.

In every case, make sure your lease provides that any fixture or improvement made by the tenant becomes your property, that it is the obligation of the tenant to maintain these new items or improvements under the terms and conditions of the lease, and that unless specifically indicated, the tenant may not remove the improvements or items at the termination or cancellation of the lease. The nonremovable provision is critical because even a simple removal of a piece of machinery can leave gaping holes in floors, ceilings, or walls or all three that can be very expensive to repair.

Storm Damage.   Check with your insurance agent to make sure that you have good coverage on the building, then be sure to include in the lease that the tenant must insure for their own window damage due to storms or vandals. Some tenant's insurance will cover these items only if the lease requires the tenant to provide that insurance.

Whenever you require a tenant to provide insurance of any kind, make sure they do the following:

1. Include you as co-insured.

2. Cover adequate minimums.

3. Have a deductible no greater than the damage or security deposit you are holding.

4. Send you a copy of the insurance policy, and evidence of each renewal payment (or new policy each year).

Uncleaned Appliances.   Until you have a midnight mover leave you with a refrigerator full of rotten food and an oven that could be used as a test lab for creatures from outer space, you do not know what *unclean* really means.

Perodic inspections, prompt use of damage or security deposit to rectify the problem, and then replacement by the tenant of that deposit is the only way to get your tenants to clean up.

Unreported Casualty Damage.   Tenants may not report damage because they are afraid you will charge them for the item. When there is another violation at hand, for example, the failure to maintain required insurance that would have covered their loss, the tenant will be doubly wary of informing you of the damage. Inspections are the key to finding this problem before it grows.

Unruly or Dangerous Pets.   To prevent a costly legal action from another tenant who has been bitten by an unruly or dangerous pet, scared by escaped snakes, or disgusted by piles of animal waste on the walkways, make sure you have strict pet rules and regulations. One way to put some muscle in this part of your lease is to have a special and costly animal deposit that can be used by you to clean up animal clutter, repair damages to the apartment, clean carpets, drapes, etc.

When tenants move in and do not have a pet, make sure the lease provides that should they get a pet in the future that has been approved by you in advance (you can limit the size), that the tenants have preagreed to the pet rules and regulations in advance and will pay you the added pet deposit.

Unruly Children.   Both working and nonworking parents can have unruly children who can create havoc in an apartment complex. Strict hours of outside play and limitation to areas for such play should be imposed with penalty promptly levied when violated.

Use Does Not Conform to Lease.   When you discover that a tenant is using the rented space for a use that does not conform to the original use stated in the lease, even though the use is legal, you should act quickly to notify the tenant that the violation causes a breach in the lease agreement and that if the "use" does not conform to the lease, then the tenant must vacate the facility.

13

How to Pay the Least Capital Gains Tax and Other Real Estate Tax Matters

107. How Does Owning Real Estate Help Me Save on Income Tax?

There are direct ways that you can save on income tax through the ownership of real estate. They are listed below.

The Seven Ways Real Estate Can Reduce Your Income Tax

1. Paper deductions from real income
2. Untaxed appreciation
3. A Section 1031 "tax-free exchange"
4. A Section 1034 zero tax change of residence
5. A one-time exclusion of $125,000 of capital gain
6. An installment sale
7. Untaxed benefits

Paper Deductions from Real Income. The IRS term is *depreciation*, and this is a paper deduction of a portion of the value of an asset as it grows older and, likely, less valuable. Prior to 1986 depreciation was the major reason that many people invested in real estate. The goal was to "shelter income" and the investments were called *tax shelters*. The idea was to use money that was going to be paid to Uncle Sam as income tax for the down payment on a property that would generate sufficient tax deductions to offset the investment. As the investor was now an owner of real property with no real cost, the investment could be rather risky, which might mean big gains. There was little or nothing to lose.

The rules for sheltering income changed, and due to changes in the amount of depreciation that can be taken, the tax shelter business is no longer the way to get into real estate risk-free.

However, depreciation still exists, and the opportunity to shelter income remains a benefit to property ownership. Here is how it works.

If you purchase an apartment building that is worth $250,000 and the land portion is worth $50,000, you would have a depreciable value of $200,000. The depreciable portion of the total value is made up of the building and its contents, as the land cannot be depreciated. Each item of the building and its contents would have a life of economic value. (Groves and orchards, for example, have a tree life for which there is a similar depreciation available. Also, if a mineral or other item is mined from a parcel of land that value would eventually be depleted, but the basic land cannot be depreciated.)

The IRS publishes standards for the different items that make up the building, giving each a minimum number of years over which you would be allowed to deduct the total value. It is possible to spread out the depreciation over a longer period of time, say, to take a straight-line deduction of the whole $200,000 over 40 years, giving you an annual deduction of $5,000, or to separate each item into its minimum life terms thereby increasing the early years of depreciation.

The method you chose should be designed to match your investment plan. Clearly, if you do not need the depreciation now but anticipate increased income in your later years, you would want to push the allowed depreciation to the period of time when it will be most important to your tax savings.

Depreciation as a tax shelter is, however, a temporary situation. The deduction is allowed as an expense from your otherwise taxable income, but it also decreases your tax basis (book value of the property), and when you ultimately sell the property you will have a capital gain, which will be taxable. This capital gain is the total amount of proceeds from a sale less the cost of the sale and your tax basis. Therefore what you do not pay tax on now you will pay tax on later. However, the best part of this is that you chose when you make the payment by determining when to sell the property, and if you chose wisely, the tax you pay could be less on the same amount of gain due to a lower tax bracket at the time you elect to make that payment.

Untaxed Appreciation.   If you put $100,000 in a bank and let it appreciate through the interest it earns, you will report that interest every year as a taxable income. This is an annual event and applies to savings deposits, bonds, mortgage interest paid to you, and any other form of interest you earn regardless if you take it out of the bank or not.

Real estate, just as stocks or that rare stamp or coin, may go up in value, and that value, unless realized (through a sale or other taxable disposition), is not taxed. Therefore, the value you invest in real estate appreciates without hindrance from any deduction for income taxes.

A Section 1031 "Tax-Free Exchange."   A Section 1031 tax-free property exchange allows you, under the right circumstances, to exchange your investment real estate for another investment property. This type of exchange is greatly misunderstood and is often called a *like-kind* exchange. This term is part of the reason a Section 1031 exchange is misunderstood. *Like kind* does not mean that you can take advantage of this IRS-approved transaction only by swapping a farm for a farm or an office building for an office building; *like-kind* signifies that an investment property must be exchanged for another investment property.

A Section 1034 Zero Tax Change of Residence.   A Section 1034 property exchange, or sale and purchase is another IRS-approved transaction that allows you to take advantage of a gain without having to pay any tax on it. The Internal Revenue Section 1034 outlines the method that allows you to sell or exchange your present legal residence and to obtain another legal residence. When done properly it is possible to move up in value from one property to another and not cause a taxable event. For example, if your tax basis (book value) in your present home is $50,000 but its real value is $150,000, then you would have a potential gain of $100,000. If you were in a 20 percent income tax bracket, your tax liability could be $20,000 or more, taking into consideration that this lump sum taken in one year could trigger an increase to a higher tax bracket.

Under the provisions of IRS Section 1034, if you sold or exchanged this home and within 24 months (before or after) of the date you acquired another residence to replace it that was worth the value of your old home or more, then you would have no tax due. If the new residence is less valuable than the one you sell, then the difference between the values would be taxable.

A One-Time Exclusion of $125,000 of Capital Gain.   The one-time $125,000 exclusion of capital gain is a great benefit to your potential savings if you qualify. Under this provision the IRS allows you to deduct the first $125,000 of a gain on the sale of a residence. This is not a mandatory rule, and you can chose when to take it as long as you meet the qualifications, which are the following.

1. You must have passed your 55th birthday.

2. You must have owned and lived in the property for at least three out of the past five years.

3. The property must have been your principal residence during those three or more years.

The one-time $125,000 exclusion of gain is an all-or-nothing event; you cannot elect to take part of it now and the rest later. It is possible to lose an opportunity if you are about to marry and each of you own a home you decide to sell so that you can acquire another. If neither you nor your spouse-to-be have used the one-time extension and you both qualify separately, then sell first and marry later to preserve the right to two exclusions. Otherwise Uncle Sam will take away one of those opportunities.

An Installment Sale.   An installment sale is a method of selling where you hold a mortgage for part of the proceeds of the sale. This form of sale works for any kind of real estate and is not limited to your residence as is the one-time exclusion of $125,000 and Section 1034. Under this provision the percent of gain to the overall price establishes what would be taxable in the sale. For example, if your basis was $50,000 and the value $150,000, the ratio is 50/150,000 or 1/3 basis and 2/3 gain. If a buyer paid you $50,000 cash and you held a $100,000 mortgage, two-thirds of the cash down would be treated as a gain, and two-thirds of every principal payment against the mortgage balance would also be gain and taxable as such. However, nothing requires you to write a mortgage that contains principal payments, and in a situation where the seller wants to maximize interest income, an interest-only payment schedule may accomplish those goals nicely. Only when the mortgage is paid off would the gain be taxable.

Even when the mortgage has a more normal amortization of principal, it may be advantageous to the seller because it will spread the gain over several years, and thereby avoid having the proceeds of the sale push that taxpayer into a higher tax bracket.

The above discussion shows briefly how the these IRS-approved provisions work. As with any IRS rule or regulation, there are apt to be changes in the mechanics of the rule, so it is wise to check with your accountant well in advance of contemplating any tax-related event.

Untaxed Benefits.   Any benefit you get that you would normally pay for out of earnings on which you pay taxes becomes an untaxed benefit. For many people this becomes the single most important bonanza to ownership of real estate.

Consider the family-owned and -operated motel or small hotel. The property cannot only support wages for many members of the family, it can also provide food and housing, transportation via the company car, insurance through usual fringe benefits, and so on.

108. How Do I Keep Good Tax Records That Will Help Me Survive an IRS Audit?

Just the mention of those three letters, *IRS*, can cause a CPA's heart to flutter with anxiety, so why should you be different? The key to dealing with the IRS is simple and painless. Follow these five key steps for your tax records and you will be on solid ground during any audit.

The Five Key Steps to a Painless Tax Audit

1. *Record everything in detail.*   It will be the exactness of your records that will enable you to get maximum deductions on all your expenses. Many peo-

ple overlook small items or improperly document medium-sized payments. Even though those expenses were deductible, they lacked the background data to support the deduction, and in a nitpicking audit the deductions may be disallowed.

2. *Cross-reference checks and bills as a clear pathway to the items paid.* At the time you or your accountant gets a bill, make a note on the bill, and on the check write down the details about what the payment was for. A bill with the heading "Lacore, Inc." for $2,500 without a clear notification as to the purpose for the bill could be for just about anything, and at the IRS audit the agent may set that aside for a closer look. However, if the bill and the check both indicate "repair to office building boiler," then it is less likely to become an issue. Such cross indications will be helpful to you when you need to check on something for your own use as well, so get in that habit.

3. *Keep a running adjustment of your tax basis.* This is important for any kind of real estate you own because if you eventually sell it, your gain will be determined by deducting this basis from the realized proceeds of the sale. As your basis can go up and down, depending on factors such as depreciation or demolition to reduce your basis and improvements to increase the basis, a separate file should be kept to support each deduction and addition to your basis. It is important that you include every possible increase to the value, even if you are not sure the expense at the time spent would qualify as an addition to your basis. At a later date, when it becomes essential for your basis to be accurately determined your CPA can sift through the amounts (even years of such additions) to eliminate those that may not qualify.

4. *An honest approach is the best approach.* This works when you understand that this approach allows you to take every cent of the deductions you are allowed, provided that you document those expenditures properly and that they were genuine.

5. *Do not fear the IRS.* While IRS agents may feel the power and revel in the intimidation their office can provoke, there is no reason to be frightened by them. However, regardless of how honest a person can be, there are some people who are intimidated and who sweat profusely without real cause. If you are one of those people, then make sure you do not attend an IRS audit—let your accountant go for you.

109. What Is the Tax *Write-Off* That Most People Overlook When Selling a Property?

Take a look at item 3 in the answer to question number 108. Keeping an accurate account of increases to your tax basis for any property you own makes this the most overlooked of all the available deductions. One reason for this is the fact that there is no immediate deduction at the time of the expenditure, so the record may be nothing more than a bill and the corresponding check that satisfied the account. All of that got filed away, then after a while (three or more years later) was thrown out to make room for new years of tax data and records.

Twenty years or more of improvements to a property can add up to substantial sums of investment in the property you own. All of these qualified expenditures will increase your tax basis by the same amount, and in turn will reduce the capital gain you have at the time of a sale.

The items that add to your basis are many and include obvious capital expenditures for items such as a swimming pool, awnings around the pool, a dock on the lakefront part of the property, etc. These are obvious and can be recorded and then placed in a separate and very permanent file that you keep until you sell, exchange, or otherwise dispose of the property. However, there are other expenditures that should end up in that file as well—some that are less obvious, such as the fee to the designer who drew the plans for the pool and the gardener who had to remove plants and lawn to make way for the pool. Each of these is a cost related to the capital improvement.

You should, on an annual basis, ask the person who prepares your income tax for a current list of what qualifies as a capital expenditure to increase your basis. If you do it yourself, ask the IRS to give you a guide on these allowable items. The following form should be completed at the end of each year, or at least, while you are preparing your income tax return for that year.

Adjustments to Property Tax Basis

Year end: _____

Property address: _____

Basis at the start of the year: $ _____

   Plus all capital improvements:

_____ Check # _____ $ _____

_____ Check # _____ $ _____

_____ Check # _____ $ _____

_____ Check # _____ $ _____

     Less depreciation, demolition, reduction:

_____ $ _____

_____ $ _____

_____ $ _____

_____ $ _____

   New basis $ _____

---

110. What Is a Capital Gain?

Capital gain is any gain in the amount of a sale of a property that exceeds the combination of your adjusted basis and the cost of the sale. Anything you purchase may be subject to a capital gain if the value of that property increase to an amount above what you paid for it, plus the added investment you have made to improve it. Because there are several ways to reduce the amount of tax you may ultimately pay, it is beneficial for an investor to plan an effective use of those reduction methods to convert earned income, which would be taxable, into a present tax-free income with a future taxable event at a lower tax.

Recent changes in tax law has increased the maximum tax rates for earned income which has made the tax rates on capital gains more favorable to the investor. This is a major benefit to ownership of real estate.

111. What Is Mortgage Over Basis, and How Does That Affect My Tax Liability on a Sale or Exchange?

When you have a situation where the amount owed on a mortgage exceeds your tax basis in a property, the excess sum above the basis will be treated as cash in the event of a sale or exchange.

This situation frequently occurs when a property that has been owned for a long period is refinanced. For example: You own an office building that is currently worth $500,000. However, because you have owned the building for nearly 30 years you have depreciated the book value down to only $100,000. Two years ago you refinanced the building with a new first mortgage of $300,000 to generate the cash you needed to buy another property (or take a vacation to Europe; it does not matter how you spend the money).

Now you sell the building for $500,000 net of all cost of sale and take $100,000 down and hold a second mortgage for the balance above the first mortgage of $300,000. The transaction looks like this:

Price	$500,000
Down payment you get	100,000
First mortgage buyer assumes	300,000
Second mortgage you hold	100,000

Your tax liability at a 25 percent tax bracket is as follows.

Sales price net to you	$500,000
Less your adjusted basis	−100,000
Total taxable gain	$400,000
Tax liability (25 × 400,000)	100,000

(Continued)

Installment Tax Treatment

Amount received at the closing	
Cash	$100,000
Existing mortgage over basis	200,000
Total constructive receipts	$300,000
Ratio of gain to net proceeds of sale	
Gain:	$400,000
Net proceeds:	400,000
Net proceeds calculation:	
Cash	$100,000
Mortgages held	100,000
Mortgage over base	200,000
	$400,000
Ratio: 400,000/400,000 =	100 percent
(for every $10.00 received $10.00 is gain)	
Taxable gain at closing	$300,000
Tax due the year of closing	$ 75,000
(25% of gain received at closing)	

You can quickly see in a transaction where you got $100,000 down, that due to a recovery of mortgage amount that exceeds basis, your tax liability will be at least $75,000. Be aware that a large lump sum of income added to your other income may move you up into a higher tax bracket and that without other deductions to offset this additional income, your tax could jump to the maximum amount allowable.

The reason why mortgage amounts that exceed your tax basis are treated as cash at the closing is for three basic reasons.

First, the mortgage may have been a purchase money mortgage that you took out or assumed when you acquired the property. At that time the basis would have exceeded the amount of the mortgage because any debt at the time you acquire a property plus the cash or other equity you add goes to increase the equity. If you depreciate the property faster than you pay off the mortgage, then the basis can drop below the amount of the mortgage. In essence you have taken advantage of tax deductions from your past income. You did not pay tax on those sums then, so they will be treated as income now.

The second reason is that you may have exchanged into the property with a lower basis from another property. This situation occurs all the time when people do a Section 1031 exchange whereby the basis of their old property moves with them to the new property. As the Section 1031 exchange may have been free of any gains tax due, when the property is ultimately sold the tax will be due now.

For example, you bought a warehouse where you traded a $175,000 value lot as a down payment and assumed a first mortgage of $450,000. If your original basis in the lot was only $10,000, your adjusted basis (without any other considerations) would be $460,000 at the end of the exchange. It would be relatively easy for you to depreciate the building below the mortgage quickly.

The third reason is that if you refinance and pull cash out of the property, for whatever reason other than putting it back into the property as improvements (improvements would increase the basis by the same amount), you paid zero tax on the proceeds of the mortgage at the time you took out the loan (even if you did that 20 years ago and have been paying interest only all this time). Now those proceeds will be taxed.

Warning: If you had sold the property for less than $75,000 down under the same situation as indicated above, you may have a tax due that exceeds the cash you get. It is important that you know what your tax implication will be before you agree to accept a purchase price. Make sure the person giving you advice knows all the details surrounding your ownership, including your tax basis.

112. Should I Take the Maximum Depreciation Available?

Depreciation, that great paper deduction that can reduce your income tax, can be molded to best fit your specific investment plan. There is no absolute requirement that you take any depreciation at all.

If your investment plan indicates that your adjusted gross income will increase over the next ten years, then it would be prudent for you to anticipate setting up a depreciation schedule that would spread out your available depreciation so that you can use as much of it as possible when you are in a higher tax bracket.

There are trade-offs to this reasoning, such as a potential sale of the property within a shorter period of time or a tax-free exchange in the future. It is important that you have an investment goal and work toward that goal in every way. Planning to maximize your tax deductions can be an important part of reaching your goals as quickly as possible.

113. How Does Depreciation Affect My Income Tax?

The paper deduction obtained through depreciation of your real property assets gives you instant (in the year you take it) reduction of your income tax by the percentage of your tax bracket times the amount of the deduction. This is the fundamental reason that real estate may be called a *tax shelter*.

One of the side benefits is that because this deduction is not an actual *cash outlay* on your part, the deduction can move your adjusted gross income into a lower tax bracket without your actually having that cash expense.

114. What About My Home Office—Should I Depreciate It?

With the trend the IRS is taking on the issue of home offices, unless the office is a substantial part of the total residence (square footage ratio) and you are able to meet all the rules that establish the office as a depreciable item, then my recommendation would be not to use the home office as a possible tax shelter.

Where office depreciation is meaningful, however, then the tax deduction should be taken only as long as it fits the overall investment plan. When you establish a portion of your home or apartment as a *commercial event*, you lose your other rights that would apply to a residence only. If you were to attempt a Section 1034 (residence-for-residence exchange or residence-for-residence sell and buy), the value that applied to the office would not be applicable to the Section 1034 rules.

The one-time $125,000 capital gains exclusion would equally not apply to the portion of your home that was classified as an office. All of these matters need to be reviewed prior to taking the depreciation of a couple of hundred square feet of your home. Remember too, worst of all, the IRS looks for depreciation of home offices as a trigger for a possible selection for audit. You may not want that to happen even if you emerge from the audit owing nothing.

115. Are there Techniques I Can Use When Selling That Will Reduce or Eliminate the Capital Gains Tax?

The answer is "yes." For example, you own a motel worth $500,000 and along comes a buyer who wants to buy the property at a more than fair price. All you have to do is agree to hold a second mortgage for part of the transaction.

The problem with this is your tax basis is only $200,000, so you will have to pay a major tax on the $300,000 gain (in your case around $80,000).

A tax-free IRS Section 1031 real estate exchange can accomplish this task if you qualify. One key to a Section 1031 exchange is to remember that if the property is an investment property, then you can find a buyer, put that buyer on hold, or close under the IRS provisions of a deferred exchange (Starker exchange), and then acquire a replacement property without having any tax to pay (if all the rules work in your favor).

Another technique that can reduce the gains tax due is through an installment sale, which allows you to postpone some of the gain tax by spreading out the constructive receipt of the funds over several years.

A very creative approach would be to split the property into two different values: one value for the land, another for the building.

When you sell, establish a land lease on the land, and sell only the leasehold interest or, in effect, the building. Take the motel you own as an example. If the land was worth $200,000, then the building portion of the total price would be $300,000. By keeping the land and leasing it to the owner (with or without an option to buy), you maximize your return on that portion of the would-be sales proceeds because you have not sold the land, paid tax on the gain, and tried to reinvest the proceeds for a decent return.

116. How and Why Is Real Estate Taxed?

Your annual real estate tax as imposed by the local government can be a real shocker if you are used to renting and not owning property. As a tenant you may not have been aware that in some tax areas of the country, rent from one out of every four apartments in a complex is used just to pay the annual real estate tax for that property. Luxury homes can amass a large tax levy, and it is not uncommon for annual real estate tax to exceed three cents per hundred dollars of the tax appraisal value of the property.

What this means is that if that office building you own is appraised at $600,000 and the taxing authority has a combined millage of 30, then the annual tax for that property would be $18,000 (0.030 × $600,000 = $18,000).

A county tax bill is usually made up of the different community charges that are added together to make up any specific property tax amount. These charges can include the following.

Property Tax Bill for Rain County, Florida

Taxing authority	Taxes from this authority
County	$ 600.65
Schools (state)	40.04
Schools (county)	380.21
City	580.00
Water Management	120.66
Special districts	90.31
Touristry	40.09
Convention	20.48
Total tax due	$1,890.44

It is your obligation to understand exactly where this money charged to you is going and to be watchful of the local hearings and meetings where the public has the opportunity to voice their opinions before the elected officials that impose these taxes.

117. How Can I Reduce My Real Estate Tax?

It is possible to reduce your taxes by having the tax assessment that has been made of your property reduced. To do this will require you to take the following steps.

The Ten Steps to Reduce Your Tax Assessment

1. Get a copy of the local procedures to petition for a reduced tax assessment. A call or visit to the county tax assessor's office will produce these results.

2. Obtain a printout of the tax assessments of all the property within three blocks of your area. These data can be obtained from the county property records office, your computer-equipped realtor, your lawyer, or the tax sssessor's office.

3. Obtain data on tax assessments of similar property to yours in other areas of the county. The source for this is the same as item 2, but be sure you have specific addresses of properties that match or are similar to yours around town.

4. Pick specific examples of "similar" property that illustrate your position for a reduced assessment. Out of many different properties pick less than a dozen to show as specific examples of similar properties that are assessed lower than yours.

5. Take one photograph of each property you plan to show as a similar property. There is no need to show the property in its best light; the idea is to downgrade value rather than create a "For Sale" brochure.

6. Include one or more similar properties that had sold in the past year and indicate the sales price, as long as that information is favorable to your position. A property similar to yours that has sold less than your tax appraisal, for example, would be to your advantage.

7. Obtain realistic estimates from two or more local realtors in your area showing the price your property would quickly sell for, as long as these numbers show a relative reduction of value over past years or are in a favorable ratio of the usual tax appraisal to market value. It is rare for the tax appraisal to equal the market value. Therefore, if you can illustrate through comparisons of several sales of similar properties in your area that the norm of the tax appraisal is 70 percent of the market value, then a market value of $200,000 would suggest that a realistic tax appraisal should be around $140,000. If it is greater by a substantial amount, then this would be a favorable indication for a reduction.

8. Build a professional-looking presentation: neatly typed, put in a professional folder, and given with the required copies plus one. If you do not type, take all your material to a "Quick Print" shop—you will find one kind or another not too far away—and let the printers help you put it all together.

9. Indicate the appraisal you expect, and why. If you feel the appraisal of $188,000 is too high and that your calculations point to $140,005, then indicate that and in clear and concise terms indicate why. Reference your examples of "similar properties" show a pattern that will allow the examiner of your petition to have an easy way to approve your material. Avoid statements such as "you idiots do not know what you are doing...," even if you strongly feel that way about it.

10. Do not take "no" for an answer, and even if you get a reduction, apply for another reduction next year.

118. Are There Other *Tax Reduction* Methods I Should Be Aware of?

Each state may have different types of exemptions from taxes that could apply to you or be made to fit one or more of the properties you own. To get a list of these exemptions, pay a visit to your tax assessor's office after making an appointment to see one of the senior tax appraisers. Some of the exemptions that may allow you to reduce or avoid tax altogether are as follows.

Homestead exemption

Agricultural exemption

Nonprofit exemptions

Church and school exemptions

Recreational land exemptions

Handicapped ownership exemptions

119. What Happens If I Do Not Pay the Assessed Real Estate Tax?

Each state may have a procedure that differs, but for the most part the results will be similar to that of Florida. To learn about the actual process as applied to your community, call the tax collector's office and ask for the delinquent tax department. Have this department give you the details for your area.

In the meantime, for Broward County, Florida, the following procedure applies.

Real estate tax bills are sent out in October of the taxable year with a March due date. To encourage early payments, there are discounts for payments made prior to the month of March. These discounts are based on the March amount and are 4 percent for payment in November, 3 percent for December, 2 percent for January, and 1 percent for February. Payments made in April through the last working day of May would have a penalty of 3 percent plus a $3.50 advertising fee. After the end of May, the tax certificate is sold.

A tax certificate is a document that is evidence that the holder has paid the tax and other costs due for that specific property. These are sold at a public auction and in Broward County, Florida during the first week of June (usually the first Monday of June).

Florida limits the maximum interest the buyer of the certificate can earn to 18 percent. So, when a certificate is sold the bids start at an 18 percent return and go down. Unlike other auctions where the ultimate buyer has bid the most, the tax certificate is sold to the investor willing to "earn" the lowest yield on the amount that investor had to pay the county for the taxes and cost due.

The holder of the tax certificate must remain in possession of the certificate for a minimum of two years and not over seven years. At the end of two years the holder can petition the county for a *tax deed*, which will ultimately force the sale of the property unless the unpaid tax and cost have been paid prior to the sale.

Some states have vastly different views on this matter, and the actual yield minimums in your state could be much greater than the norm for Florida. If you have not made a payment for a past year's tax, you should find out your rights as soon as possible and what you may have to pay to make your account current.

120.   What Can I Do If a *Tax Certificate* Has Been Sold Against My Property?

In the case of Broward County, Florida, tax certificates are sold the first week of June following up to four weeks of public advertisement giving notice of this pending event. All legal descriptions and/or property addresses would be advertised. Copies of the list of all properties in question would be available for viewing at the tax collector's office.

Once the certificate has been sold, the only way to remove it as a lien on the property is to pay it off, along with the interest that is due that certificate. The interest due will depend on the amount of return the buyer was willing to accept when he or she bid for the certificate. There may be other costs imposed by the tax collector to handle the paperwork involved.

If there has been an application (by the holder of the tax certificate) for a tax deed, then time is growing short for the certificate to be redeemed. The application for the tax deed will lead to the eventual auction of the property by the county. The property owner can "buy" the tax certificate any time up to the auction, but the cost increases as the county is spending money to prepare for the auction.

Keep in mind the chain of events can proceed quickly from the date the tax is due to the sale of the tax certificate. At that point there is a period when things slow down (in Florida at least), and until twenty-two months pass, the tax deed cannot be applied for and would not be issued for at least another two months.

121.   What Happens to the Mortgage Holder When the Property Owner Fails to Make the Mortgage Payment as well as the Real Estate Tax Payment?

When both a mortgage and a tax liability are in default, the tax lien must be satisfied first. In the case of real estate tax, as mentioned earlier in the answers to questions 119 and 120, continued default on the annual real estate tax due will trigger the sale of a tax certificate that may lead to the ultimate auction of the real estate itself.

Most delinquent tax departments indicate that every reasonable effort is made to notify a mortgage holder of record of the pending events. This may give the mortgagee the right to foreclose on the mortgage and give the county a payoff of any tax due prior to a tax certificate sale, or at least to allow the mortgagee the right to protect his or her interest in the property before the county sells the property at auction.

Even if the property went to auction, any proceeds over and above the tax and interest due (to the owner of the tax certificate) plus the advertising costs and other pre- and postsale costs would go next to satisfy any other tax liens that may be against the property, then to pay off recorded mortgages. Any balance is paid over to the previous owner of the property.

Keep in mind that there can be circumstances when this pattern would not fit, for example, if the property had been confiscated by the federal marshall's office in a case involving drugs, as well as other situations that can occur due to changes in the current laws governing these matters.

14
All about Foreclosures

122. How Do I Foreclose on Someone?

Foreclosure is the procedure you, as a mortgagee, would initiate against the mortgagor when the loan terms, as described in the note and mortgage, have been breached and the loan is in default. The usual term that is breached is the payment of the loan installments in a timely manner.

When the person you lent money to fails to meet his or her obligations to you, according to the terms of the loan agreement they are now in default. Default allows you to demand immediate payment of the past due payments, as well as to *accelerate the mortgage*, which would require the borrower to pay back the entire amount owned. If you are not paid as you demand, you could begin an *action of foreclosure*.

The action of foreclosure follows a fairly standard procedure regardless of which state you live in or which state the property that secures the loan is located in. However, as with all laws that govern property rights and actions against breach of contract, each state generally has its own specific set of laws, and these can vary among states. Nonetheless, the actual steps leading up to the foreclosure are indicated below.

The 14 Steps Leading up to a Foreclosure Sale

1. Mortgage or loan agreement in default
2. Notice of pending legal action
3. Final notice before legal action starts
4. Title search by the lender

5. Notice of foreclosure

6. Decisions on tenants

7. *Lis pendens* filed

8. New title search

9. Final chance to halt the foreclosure

10. Foreclosure sale advertised

11. Sale held

12. Buyers bid at the auction

13. Right to redeem

14. Deficiency judgement awarded

A Mortgage or Loan Agreement in Default.   The mortgagor (persons who borrowed the money) has breached the mortgage contract with the lender (the mortgagee). Usually this occurs by way of a default in the required mortgage payments but is not limited to those terms or conditions. Any form of breach or default can cause the lender to accelerate the mortgage and, if not then paid in full, to file for foreclosure action.

Notice of Pending Legal Action.   Notice of pending legal action is usually sent to the lender. Most lenders would rather not go through the process of foreclosure and try to work with the borrower if at all possible so they will usually take steps to attempt to collect past payments without resorting to a foreclosure action. Lenders know that many different situations can occur that would cause a good credit risk to suddenly miss several payments and want to avoid the time and expense of legal proceedings. The initial notices to the borrower are usually letters, and these may come in several stages, each letter building in intensity. A collection agency or department may also call on the phone or even pay for a personal visit to try to motivate the borrower to make the mortgage current. It is important to recognize that this step may not be necessary or legally required. Some lenders may take the position that they would like to get the property back, or an investor who has purchased the mortgage did so just to have the opportunity to attempt to foreclose on the property to get title. If this is the case then the moment the mortgage is in default, the foreclosure process can start.

Final Notice before Legal Action Starts.   Final notice pending the foreclosure action is sent to the borrower. There may, of course, be several "final notices," but sooner or later the lender's patience will have been exhausted and the procedure will advance to the next stage.

Title Search by the Lender.   To ascertain the chain of title and find who the interested parties are, a title search is ordered by the lender. Most state laws will provide that the borrower must join with other creditors of record and that all persons who have any interest in the property are made parties to the action.

Notice of Foreclosure.   Notice is sent to interested parties informing them of the initiated action. Such notice is initiated by the lender naming them as parties to the suit and serving them a summons to that effect. This summons must be served according to the laws of the state (either in person or by proper notice and advertisement or both), but if the lender intends to demand a *deficiency judgment* to collect the proceeds of a foreclosure sale that is short of the needed payoff of the delinquent debt plus expenses, the notice to the borrower must be delivered in person.

The lender need not, however, name as a party to the suit a holder of a superior lien. Such would be the case if a second mortgage holder was filing suit for foreclosure action and there was an existing first mortgage. The rights of the first mortgage would not normally be affected by the foreclosure action of the junior mortgage, as a purchaser at a foreclosure sale would acquire the property with the mortgage in place, unless a superior mortgage has also filed for foreclosure action.

In any event, unless a junior lien wishes to dispute the validity of a superior lien there may be no advantage to joining them as parties to the action.

Decisions on Tenants.   If there is a tenant, and the tenant's lease precedes the mortgage without being subordinated to that mortgage, then the foreclosure action may have no effect on the rights of the tenant. However, this is a function of law and the circumstances. Even if the lease was written after the mortgage or subordinate to the mortgage, the lender seeking foreclosure action may wish to keep the tenant in place as that tenant could be an asset to the ultimate sale of the property, in that event the lender may choose to name the tenant as a party only for notice purposes.

Lis Pendens Is Filed.   A *lis pendens* is filed and recorded. The *lis pendens* or *notice of the pendency of the action* is a legal device that results in the automatic joining in of any party who acquires any interest in the property after the notice is filed. This action is a legal notice that appears in the county property records and has the ultimate result of putting anyone who may want to buy, lease, or otherwise obtain an interest in the property of a pending legal action. It would be rare for anyone to buy or rent (for a long term) under these conditions.

New Title Search.   A second title search is made. This is to ensure that everyone necessary has been given proper notice and joined in as parties to the action. The second title search also double checks that the owner has not made a midnight sale of the property in an attempt to complicate the matter.

Final Chance to Halt the Foreclosure.   This is the final opportunity for negotiations between lender and borrower. Up until the moment of the foreclosure sale the owner of the property may attempt to negotiate with the lender to reactivate the original loan, to obtain new and more attractive loan terms, or just to get out of the property by deeding the property back to the lender by way of a *deed in lieu of foreclosure.*

Foreclosure Sale Is Advertised.   Most states require that the foreclosure sale be advertised in advance. This is to ensure that the public is given an opportunity to come to the sale and to bid for the property. These advertisements frequently appear in legal journals or professional newspapers whose subscribers are mostly lawyers, title companies, and a few investors who specialize in the many different opportunities that come from dealing with legal evolvements. Many local newspapers have a legal section, often part of the classified news section, where these notices are placed.

Sale Is Held.   The sale itself may be administered by the court or an officer of the court, such as a judge, sheriff, or other party. In some states there are laws that allow the lender to administer the sale, but that is rarely the case. Foreclosure sales are usually an absolute auction where the highest bidder becomes the buyer. Care must be undertaken to ascertain if there are any obligations that must be assumed (superior existing debt, construction problems, city, county or other governing agency violations or penalties, etc.).

Buyers Bid at the Auction.   Anyone can show up and bid at the auction, and parties who have recorded liens or judgements can use those as value sums to bid. If there is a first mortgage of $100,000, the lender holding that lien does not have to bid at all and can wait to see if there is anyone else who will bid sufficiently to cover the cost of the foreclosure sale (court costs, advertising, etc. come off the top), and tax liens that would be superior to the first mortgage. If the highest bid seems to be settling around $80,000, which would leave $75,000 for the payback of the first mortgage, the lender would have to decide to bid or take a loss on the sale and attempt to collect a deficiency judgement from the borrower.

Right to Redeem.   The previous owner may have a *right to redeem* both before and after the sale. In some states the mortgagor has the right to redeem before and/or after the sale. The period following the sale may be very short or not available at all under the circumstances.

Deficiency Judgment Awarded.   A deficiency judgment may be awarded to the lender. If the loan document called for a personal liability on the part of the borrower, then the lender may want to have the foreclosure suit include a deficiency judgment. This usually requires that a personal notice be delivered to the party or parties, and failure to make personal contact can thwart the procedure altogether. This factor is why many banks are reluctant to make loans to people who have primary residences outside the reach of such legal summons. Courts vary on their decisions governing deficiency judgements even within the same jurisdiction.

Warning: It is not wise for a property owner to "play around" with the potential results of a foreclosure sale. I have seen property owners threaten their lenders with statements such as, "If you can't give me a lower interest rate, then I'll be glad to give you the property." This might sound good in the movies, but does little to win friends at your favorite lending institutions.

Because of the complexity of many mortgage documents, and the fact that many old savings and loans institutions are now defunct, most lenders are quicker to react, act tougher than they should, and often are so remote to the situation that there is little or no personal attention possible. These circumstances make it difficult to have that chat across the desk to work everything out.

123.   If I Get Behind in a Few Mortgage Payments, What Can I Do to Keep from Facing a Foreclosure Myself?

The steps you might consider in this situation would vary depending on the nature of the loan and the lender. Some mortgagors actually *want* the lender to foreclose and force the issue. This is rare and generally occurs when the foreclosure action will cause an ultimate benefit to the owner. One such event would occur when the property owner wants to refinance the existing loan that is at a high market rate in comparison to the interest rates available for a new loan, but the owner would be forced to pay a penalty for early retirement of the loan. Many institutional loans and most private mortgages have such provisions as standard clauses in their loan documents. Even with the cost of the foreclosure action the owner may find that route the best direction to follow. Of course, the whole ploy might be used as a negotiating tool, as many lenders would quickly negotiate for a payoff at a reduced penalty or waive the penalty to avoid a legal action where they would benefit little in the long run.

Another mortgagor-initiated foreclosure situation would be when the property was financed by municipal bonds or other public bond issues that imposed restrictions on the property and the lender. These bonds may restrict the use of the property or limit the nature of tenants that can be housed in the property. Time restrictions can be binding for a minimum period of years *even if the bonds are paid off early*. A foreclosure may circumvent that minimum time period.

If, on the other hand, you are simply caught in an economic bind, have gotten behind in mortgage payments, and want to do everything you can to catch up so you do not face the ultimate foreclosure sale, then follow these steps.

The Four Steps to Negotiate Avoidance of Foreclosure

1. *Know your documents*. Get complete copies of your note and mortgage and read them over carefully. Make sure you understand all the terms and what your obligations are under those terms and conditions.

2. *Know your legal rights.* Spend an hour with a good real estate lawyer who is familiar with foreclosure actions. Have him or her advise you about your rights and exactly what you can do to prevent the foreclosure or the lien holders to force a sale and to remove you from the property. Knowing this can be essential because this is your leverage even if you never mention or threaten to exercise those rights to the fullest extent.

3. *Negotiate with a decision maker.* This may be harder than you think. We live in a world of computers and in the case of institutional lenders, service companies that could not function without them. Your lending savings and loan association that made the loan might be just around the corner, but the loan service company could be 2000 miles away.

Mortgage service companies can be very impersonal, not trained in anything other than the mundane tasks they perform. My personal experience is that they may promise you anything but not have the authority or any initiative to follow up. You may not be able to negotiate with these people, but try anyway. Sometimes their utter impersonality works in your favor.

But if you still get nasty letters threatening to expose you to the world of bill collectors, then push to get to someone who actually works for or represents more closely the holder of that mortgage.

4. *Have a proposal ready.* This is an important step. Your success in any form of negotiation improves if you can illustrate to the other side of the dispute that what you are asking them to do should be acceptable to them. Be quick to explain that you want to live up to your obligation, but need assistance, time, understanding, and forgiveness from the lender. If you can then follow that up with some positive action, such as a check for one or two past payments, then you should be met with a willing response.

124. Are Foreclosure Sales a Good Buy and Where Do I Find Them?

In general, the foreclosure market is the same as any other marketplace. There certainly will be opportunities, but these opportunities take special skills to locate and special attention to deal with. However, there are people who swear by the foreclosure market, and it is possible that your community offers some great bargains.

Buying a property at a foreclosure sale may require you to have a sizable cash or cashier's check ready for an on-the-spot deposit. You may have a short time to get your financing in order, and if you fail, you will most likely lose your deposit.

Prefinancing qualifications with the mortgagee who forced the sale would help, but having your own bank behind you is the ultimate answer.

Look at the list of foreclosure sources in question number 25. A quick check in your local phone directory should produce phone numbers and addresses.

125. How Can I Find Out about Foreclosure Property?

Every community will have its fair share of foreclosed properties. If you are unsure about getting into this area of the market, start slowly by attending a few foreclosure sales. Talk to the loan officers and department heads of the sources for foreclosed properties listed below. You will find that almost everyone will be helpful to you in your learning process—after all, you may buy one of their properties in the near future.

Four Places Where You Can Find Foreclosed Properties for Sale

1. Subscribe to the local legal newspaper. Most communities have one. Find out by calling any local lawyer or title insurance company and ask them for the name and phone number of the paper they subscribe to. This is where most foreclosed properties in your area will be advertised.

2. Contact the local or closest office of the Veterans Administration. This association may have a list of properties that they have taken back in foreclosure and will sell to you directly. Usually the down payment is very low and good financing is available.

3. Contact the local or closest office of Federal Housing Administration (FHA) properties. The FHA has its own properties they have taken back in foreclosure and like the VA can offer you good financing with low down payments.

4. All institutional lenders in your area usually have departments that handle their real estate owned (REO). Some lenders give these foreclosed properties interesting names such as *Special Assets* or *Seasoned Properties*. In all cases, when the lender has taken back the property on which a foreclosure action was initiated, it is because no one bid high enough to satisfy the lender's position or because the lender took the property as a deed in lieu of foreclosure. In virtually every case the lender does not want to own the property—they want to lend money. Make a few phone calls to the *Special Asset* or REO departments of some of the bigger lenders in your area and get on their mailing list. You may also want to become prequalified for a loan in the event you see exactly what you have been looking for.

126. What Are the Major Pitfalls of Buying Foreclosed Property?

Any property that has an economic problem attached to it may end up having several or all of the following additional problems.

The Five Major Pitfalls of Foreclosed Property

1. Deferred maintenance
2. Hidden liabilities
3. Lost market potential
4. Financing problems
5. Long recovery time

Deferred Maintenance.   One of the first things a property owner does when short of funds is to stop the usual upkeep to a property. If the mortgagor is trying to take advantage of the property, sometimes right up to the time of the foreclosure sale, you can be sure that even serious repairs may not have been done.

Sometimes a lender will attempt to "spruce up" a property pending a foreclosure sale, provided they have gotten some control over the property by having a receiver appointed or through agreement with the property owner (who should not object to the lender spending their own money), to increase the potential sale proceeds. Often this "spruce up" procedure is just a cosmetic coverup. Very detailed inspections are essential to protect your interest.

Hidden Liabilities.   If the state law allows the mortgagor to redeem the property, then there could be problems even after the sale. Even if that is not a potential problem, this kind of sale has other latent problems that can occur. Tenants' rights can be affected, or a legal action can occur for little or no real reason other than to take advantage of your "new position." Never take title to any property from a foreclosure action sale unless you have had a title company or lawyer review and agree to *insure* your new title and give you a written list of any conditions or exclusions in their policy. The fact that they include exclusions may not be bad, but make sure you know what they are and that the risk those exclusions impose are acceptable. A usual exclusion would be any potential liability that a recent survey would have uncovered as a potential risk. The term *recent* need be defined, and if the survey you are given is not recent enough then request a current one from the court or the seller. If possible, you should strive to have all exclusions removed that produce even a marginal risk on your part.

Lost Market Potential.   If the property is in an area where there are many foreclosed properties, the neighborhood can be depressed. Sometimes the neighborhood looks like a battle zone, with builder's models abandoned, half-finished structures with their exposed walls open to the elements, and so on. This kind of area can breed more foreclosures and the market here can be headed for a sharp downturn.

Financing Problems.   Financing problems can start at the time of the sale itself, because that cash or cashier's check deposit can be a nonrefundable deposit you may not want to risk. Usually there are some escape provisions you are entitled to, such as a bad title, or a counterclaim by an interested party that will block your continuing with the sale, but unless you can get the needed financing or have it already in your pocket, financing can be a tough problem to solve.

Long Recovery Time.   If you are acquiring your dream home or the ranch you have always wanted but could never afford until now, then there may be no reason to even think about recovery. However, if you are looking at this acquisition as an investment or a stepping stone, then the acquisition of a foreclosure should be contemplated only after you have taken a careful assessment of the time it will take for you to recover your investment and the added investment of fixing up the property for a profitable resale.

15
Buying and Selling through Auctions

127. How Does a Real Estate *Auction* Work and How Can I Benefit from It?

Virtually every manufactured product can end up at an auction at one time or other, and for many items, sometimes the auction produces the highest price possible. On other occasions the auction can be a market place for real bargains. The key is to know how the auction process works and to take advantage of the *bargain* if it fits your plans. All real estate auctions follow a format similar to the following.

The Four Stages of a Property Auction

1. A property is put up for sale through an auction format because of a foreclosure action, a tax deed application, a court-ordered sale, provisions in a contract, a divorce resolution, a provision to satisfy the needs of an estate, or a method to a dissolution of a partnership or trust, or because the owner chooses the auction as a means to quickly dispose of the property.
2. The auction rules are established and the category of the auction is determined from one of the following:
   a. *Absolute auction*, in which the highest bidder will get the property regardless of how low that bid might be.
   b. Absolute when a minimum bid is reached.
   c. Subject to withdrawal at any time by the seller. When the seller does not like the amount of money bid, the seller can bid in for him- or herself or withdraw the property outright from the auction.
   d. Silent or sealed bid. Bids are made in advance and submitted for review. No one knows what anyone else is bidding.

3. In the case of a foreclosure or other court-ordered sale, state laws generally establish a period of time over which the property must be advertised prior to the sale. This serves several different goals. The most important is to give ample notice to draw prospective buyers. The other main reason for such announcement of the auction sale is to give all "interested parties" sufficient time to react to protect their interest. However, even with advance notice and advertising it is rare for an auction to draw many prospective buyers.

4. At every real estate auction the prospective buyer has been given some preinspection rights. The inspection period is usually shown in the advertising material, but not always. Direct contact with the administrator of the auction is frequently needed to arrange personal inspections

128. What Are the Most Important Steps I Should Take before Bidding at Any Auction?

There are many different kinds of auctions, but there are only three kinds of people who go to them:

1. People who go to buy
2. People who go to watch
3. People who buy when they should not have

To make sure you do not fall into category "3," review the five steps outlined below.

The Five Steps to Follow at Every Auction You Attend

1. Review your goals.
2. Look for properties that serve those goals.
3. Make thorough inspections of the property.
4. Preset the maximum amount you should bid.
5. Never exceed the maximum you set.

129. Why Is the *Absolute Sale* Auction the Best to Attend?

When a property is offered for sale at an absolute auction the audience can anticipate that the property will be sold no matter what happens. Auctions that are not absolute are subject to bids not meeting a preset level and the property then being withdrawn from the sale. If you have to incur an expense to go to the auction you want to make sure that your time, money, and effort are spent wisely.

130. What Governmental Agencies Hold Regular Auctions?

Most government agencies hold auctions of one kind or another. Some, such as the Postal Department, can be interesting if you are in the market for delivery vans, jeeps, and other vehicles used by the post office.

The Customs Department frequently has auctions to get rid of items that have been left in customs warehouses because the duty exceeded the amount the recipient wanted to pay, or items that have been confiscated by customs officers.

The U.S. Marshall's office frequently auctions off property taken as a result of drug or other illegal operations. Often these properties include some very expensive real estate.

The above-noted and other governmental agencies and departments that hold auctions will generally advertise extensively in advance of the event. Look for these advertisements in the local "legal" publication and national financial newspapers.

131. How Does a *Court-Ordered Auction* Differ from a Seller's Auction?

A court-ordered auction is the result of an event where the auction is the last resort to resolve the problem. This can be because of a defaulted mortgage, a contract dispute, or some other legal action evolving title or ownership of a property that could not be resolved without a forced sale.

The seller's use of an auction as a tool to "move" a property is an attempt to use this technique to bring a large number of prospective buyers together in an attempt to motivate them to buy something they might not normally buy and/or to pay a higher price than they would if left on their own to negotiate one-on-one with the seller.

Many land and housing tracts have been successfully marketed with this technique.

132. Why Is a U.S. Marshal's Drug Property Auction or Sale the Least Bargain?

When in the hands of a master auctioneer, and given sufficient advertising funds and the draw power of an absolute auction, the auction is likely to draw a very large audience. With this and the fact that some of the "items" are apt to be in demand by other drug dealers, the prices at the auction can skyrocket.

However, these auctions can be very interesting to watch. Be careful not to scratch your head or you may have just bought a speed boat capable of traveling 150 knots per hour!

133. What Is the Resolution Trust Corporation?

The Resolution Trust Corporation (RTC) was formed by the U.S. Government as a department to catalog, organize, and then sell off the assets of the savings and loans and other lending institutions that were "bailed out" by the Congress of the United States.

This organization was given a very difficult task to accomplish. Most real estate professionals have very little praise of the way the RTC handled the organizational stage of the process, and most banking professionals seem to have little praise of the way the RTC disposed of the properties.

The end results of the disposing of the real estate may be many years away from being analyzed, but the RTC is sure to get blamed for the tremendous real estate depression that began about the same time they started dumping real estate on the market.

134. How Can I Cash in on RTC Auctions?

The early "cash in" days are over, but that does not mean that all the bargains are gone. As the RTC finishes, there are going to be some final sales that may beat the records of selling property below its former value.

If you are careful, and do not buy just to be a part of that record, but buy because the property fits your goals or needs, then RTC property can be worth checking before you look anywhere else.

The problem is finding someone who knows something about the property, can talk to you, and be of assistance to you. One of the most difficult functions of the RTC, and a frequent complaint among genuine and very frustrated would-be buyers of RTC property, is information dissemination.

However, if you stick to it, sooner or later you will find a live person (not a phone message center) who can give you up-to-date information on what is available in your area.

135. How Can I Select an Auctioneer to Auction off My Property?

Review the steps shown below to best select an auctioneer.

**The Ten Steps to Follow to Select
the Best Auctioneer for Your Property**

1. Attend two or more different auctions.

2. Find out who the insiders to auctions are.

3. Ask the insiders who they would recommend.

4. Contact two or more of the recommended auctioneers.

5. Attend at least one auction of each prospective auctioneer.

6. Meet with your final choice of three.

7. Explain your investment goals to them.

8. Outline your expectations of the auction.

9. Ask their advice and proposed plan to auction your property.

10. Review your findings and make a choice.

136. Can I Use the Auction as a Tool to Sell My Own Property?

As the auction can be an effective method of selling property, it seems logical that a voluntary selection of this technique might produce a beneficial result to a property owner who has not been able to sell a property that has been on the market for some time.

The decision to use an auction to sell your property should come after you weigh the local market conditions very heavily. If the real estate market in your area for the type of property you own is soft and there are few "takers" for what you have to offer, then the auction could be a disaster.

On the other hand, if your property can be offered at a bargain price and your motivation to sell strong enough to allow the auction, let it proceed as an absolute auction. This kind of auction draws people because they know the property will be sold to the highest bidder, regardless of how low that price may be. When there is a strong turnout of prospective buyers, a well-run auction and a strong auctioneer may whip the crowd into a buying frenzy and entice the prospective buyers to pay more for the property then they might have were they the only buyer in town looking at that property.

16

Real Estate
Finance
Made Easy

137. What Is the Best Way to Calculate Mortgage Payments?

The real "insiders," that is to say, mortgage brokers, real estate brokers, and others in the financial end of the business, frequently rely on computers to print out amortization schedules, or own and are proficient in how to use a "financial calculator."

There are several great, and not too expensive, calculators that will serve you very well with virtually all the different kinds of mortgage calculations you may want to obtain exact answers to quickly. One of the most economical line of financial calculators is made by Texas Instruments and several of their models can be found in most discount office product stores for under $30.00. No matter what your profession, there is no need to spend more than that to get adequate results.

For quick and easy answers, there are two great publications that you may want to invest in. They are the *McGraw-Hill's Interest Amortization Tables*, which is commonly referred to as the "red book," and *McGraw-Hill's Compound Interest & Annuity Tables*, known as the "blue book," both of which are compiled by Jack C. Estes and Dennis R. Kelley. These books offer the real estate investor a fast way to determine the answers to many real estate problems. It is helpful when using these tables to have the additional help of an inexpensive calculator, but the only calculation you will do will be to add, subtract, multiply, or divide. You can order these and any other McGraw-Hill publications by calling 1-800 2-McGRAW.

138. How Do I Calculate the *Yield* on an Income-Producing Property?

Yield is an important measurement of what an investment is going to or has produced for the investor. There are several different terms that refer to yield that can be confusing or if improperly used convey a very misleading picture of the actual events.

Cash on cash return is the most basic of all yields and is often used as a guide to the immediate benefits from any investment. A cash on cash return, however, is not as informative to any specific investor as would be the after tax spendable return in which the income and other taxes have been deducted from the cash flow.

Look at the example where a mortgage was purchased for $44,145 with a demand return of 12 percent. The mortgage had 10 years to go at the time of the purchase, but was paid off at the end of one year. The total cash return to the investor was $10,222.05. The following steps will show you how to calculate the yield of this investment.

The Four Steps to Calculate Yield

1. The formula: (cash invested) × (yield rate) = (return) or (return)/(cash invested) = (yield rate).
2. $10,222.05 ÷ $44,145 = 0.231556.
3. Convert to a percentage by moving the decimal two places to the right.
4. Yield = 23.1556 percent.

This indicates that the investor had a return equal to 23.1556 percent on the cash he had invested.

Net operating income (NOI) yield is another yield that investors sometimes look at as a comparison criterion when reviewing several different properties. As the NOI is found by taking the gross income and deducting all expenses from it, any yield arrived at from the NOI will not take into consideration the cost of debt or income taxes. As NOI assumes that there is no debt (as was the case in the above example) the NOI yield can be exactly the same as the cash on cash yield.

139. How Can I Increase *Spendable Cash Flow* from an Income Property?

One of the greatest dilemmas of property management is the mystery of increasing the bottom line of a rental property. The finesse needed to accomplish this task is less difficult if the work is broken down into the individual elements that make up the truly important bottom line—the spendable cash flow.

The first step is to see the bottom line in its most important definition: *spendable cash flow*. *Spendable cash flow* is the amount of money that is left at the end of any given year, after deductions have been made from all income. This is then the amount of money that the property owner can spend once everything, including operating expenses, fixed charges, debt service (interest and principal), and all taxes have been paid.

Keep in mind that the term *bottom line* when used by itself can mean NOI, cash flow, or other accounting results that may vary, depending on the specific investor. *Spendable cash flow* is relative to the specific investor whose circumstances match the assumptions made for tax bracket and depreciation, because to arrive at this amount, income tax must be deducted from the cash flow.

The following are the seven ways to increase the *spendable cash flow*.

The Seven Ways to Increase the Spendable Cash Flow

1. Increase rental rates.

2. Decrease vacancies.

3. Decrease expenses.

4. Reduce debt service.

5. Add rental units.

6. Decrease tax liability.

7. Convert to another use.

Increase Rental Rates.   It is often taken for granted that rental rates will continue to go up, and therefore property values will increase accordingly. Anyone who has owned rental real estate during the 1970s and 1980s knows that this is not an absolute truth, nor is this factor a function of the condition of the property. Rental rates vary widely for many different reasons, but in general, the greatest effect on the amount of rent a property will bring will depend on the level of vacancies in that specific rental category. Low-priced rentals in an area may have a high vacancy factor, while upper category (higher rents and/or better clientele) rentals may have a negligible vacancy factor.

All rental properties fall into rental categories within every market area. It is possible for two identical buildings to have rates that vary 30 percent or more because of the location, condition, ease of access, and tenant makeup. Because of this, one of the best long-term approaches to increasing rental rates is to upgrade the rental category of the property if at all possible. This may take concentrated effort and expense.

If a property owner is able to increase the rents by as little as 5 percent and hold firm all other costs and expenses, an increase from $100,000 to $105,000 will have the bonus of increasing the value of this property by an additional $50,000. How so?

The value of income property is based on the ultimate return that property will generate. A rental property that generates a 10 percent cash on cash return may be considered a good investment. That extra $5,000 reflects an additional cash investment of $50,000 (10 percent of $50,000 = $5,000).

Decrease Vacancies.   Astute property manager investors look for rental properties that have high vacancies that can be reduced by good management practices and capital improvement. Because value has a direct connection to the yield, a property that is operating at only 70 percent of its maximum capability will be valued accordingly. If the investor can decrease the vacancies while holding steady the rental rates, then an income boost from 70 to 90 percent can cause a sudden and very dramatic increase in the NOI of the property. For example, a 20-unit apartment building with quoted rents of $600 per month would have a gross rent roll possible (if 100 percent occupied) of $144,000. At 70 percent occupancy it would have an actual rent roll of $100,800. If during a one-year period the vacancy factor could be reduced from 30 to 10 percent, the new rent roll would be $129,600. The increase of $28,800 in revenue would reflect a value increase of $288,000 or more.

Decrease Expenses.   Logically any decrease in expenses should increase the bottom line, and this is often the first place investors look at to concentrate their efforts for an increased bottom line. There are many opportunities to decrease expenses, and the astute property manager knows what areas of management to apply to bring about those decreases. However, most sellers are less than 100 percent accurate about their expenses, and it is not uncommon for even an astute property manager to acquire a property with the belief that the expenses can be reduced, only to find that they go up and often dramatically so.

Neglected property maintenance is often the culprit, as this is an easy area to cut back, especially if the owner plans to sell the property, and meanwhile is milking it for every dime the property will produce. Along comes a buyer who looks at the income and expense report on the property and finds several expenses that seem too high, such as travel and promotional expenses. These should be easy to cut back on, the property manager type thinks. But there is not enough attention given to the fact that over the past five years the amount of money dedicated to repairs and replacements has been pitifully low, or practically nonexistent. This property is going to need to catch up with repairs and replacements to bring it to the level it should be when purchased. These expenses cannot be overlooked.

Many weekend property owners sell because they no longer can keep up with the maintenance costs. At first they did the work themselves—a little paint here, an unplugged toilet there, and so on. But now they do not have the time, and to hire that work out for a small rental property is too expensive. If you are into owning this kind of property and can either do the work yourself or have enough units to hire a full-time person or crew to do the work, then this is one area where expenses can be reduced tremendously.

Buying a job, is a good investment, and many foreigners coming to the United States have begun their fortunes by buying a property or business that not only gives them a job but can provide jobs for their whole family. Properties that are management and employment intensive, such as hotels, motels, and restaurants, are good examples of this kind of investment. While this aspect does not decrease overall expenses, it has the benefit of keeping the cost within the family.

Reduce Debt Service.   If a property has an NOI of $144,000 and a total debt service of $100,000, the cash flow will be $44,000. If the demand rate was 10 percent, the value of this property may be assumed to be $440,000 plus the amount of the debt. If there was a first mortgage of $1,000,000 on the property (with an annual debt payment of $100,000), then the property value would be $1,440,000. However, the debt service of $100,000 may not reflect the true value of the property fairly. For example, if the outstanding first mortgage was $500,000 at 13.75 percent interest and would fully amortize in just slightly over 8.5 years, the annual payment would also be $100,000.

The NOI yield indicates value is there. Based on the NOI yield, a 10 percent demand rate on $144,000 would reflect a value of $1,440,000 and not the combination of $500,000 plus $440,000. Yet, the cash flow does not support a greater purchase price, unless the debt service can be reduced. A refinancing of the high interest rate $500,000 would be the logical solution.

Add Rental Units.   When a property has untapped potential, the logical step is to find out what it is and then obtain it. In the case of rental properties, this untapped potential may be additional units that can be added or created by remodeling the existing building.

Start by finding out what you can do. The first step in discovering this untapped potential is to review the building codes, ordinances, and zoning for the subject property. This will tell you exactly what the current laws allow for that property given your existing situation. It is possible that what you have may exceed the current legal number of rental units and that while you are *grandfathered in*, there can be little opportunity to add more units without first having the whole building conform to the current laws. Even if this is the case, however, it may be worth doing, so do not overlook any possibility. If your ultimate goal is to sell the property at a profit, the exercise to find out all the potentials available may help you sell to someone else who may want to follow those avenues.

Decrease Tax Liability.   Real estate tax can be a substantial part of total expenses. It is not uncommon for the *ad valorem tax* on a rental property to exceed 25 percent of the total expenses. Any reduction in the real estate taxes can result in a substantial jump in the spendable cash and property value.

Seven Steps on How to Get Your Tax Bill Lowered

1. Get your local realtor to print out a deed search of your neighborhood or several similar neighborhoods showing all the properties that match yours.

2. Find examples of properties similar to yours that have lower tax assessments.

3. Make a list of why your property should be appraised at or even lower than those properties.

4. Take photographs illustrating your findings.

5. File your presentation with the local tax assessing authority using the proper forms to petition for a reduction in your tax assessment.

6. Plan on doing this every year that you feel your property has been taxed higher than it should be.

Convert to Another Use. Economic conversion is the technique of taking a property and converting it to another use. This does not mean that you need to make any physical changes, but only means that the new use will give you an economic benefit following that conversion. The small apartment building may be converted to a college fraternity house, if there was a university willing to pay you more in rent than the apartments would bring and the zoning would allow. The office building may be simply and more subtlety converted to a medical center by catering to doctors only. Economic conversion can also be a long-range goal, as might be the case in the purchase of a rental apartment complex with the idea of eventual conversion to condominiums within a ten-year period.

140. What Is the *Loan To Value Ratio* and How Do I Calculate It?

The *loan to value ratio* (LTV) is the ratio in percent of the amount of a loan to the value of the property that is security to that loan. If a property worth $200,000 had a $150,000 mortgage on it, the LTV would be 75 percent. If the mortgage was $180,000 the LTV would be 90 percent. This percentage is found by dividing the value of the property into the amount of the loan. For example:

1. $150,000 ÷ $200,000 = 0.75; thus, $150,000 is 75 percent of $200,000.

2. $180,000 ÷ $200,000 = 0.90; thus, $180,000 is 90 percent of $200,000.

This ratio is important to both the lender and the borrower, as it establishes the level of risk for the lender. Because the lender will adjust his or her interest rates according to the risk of the loan, a higher LTV will usually carry a higher interest rate for the borrower to pay back.

Some lenders set loan rates to specific LTV levels. The prospective borrower would be advised to find out what those levels are and to review the result from reducing the LTV of a loan requested to obtain the lower rate. It is possible that other terms in addition to the interest rate could be favorably affected to the borrower's favor with a greater equity position.

It would be logical that 100 percent minus the LTV would be the borrower's equity. While this is the theory, in reality this is not always the case and a lender should be careful to examine the real value of any property that is mortgaged as security to a loan.

Be wary of values that have been artificially established to suggest a value greater than that a fair market would deliver. For example, in-house transactions can create leases that show income that, while actual, is temporary and unrealistically high. That high income would reflect an equal value. A prospective lender was offered a LTV of 70 percent on a loan request of $700,000; one would expect the property to be worth $1,000,000. A lease to a retail enterprise that produced a triple net (all costs covered by the tenant) to the property owner of $100,000 would suggest a value of $1,000,000 at a demand rate (interest the investor demands on his investment) of 10 percent. If, on the other hand, the real market rate for rent in the building was only $65,000 triple net, then the real market value of the property could actually be less than the requested loan of $700,000. This could be a classic example of a property owner trying to pull the wool over the eyes of a lender. This borrower would have no actual equity in the property, and the property would have zero equity above the mortgage.

However, not all zero equity transactions are bad. A builder clearly manufactures equity in a property; even when he or she borrows 100 percent of the funds needed to acquire a property and to construct a building on it, the final result should represent a value in excess of the loan.

141. What Are the Different Ways to Calculate Mortgage Payments and Why Is Each Important?

The typical mortgage that is obtained from a lender is usually based on an equal monthly payment for the whole term of the mortgage, or at least equal payments between adjustment periods for changes in interest rates. However, there are other ways to calculate these payments and the most common are shown below.

The Seven Most Common Methods to Calculate Mortgage Payments

1. Equal constant payments of interest due plus principal
2. Equal constant payments when short interest principal increases
3. Equal constant payments of interest only
4. Zero payment—principal increases
5. Equal principal plus interest payments
6. Adjustable rate mortgage
7. Graduated rate mortgage

Equal Constant Payments of Interest Due Plus Principal. This is the most common method of calculating a mortgage, and in this type of mortgage the monthly payments fixed at the same amount for term of the mortgage (or term between adjustments of interest rate). A mortgage made at 10 percent interest for 20 years would have a constant rate of 11.58 percent. A *constant rate* is a rate that combines interest and principal. If you had *McGraw-Hill's Interest Amortization Tables* (the "red book") you could calculate the constant rate by finding the payment rate under 10 percent interest for 20 years, which would be a monthly rate, take the 1,000 repayment rate and multiply that by 12, moving the decimal one more place to the left in the result. Therefore, a $60,000 mortgage would have a monthly payment of $579.00 ($60,000 × 0.1158 = $6,948 ÷ 12 = $579.00). This mortgage would then be paid out over a period of 240 months (20 years) at a constant rate of $579.00.

The formula to get this payment takes into consideration that each month's payment will be made up of two separate amounts of money: interest and principal. Of these two amounts, each year the total interest paid will be less than the previous year because of the slowly increasing deductions to the principal.

These mortgages can have a balloon payment or have an adjustment in interest rate that would cause the amortization schedule to be changed to reflect the new balance owed and the altered interest rate. When these adjustments are made, the new payment schedule changes from the previous schedule.

The important characteristic of this kind mortgage is that the principal owed will decrease slightly every month until the mortgage is paid off. If there is no balloon payment, then the mortgage will eventually amortize itself fully with this payment.

Equal Constant Payments When Short-Interest Principal Increases. Some mortgages are established with a constant mortgage payment but have a flexible interest rate that can be adjusted at periodic times. This type of mortgage differs from the first because although the payment remains constant during the term of the mortgage, the amount of principal may (and generally does) increase.

The principal owed actually increases because the mortgage payment does not fully cover all the interest due. This may not be the case in the first few years of the loan, but as interest rates are adjusted upward, the amount due for interest is greater than the monthly payment. This deficit is added to the principal due. As the principal due increases, more and more interest would be due, but as the payment does not increase the continuing short-fall increases. It is easy to see that this kind of mortgage can cause a fast growth of principal outstanding.

These mortgages can build up principal owed very quickly and should be carefully reviewed before accepting this form of repayment. A critical aspect of this kind of mortgage would be the ability of the borrower to pay principal at any time. If the loan does not allow that, or imposes a penalty for principal payments during the term of the mortgage, then the loan should be rejected.

Equal Constant Payments of Interest Only. A mortgage of payments that are interest only and do not include any principal will have the same monthly (or other period of time) payment during the term of the loan. The final payment would, of course, include all the principal due.

If the interest rate can be adjusted by the lender, the payments would remain constant and equal only for the term between adjustments.

Zero Payment—Principal Increases.   Often, as an inducement to a buyer, the seller will agree (or the buyer insist) that the seller hold a *zero payment* mortgage for a period of time. This provision can be incorporated into any mortgage at any period of time during the mortgage. In this situation the borrower makes no payment at all, and the principal owed is increased each month (or other period) by the amount of interest for that period. For example, an $85,000 loan at 12 percent interest per year with zero payments for the three years, and then seven annual payments of a constant equal payment of principal and plus interest thereafter would have a repayment schedule shown below:

| End of | Payment made | | | Principal |
year	Total	Interest	Principal	owed
1	0	0	0	$95,200
2	0	0	0	106,624
3	0	0	0	119,419
4	$26,166	$14,330	$11,836	107,582
5	26,166	12,910	13,256	94,325
6	26,166	11,319	14,848	79,477
7	26,166	9,537	16,630	62,847
8	26,166	7,542	18,624	44,222
9	26,166	5,307	20,859	23,362
10	26,166	2,804	23,362	0

The above mortgage, while it has zero payments during the first three years, shifts to an annual amortization payment for the next seven years.

Equal Principal plus Interest Payments.   This payment schedule is similar to the previous schedule, but with a significant difference. Here the principal payment remains the same, say, for example, $8,500 per year for a $85,000 loan. This would retire the debt in 10 annual payments. If the interest rate was 10%, the interest owed would decline each year as the amount owed was reduced.

| End of | Payment made | | | Principal |
year	Total	Interest	Principal	owed
1	17,000	8,500	8,500	$76,500
2	16,150	7,650	8,500	68,000
3	15,300	6,800	8,500	59,500
4	14,450	5,950	8,500	51,000
5	13,600	5,100	8,500	42,500
6	12,750	4,250	8,500	34,000
7	11,900	3,400	8,500	25,500
8	11,050	2,550	8,500	17,000
9	10,200	1,700	8,500	8,500
10	9,350	850	8,500	-0-

Notice that the total payment for the first year is nearly double that of the last year.

Adjustable Rate Mortgage.   This term, often abbreviated ARM, is any mortgage that has a method of adjustment to the interest rate built into the mortgage payback terms. This form of loan is very attractive to lenders as they are not locked into any fixed interest rate over any period of time. The mortgage can also be attractive to borrowers who may guess correctly that interest rates will go down rather than up.

ARM mortgages are generally adjusted to U.S. Treasury Bills and as there are several different types of treasury bills, the variation of rates between different lenders can vary accordingly. This type of mortgage should be carefully selected from among several lenders and all the different terms should be considered. One of the most important of such terms would be the maximum that the interest rate could be increased during any period and over the term of the loan.

Graduated Rate Mortgage.   The graduated rate mortgage (GRM) starts with payments that are below the amount needed to pay interest, and in this respect function like any of the other mortgages where the deficit is added to principal owed. This mortgage, however, has scheduled increases in payments so that eventually the payments will begin to amortize the loan fully. This form of loan is attractive to a young property buyer who anticipates a steady increase of income to handle the higher than usual payments that come with this kind of mortgage.

142. How Does a *Wraparound Mortgage Work to Benefit Both the Buyer and the Seller?*

The wraparound mortgage is a technique of secondary financing where the mortgagee incorporates existing debt into the mortgage structure to effect a payback schedule that can leverage up the return to the mortgagee of the wraparound funds while establishing an overall rate and payback program that is satisfactory to the borrower.

Wraparound Mortgage Example

Assume you are the seller of a 6,000 square foot office building that has a fair market value of $360,000 and is supported by the $38,000 NOI that the property honestly reports each year. Against this value you own two existing mortgages:

$120,000	First mortgage at 8 percent interest, 10 years remaining. Monthly payment: $1,455.90.
$ 80,000	Second mortgage at 7 percent interest, 10 years remaining. Monthly payment: $928.90.

This gives you a total existing debt service of $2,384.80. Along comes a buyer who is willing to pay your price, but he wants to invest no more than $100,000 down and expects to earn a cash flow of $10,000 (demand rate of 10 percent) each year. Current market rates for this type of property are at 9.5 percent interest rate.

Conventional Solution. The buyer goes to a local lender and refinances the loan for a new mortgage of $260,000, providing all the funds to pay off the existing debt and to pay you the difference of $60,000. That plus his $100,000 closes the deal. At 9.5 percent over a 23-year payout his debt service will be $27,860.80 per year and without any increase in the NOI his desired return of $10,000 seems to be preserved.

Problem with the Conventional Solution. The cost to the lender can be as much as $8,000. In addition, many current lenders will not consider a payout over 23 years, and many want a balloon at the end of 7 or 10 years.

Wraparound Mortgage Solution. As seller you agree to hold a wraparound mortgage in the amount of $260,000. This amount takes into consideration the existing debt, which consists of $200,000 and the new money portion of the wraparound of $60,000. The terms you establish are 8.75 percent interest with an amortization based on a 18-year schedule with a balloon at the end of 10 years. As this is a wraparound mortgage, you will continue to make the payments for the existing first and second mortgages out of the money paid you from the buyer. The buyer need only be concerned with one mortgage schedule and one monthly payment of $2,394.30.

A quick check at the combined payment on the first and second mortgages will show that these mortgages total $2,384.80, so there is not much of a difference each month—so little, in fact, that for the rest of this example we will forget about the $9.50 left over.

However, at the end of 7 years you will no longer need to make the payments on the second mortgage, so that $928.80 starts to stay in your pocket, and does so for three years.

At the end of the tenth year, your wraparound will balloon and the owner will have to pay you off. The balloon payment will be $164,888.20, all of which will stay in your pocket because the existing first mortgage has self-amortized and has been paid off.

Here is a summary of the total benefits:

$9.50 each month for 120 months	$ 1,140.00
$928.80 each month for 36 months	33,436.80
Final balloon payment	164,888.20
Total benefits and payback	$199,465.00

All this is your return on the new money portion of the wraparound mortgage that was originally $60,000.

The primary benefit for the lender is the leverage over the existing debt, as the interest rates on both the first and the second mortgages were less than that of the wraparound. As the borrower paid 8.75 percent on the total of $260,000, he was in essence paying 0.75 percent overage on the first mortgage of $120,000 and 1.75 percent overage on the second mortgage of $80,000.

The primary benefit to the borrower is the relative ease in which this transaction can proceed to close, and that his overall payment, mortgage terms, and interest rate are *below* what the current market rate would have been.

143. How Does the *Cost of Living* Adjustment Work?

Cost of living is a term that is primarily used as a basis for adjustment of leases and purchase contracts. The U.S. Department of Labor maintains a series of indexes that keep track of the cost of living. These indexes are published with specific references to areas of the country, and by sending a request to be put on their mailing list you can receive the index with both national and local references. Send your request to The U.S. Department of Labor, 1371 Peachtree Street, N.E., Atlanta, Georgia 30367. A sample of the index is shown on page 198.

Example of How the Cost of Living Index Adjustment Is Made. Assume a lease provides for an annual adjustment to any increase in the cost of living All Items index for All Urban Consumers. Such a provision may require the adjustment to be on an annual basis or any other period of time. In this example, the adjustment is to occur each year to a base rent of $600 per month.

Find the appropriate index in Figure 16-1 on page 198. It will show the present All Items index for the month of April 1993 to be 144. This represents an increase in the All Urban Consumers section of 3.2 percent over the past 12 months, and 0.3 percent over the previous month.

To find an annual increase (April 1992 to April 1993) in a base rent of $600.00, with the All Items index as the formula provided for in a lease, you would multiply the rent of $600.00 by 103.2 (100 percent plus 3.2 percent) to give the new rent of $619.20.

As you can see from the index, there are other items taken into consideration, and that the specific increase (or decline) in the cost of living will vary between item and location of the study. There is no set rule that the "all items" indicator be used. In fact, some leases are far more specific and are tied to factors that may be more representative of the type of tenant, such as tieing a doctor's lease to the Medical Care index.

All contracts that have a cost of living adjustment provision should carefully spell out which index and which local chart is to be used.

144. How Do I Calculate Real Estate Depreciation?

Depreciation is the paper expense that is allowed by the IRS. The term *paper* is used because you take a deduction from income of an expense of which you did not have to make an actual payment.

News

For Release:
8:30 A.M. . EDT. Thursday.
May 13, 1993

BUREAU OF LABOR STATISTICS
SOUTHEASTERN REGIONAL OFFICE
ATLANTA. GEORGIA
TELEPHONE: 404-347-4416

CONSUMER PRICE INDEX
(1982-84=100)
April 1993

Group	All urban consumers			Wage earners & clerical workers		
	U.S. City Average	Percent change Apr. 92 Apr. 93	Percent change Mar. 93 Apr. 93	U.S. City Average	Percent change Apr. 92 Apr. 93	Percent change Mar. 93 Apr. 93
All items (1982-84=100)	144.0	3.2	0.3	141.6	3.1	0.4
All items (1967=100)	431.2	.	.	421.6	.	.
Food and beverages	141.4	1.9	0.4	140.9	1.7	0.3
Food	140.6	1.8	0.4	140.2	1.8	0.4
Food at home	140.0	1.9	0.4	139.3	1.8	0.4
Food away from home	142.7	1.8	0.2	142.5	1.7	0.2
Alcoholic beverages	149.7	1.7	0.2	149.3	1.5	0.2
Housing	140.4	2.9	0.1	137.7	2.8	0.2
Shelter	155.0	3.2	0.1	150.8	3.1	0.2
Renters' costs 1/	164.9	3.0	-0.2	144.3	2.6	0.0
Rent, residential	149.7	2.4	0.4	149.3	2.4	0.4
Apparel and upkeep	136.9	2.7	0.5	135.2	2.3	0.3
Transportation	129.4	3.4	0.3	128.4	3.5	0.5
Medical care	199.4	6.0	0.4	199.0	6.1	0.4
Entertainment	145.3	2.3	0.3	143.5	2.1	0.3
Other goods and services	192.4	6.7	0.2	192.8	6.9	0.3
Purchasing power of the dollar: 1982-84=$1.00	$.695	-3.1	-0.3	$.706	-3.2	-0.4

Group	All urban consumers			Wage earners & clerical workers		
	All Items	Percent change Apr. 92 Apr. 93	Percent change Mar. 93 Apr. 93	All Items	Percent change Apr. 92 Apr. 93	Percent change Mar. 93 Apr. 93
South (1982-84=100)	140.2	3.2	0.4	138.8	3.2	0.4
Less than 50,000 pop	137.7	2.7	0.5	137.8	2.7	0.6
50,000 - 450,000 pop	139.3	3.1	0.5	139.3	3.3	0.6
450,000 - 1,200,000 pop	141.9	3.3	0.2	138.6	3.3	0.3
1,200,000 or more pop	140.8	3.5	0.3	138.8	3.1	0.2
South (Dec. 1977=100)	227.5	.	.	224.7	.	.
Less than 50,000 pop	223.7	.	.	223.1	.	.
50,000 - 450,000 pop	225.5	.	.	225.5	.	.
450,000 - 1,200,000 pop	231.6	.	.	224.6	.	.
1,200,000 or more pop	227.3	.	.	224.9	.	.

1/ Base year is December 1982 for CPI-U; December 1984 for CPI-W.
NOTE: Annual averages available upon request
NOTE: Because they are based on smaller samples, local area indexes are subject to substantially more sampling and other measurement error than the national indexes. BLS strongly urges users to consider the use of national indexes in escalator agreements.

CPI HOTLINE NUMBER IS 404-347-3702

Figure 16.1

For example, you have just purchased a five-unit apartment building for $100,000. Your accountant sets up an initial tax basis at $100,000 with a division between land and buildings. If the buildings are worth (from depreciation point of view) $80,000, then your accountant should review your income and expenses for the past several years, ask you about future income and expenses that may be different from that past, and establish a depreciation schedule that fits your needs for this paper loss.

The IRS publishes guides that will indicate the term of years and the method of depreciation that you are allowed to take. In general, depreciation only applies to *income-producing property*, although you can depreciate property you use as a part of your own business, such as a home office.

The land cannot be depreciated as a general rule. If the property has mineral rights that are being used up, there is an allowable depletion allowance that is much the same as depreciation. However, only buildings and other improvements that fall into capital improvements or capital costs can be the basis for your depreciable asset.

Real estate tax assessment may be the logical division of values between the land and improvements, but if you have just purchased a property that has an assessed value of $500,000 and the local taxing authority assigns 20 percent of the value to the land and 80 percent to the building and you believe it should be different (with respect to the IRS), then you should be ready to justify that change.

The *tax basis* is important because this is the taxable value of your real estate at the time of a taxable sale (or other form of disposition). Your tax base in any property is increased by capital improvements you make to it, and decreased by demolition and depreciation. This is where depreciation becomes an important factor, because while you get the tax deduction the year you take it, that same year your property tax basis is reduced by the amount of the depreciation (not the tax), so that when you have a taxable sale you may be liable for tax on the proceeds of the sale that exceed your tax basis. This is the IRS's opportunity to tax you for the accumulated depreciation you took over a period of time.

Annual adjustments to the tax basis are essential to ensure that you take advantage of every capital improvement you make to your property.

145. What Are the Most Important Steps When Making Income Projections?

Any prospective purchaser should review these seven steps prior to making any purchase. The first three steps should be maintained in a "ready alert" status, that is, investors should be continually updating these three steps so that when opportunities are presented, the investors will recognize them to be genuine opportunities that will fit their goals.

The Seven Steps to Making Meaningful Income Projections

1. Know investment goals.
2. Review the levels of risk acceptable.
3. Know the standards for the area.
4. Make general assessments quickly.
5. Tie up the property.
6. Complete due diligence.
7. Keep projections realistic.

Know Investment Goals.   Every investor should have a clear set of goals. These goals become the focus of everything the investor does, and for every property considered the question "does that property move me closer to my goals?" should be answered in the affirmative. If the answer is "maybe," then additional time may be devoted to study the possibility, but if the answer is a clear "no," then no more time should be devoted to that property and the investor should move on to other properties.

Review the Levels of Risk Acceptable.   There are two elements that determine acceptable risk. The first is the investor's ability to handle a specific property. By *handle* I mean the ability to deal with everything about the property. If the investor is comfortable owning and operating small apartment buildings, that does not mean that same investor should jump up to a 200-unit complex. The second element that determines acceptable risk is financial capability. If the transaction is marginal and the complexity of the property at the upper limit (or beyond) that of the investor, then risk increases substantially.

All investors need to make continual adjustments to decrease risk by expanding their abilities and capabilities. Management, accounting, legal, and building trade skills, etc., are all factors that can be learned to advance investors' comfort with any specific type of property. As this learning progresses, investors can take on larger and more complex properties without increasing their level of risk.

Know the Standards for the Area.   Every local area has its own standards for income and expenses. While there may be similar comparisons among different areas of the world, the data going into income and expense calculations can vary widely. You will be able to learn the standards for your area by getting the facts first hand from other real estate insiders. The real estate tax accessor's office often has information that can be used to build your own file of standard income and expenses. Often that department publishes its findings that give rather detailed information about income and expenses for different kinds of rental property.

Make General Assessments Quickly.   Many prime opportunities are lost because the prospective buyer has spent too much time making studies of the property only to find another buyer has snapped it up. The key to successful acquisition of real estate is to see the opportunity and buy it before someone else does. It is a very simple concept, and absolute. If you can do that, you are bound to succeed.

Tie Up the Property.   Once the general assessment that the property fits the pattern for the goals and is within acceptable risk levels has been made, then the property should be tied up so that additional studies can be made, without fear of losing the property.

There are many different techniques that investors use to tie up property with little or no risk of capital. Letters of intent that lead to formal contracts can be accomplished without any initial deposits, and sometimes the deposit itself can be a promissory note (promise to pay), or the contract may be a real estate exchange proposal that does not require any deposit at all.

Once the property has been tied up, the investor can proceed to the next stage.

Complete Due Diligence.   Adequate homework can only be accomplished with full and complete information. Once you have tied up a property, the needed information to complete your property analysis will be easier to obtain and will be more meaningful to you because you know your time is directed toward an attainable end. This is the time to take a deep breath and look hard at everything.

When reviewing the material given you about the subject property, look for expenses that are both excessive and insufficient. Each of these two areas can tell you a lot about the present owner.

Keep Projections Realistic.   When you review the information and make your own projections on what you can do with the property, be sure to remind yourself that those projections should be both realistic and conservative and suit your abilities.

17

Insider Secrets for Creative Investing Techniques

146.   Are Those "Get Rich Quick through Real Estate" TV Programs a Realistic Way to Learn Real Estate Investing?

No. The task of becoming a successful real estate investor cannot be learned from any single source. The real insiders in the real estate investment game have learned the secrets to success by becoming an expert in their comfort zone.

Any program that begins with the premise that all you have to do is buy "right" and then sell for more than you paid has missed the target. While learning techniques can be very helpful in structuring a creative deal, the fundamental truth about real estate is that you will be successful because you recognize the opportunities within your comfort zone. You reduce risk by knowing what not to buy, and you ultimately buy because you see the clear path to a profit before you close the deal. The problem with most of the TV real estate "get rich quick" programs is that they teach you techniques that can actually help you buy real estate. However, using a technique without knowing where to use it can create economic disasters. The guy who teaches you how to buy without using any of your own money is taking advantage of you. The trick to success is not to buy anything without using your own money, but to buy the right property for you.

To build your wealth to the point where you achieve financial independence is a worthy goal that you can attain. The road to that end is not possible overnight. It will require time, effort, and the willingness to overcome obstacles, expand your own sphere of reference, and make sacrifices. You will need to follow the examples set by those who have already made those same choices and have succeeded. You must strive to develop your own *comfort zone*. The steps to achieve this are available for you from masters who have spent their lives experiencing it, and these masters make this knowledge available to you in their books that are free to borrow in any well-stocked library in America. Take advantage of those sources and that kind of experience instead of using any get rich quick plan or program that you have to pay *big* bucks for.

Build your own library of material from other authors who have written their experiences for you to learn from, and dive into the world of real estate. You will soon become an insider yourself. The effort must come from you.

147. Is There at Least One Easy Way to Invest in Real Estate without Risk?

Yes. My recommendation to all first-time real estate investors is to attempt their most basic of needs while at the same time move closer to their overall goals. For most people this means acquiring a place to live. If you are now renting, you are actually in a loss situation every month. There is no equity being built up, no appreciation, no tax write-offs, and so on. All the benefits of real estate are in the hands of someone else: the person you pay your rent to every month.

The United States is full of small rental properties that are affordable to millions of first-time buyers. If you are able acquire one of these income properties you can satisfy your housing needs, while at the same time get other people's money (OPM) on your side of the investment game. Using OPM for a change, instead of being one of those other people and paying, will enable you to build your wealth.

It might be true that your first small apartment building will not be in the neighborhood where you eventually want to own a home, but it will move you closer to your goal of financial independence than contining to pay rent.

148. When Using Other People's Money, What Are the Most Important Questions I Need to Ask First?

Using OPM gives all investors the opportunity to acquire something that they would not be able to afford otherwise. But OPM does not grow on trees, and the use of someone else's funds is not free. The overall price for getting a mortgage, for example, can be more costly than the property or the investment can support. Many investors end up in deep trouble with debt they cannot pay back.

Part of the solution to this problem is to know what questions to ask *before* you obligate yourself to any mortgage and how to evaluate the answers you get. The following is a list of the 21 most important questions you should have the answers to before you go into debt.

The 21 Most Important Questions
to Ask before You Go into Debt

1. What are the current *market rates* for similar mortgages?

2. Who are the lenders?

3. Has the lender or the lender's agent asked for a nonrefundable deposit?

4. Are you required to sign personally on the note?

5. Are co-signers required, and what does that mean?

6. Does the lender ask for *cross-collaterized* security?

7. What will you lose if you cannot repay the debt?

8. Can the debt be assumed by a future buyer or other party?

9. What are the repayment terms of the debt?

10. Can the interest rate go up?

11. Is there a balloon payment?

12. Does the lender have any *equity kickers* in the loan agreement?

13. Is there a penalty for early repayment of principal?

14. What are the *notice dates* and why are they so important?

15. Can you *substitute security* to the loan?

16. Does the mortgage require the lender to *subordinate* to other debt?

17. Is any part of this mortgage a *wraparound*?

18. Do you have any *releases of security* from the mortgage?

19. Do you have the right to obtain secondary financing?

20. Are there provisions that trigger sudden payback of the debt?

21. Can I meet the obligations of this debt?

Market Conditions for Debt Are One of the Guides to Successful Negotiations to Acquire the Property.   If you are in the middle of a heated offer–counteroffer situation, the transaction may hinge on how the debt is structured. When you are asking the seller to hold debt, you need to make sure that you do not overpay for that debt. At the same time, you should be aware of the cost of the usual charges to obtain market loans so that you appreciate and take into consideration what you are saving by using seller-obtained or other less expensively obtained debt.

Who Are the Lenders?   It can be helpful to know who you might have to deal with should you anticipate or need to make a change in the repayment terms. A mortgage held by a previous owner, for example, can have far more flexible terms than one held by an insurance company. The larger institutions may not be accessible to discuss even the simplest of mortgage terms with you. Private parties generally are more motivated to keep the loan in place or to seek an early payoff at a discount. However, when you discover who the lender is, find out if this person (or company) has made a habit of selling and then foreclosing on the same property. This does happen, and you do not want to be the next victim.

Nonrefundable Deposits before the Loan Has Been Committed May Be a Clue to Move On.   Many lenders ask for an application fee for them to run a credit check or handle some basic paperwork. However, when lenders or persons who represent themselves as agents for the lender ask for a substantial nonrefundable deposit, beware. Mortgage agents, people who pretend to be mortgage brokers, and even companies that claim to be genuine insurance companies, banks, and other sources of money exist and make their living (and a very good one at that) from the deposits they take for loans that never are obtained—loans that never were intended to be obtained.

A very simple step to take to avoid this problem is to ask for references, check with the Better Business Bureau, and ask the reputable lenders in the area for verification (do all three). If you cannot get any references because the agents "never give out the names of their clients," then move on and do not give them a deposit.

Many Loans Require Personal Signatures.   Your personal signature on a loan may not increase your immediate risk to the transaction, but it can place a burden on your ability to obtain other credit.

Virtually all savings and loan mortgages and other similar institutional loans will require your personal signature. If you can acquire a property subject to another loan without your having to assume it or give your own personal guarantee, that fact may make the property easier to sell.

Co-Signataries May Be Needed If Your Credit Is Weak?   Some first-time buyers discover that the lenders want additional security to make the loan, and one way to obtain that is to have a partner, friend, or relative co-sign. This is a risky situation for the co-signor, and they may want (or be entitled to) an interest in the property or some other consideration. As a co-signor to a mortgage you would want to know what you would stand to lose if your friend, partner, or relative did not make the payments.

Cross-Collaterization Is Another Way to Increase the Lender's Security By Giving Them an Additional Property or Other Item of Value as Security.   Lenders may ask what you can add as security to a loan because they are not satisfied with your ability to repay the loan and they do not want to be at risk without additional security. When you give some other valuable item or property, the loan becomes cross-collateralized with this additional security and that other property or item is locked into the loan until the loan is repaid or the borrower obtains a release of that security.

What do You Risk If You Cannot Repay the Loan?   Many borrowers do not put this question in the proper time frame. For example, if you buy a property with $10,000 down and get plenty of help from friends to fix it up, remodel it, and get it rented, do you only have the $10,000 at risk? No. The correct answer is that you have a lot more at risk because of the invested time and effort. If you increase the value to double what you paid for it, then the new value is still not all that you have to risk because you may also be personally responsible for eventual payback on the loan. At the time you bought the property your total "other net worth" may not have been substantial, but what about ten years down the road? What if the seller holds the mortgage and there is a balloon payment and the whole amount you borrowed becomes due and payable at a particular time? At a future point in time your increased fortune can be at risk to early decisions. It is important for you to look at the level of risk over a period of time, particularly as the due date of any balloon payment approaches.

Assumption of Debt by a Future Buyer or Other Party Is Important. Anytime you are able to include an assumption provision in a loan you are obligated to, your opportunity to sell the property in the future increases. This occurs because the loan you have at closing when you purchase may have a much better term and interest rate than what might be available in the future, even the near future.

But be careful of loans that look like they are assumable but are not. Some lenders give the impression that their loans are assumable by incorporating phrases such as "this loan may be assumed by a future party on approval from the lender." The lender may mean that a new buyer will have to apply for assumption as though he or she were taking out a new loan (with the additional expense of appropriate points and other costs). That kind of assumption is very misleading.

Every Borrower Should Know *All* the Repayment Terms. This means carefully reading the mortgage and the mortgage note. Do not rely on what the lender tells you about the loan, as the lender's representative may not actually know what the loan provisions actually call for. This is not uncommon today as many savings and loans institutions have sold their loan portfolios to other lenders, some from other states. The loan documents may vary among lenders, and the exact details contained in the document itself are important. Read and make sure you understand what it says.

Adjustable Interest Rates Are Common, But How Adjustable Are They? Adjustable rate mortgages (ARM) are very common both with institutional and private loans. The amount of adjustment and how the adjustment is made can vary greatly, and you should be award of all the details that pertain to those calculations. If the loan interest rate can be adjusted up, why not down too? You should insist on the following provisions:

- Adjustments that can go down as well as up tied to the same criteria
- A maximum that the rate can be adjusted in any year
- A maximum that the rate can ever adjust upward

Balloon Payments Can Sneak Up on You.   When the mortgage has a balloon payment, which is a scheduled repayment of some or all of the principal owned, you must be very careful to keep track of these due dates. Some loans have a *call date* that gives the lender the right to require you to repay the principal or to renew the mortgage for another term at an adjusted interest. If the lender decides not to renew, then the mortgage has a sudden balloon. Other balloon payments are planned, and when used properly can be an effective technique by the buyer to obtain an easy payment schedule for a period of years leading up to a refinance of the property. Smart borrowers make efforts to refinance their mortgages a year or two in advance of a balloon payment to ensure they have sufficient time to get the needed financing.

Some Lenders Require *Equity Kickers* to Increase Their Return.   Often these are provisions that give the lender a percentage of the income over and above a set amount or that give the lender a percent of the profit on a future sale. Whatever the kicker, make sure you understand the exact formula that is used to calculate it. Many buyers use equity kickers as a tool to entice a seller to give good terms or accept a lower price. As with most financing terms, offering kickers can be beneficial to both the borrower and the lender when used correctly.

Prepayment Penalties Often Exist.   When a lender wants to make sure that they will have a set return for a minimum period of years from the loan, they may insert a prepayment penalty in the mortgage document. This can cause many problems in the near future if you suddenly are able to refinance at a much lower rate or have a buyer who wants to pay off the high interest mortgage. If you find such a penalty, do not automatically assume that the lender will impose it. If you are assuming a mortgage at a closing, attempt to get the lender to remove that provision.

Mortgages Often Contain *Notice Deadlines* That Can Cause Havoc If Not Met.   When a mortgage has a provision that requires a specific notice be sent to the lender, it is critical to make note of the deadline dates. For example, if the mortgage allowed partial repayment of principal at a specific time, say, every January of every other year, but only if notice had been sent 60 days earlier, a failure to send the notice could make it impossible to make the repayment without penalty until the next period came along. Other important notice dates may trigger mortgage extensions or releases of security.

Substitution of Security Is a Great Buyer's Technique Because It Allows You to Move the Mortgage to Some Other Property.   Most home mortgages or other institutional mortgages do not allow you to replace one security for another, but within private-seller-held financing this can be a good tool to use. The right to pledge a different property as the security to the loan could allow you to take advantage of the good terms of a seller-held second mortgage while refinancing the property with a new mortgage that might not be possible without otherwise paying off the second. If you are ever asked to give this provision to a loan you are holding, make sure you have right to approve the substitution property.

Subordination of Debt to New or Other Debt Is Another Buyer's Technique.   This is a good provision that allows you to refinance or obtain additional financing without having to repay the existing debt. When a lender subordinates their position, they give up the right they have in line to the security pledged on the loan to another. A simple and very common form of subordination is where the owner of the land that is leased to the building owner agrees to subordinate to a first mortgage. In this situation the first mortgage now has a right to lien the land ahead of the property owner, even though the lease may have been in effect prior to the loan.

Wraparound Mortgages Should Be Reviewed Very Carefully and All Underlying Mortgages Read and Understood.   When there are existing or new wraparound mortgages on a property, the buyer's contract may show obligation to make the wraparound mortgage payment only, with the underlying mortgages being paid by the seller. However, if the seller does not make the payments on the underlying mortgages, then the buyer can be in default and lose the property even though all required payments on the wraparound have been met. One way to solve this problem is to make sure that the wraparound mortgage sets up a trustee or other collection agency that takes the required payments from the buyer and before giving any money to the seller makes the necessary payments to the underlying mortgages. For example, if you buy an office building and are obliged to make a $20,000 per year payment on a $180,000 wraparound mortgage, make sure that the collection agent (a title insurance company, escrow agency, real estate agency, or lawyer) takes your money and then pays out on the existing first mortgage of $80,000 and the second of $40,000 before giving the seller any return on his or her "new money" portion of the wrap ($60,000). Then you can be sure that the first and second mortgages do not go into default.

Releases of Security Can Be Critical in Land Deals, But Are Important Whenever Multiple Security Is Given.   The typical release of security is when a land developer buys a tract of land and then sells off or builds on individual lots he or she carves out of the tract. Without the ability to release those lots from the overall security of the mortgage, the mortgage would have to be paid off, or the new buyer would have to accept the risk that if the developer did not continue to pay on the mortgage, the lot could be lost. In the case of a loan where the lender had originally required a co-signer or cross-collaterization, you should insist on the right to release that additional security once the loan has been paid down to an agreed to level.

Secondary Financing Can Be Helpful or a Needed Part of the Picture, Either Now or in the Future.   However, some loans have provisions that do not allow you to increase the amount of debt against the property. If this is the case, make sure you understand the full ramifications of this provision, and seek to limit its scope or to have it removed completely.

Acceleration of Payback Can Mean Disaster.   Most loans have provisions that allow the lender to accelerate the repayment of the debt. The usual situation is a *due on sale* clause that gives the lender the right to call the loan if you sell the property. Other provisions can be tied to long-term leases, exchanges, sale of partial interest, replacement of management, and other conditions that the lender believed important when the loan was originally made. A default on your part of any of the mortgage terms may also give the lender the right to trigger this demand for payment, so it is important to look for any provision that ties one clause of the mortgage document to another.

Can You Meet the Obligations of This Debt?   Do not view this as a borderline situation where you might be able to pay if everything goes well for you. What I am talking about is the absolute ability to make payments when due. If you lose a few nights' sleep thinking about the debt, odds are you are going to lose much more sleep worrying about making those monthly payments until the day you lose the property.

If the mortgage is on nonincome-producing property, then you will need other income or savings to draw against to meet the payments. This is okay if it fits your goals and the plan to reach those goals. If the property you are buying produces income, then that income plus your other income sources will be at risk. Can you handle it, or are you right on that thin edge that comes with highly overleveraged investments? If you are on that edge, have some inside information, trust in the luck of the Irish (if your name is O'Hara), and have a silver spoon tucked away somewhere, then you are okay. Otherwise go back to the drawing board and reconsider this investment and the debt you are about to go into.

149. How Can I Maximize My Negotiating Leverage with Any Seller?

Savvy buyers learn negotiating techniques that work for them. What you do may be different from the next successful buyer, but your overall strategy will be improved if you keep the following twelve steps in mind.

The 12 Key Steps to Negotiating with Sellers

1. Have your real goal firmly in sight.
2. Remember that the seller is not your enemy.
3. Learn all the facts you can about the property.
4. Attempt to discover the real reason why the property is for sale.
5. Meet with the seller on the seller's turf and be observant.
6. Make an informed offer.
7. Do not respond quickly to a negative reaction from the seller.
8. Make sure the seller has fully understood your proposal.
9. Do not appear anxious.

10. Have an intermediary who can be anxious.

11. Be ready to give and take to close the deal.

12. Close on small items, never big ones.

150. What Are the Steps for Negotiating with Buyers?

Buying and selling real estate is an essential part of making real estate a source of income and wealth. The smart seller knows how to deal with buyers to move property in tough times and how to make deals that work and do not fail. The following ten steps will improve your chances of being a more successful seller.

The 10 Key Steps for Negotiating with Buyers

1. Have your *real* goals firmly in sight.

2. Remember the buyer is not your enemy.

3. Do not be insulted by any offer.

4. Look for the smallest "meeting of the minds."

5. Build on every agreement.

6. Do not accept or decline any segmented offers.

7. Do make counterproposals.

8. Use a real estate agent to absorb the heat of the deal.

9. Be open to creative ideas.

10. Keep your social activities with the buyer to a minimum.

151. What Is a *Letter of Intent* and When Should It Be Used?

A *letter of intent* is a simple proposal to a seller drafted in a letter from the buyer or the buyer's agent outlining the basic terms and conditions under which the buyer would enter into a contract with the seller. The letter is not a binding contract and does not cover all the legal aspects of a contract. It generally deals only with the most important points to a purchase.

A *letter of intent* is effective in many situations ranging from very complicated and very expensive acquisitions to simple deals that may not involve more than a few thousand dollars. Advantages and the disadvantages of this format are as follows.

Advantages of Using a *Letter of Intent*

1. Quick

2. Not binding

3. Deals with important issues only

4. Not in legal language

5. Easy to respond to

6. Less costly than formal legal proposals

Disadvantages of Using a *Letter of Intent*

1. Not binding

The following is an example of a letter of intent that is a proposal to acquire a 50-unit apartment building. The seller is asking $1,650,000 for the property, all cash to his first mortgage of $300,000.

LETTER OF INTENT

March 3, 1994

Dear Mr. Seller,

This letter is to express the intent of the undersigned, Jack Cummings, acting on his own behalf, to enter into a contract to purchase the SUTTON HILL APARTMENTS, located in Plantation, Florida, owned by you.

If the basic terms and conditions outlined below are acceptable to you, then I shall cause to be drafted a formal agreement along those lines for your review. Please understand that while this letter is not a binding contract, it is a sincere attempt to arrive at a meeting of the minds as soon as possible so that we can proceed to acceptance of a formal and binding agreement.

TERMS AND CONDITIONS

1. Price: $1,375,000
2. Deposit: A $200,000 deposit will be made with the signing of the formal contract.
3. Payment Terms:
   a. $700,000 cash at closing, of which the deposit is a part.
   b. Assumption of the existing mortgage of $300,000.
   c. A purchase money mortgage in the amount of $375,000 payable over 10 years at prime plus two percentage points.
4. Closing: Within 30 days following a 45-day inspection period.

Kindly direct your reply to my Fort Lauderdale office, and should you have any questions please call me directly.

Sincerely,

Jack Cummings

The above letter of intent may seem to be very simple and basic, but that is the whole idea.

When Would You Use a *Letter of Intent*?   The usual application of this format is for a more complex type of transaction. The deal in question need not be a purchase, as the letter of intent works just as well for leases, exchanges, etc. One word of caution: most real estate brokers and salespeople do not want to use the letter of intent format because they are trained to "get the buyer and seller to sign on the dotted line." That kind of sales procedure works very well with contracts that become binding the moment they are signed, but not too well for letters of intent.

152.   What Is a Standard Deposit Receipt Contract?

Standard contracts can be found in just about every office supply store and many well-equipped drugstores, and they can cover everything from leases to Power of Attorney. However you should avoid the office standard real estate contract sold at office supply stores. Instead, pay a visit to the local Board of Realtors or any realtor's office and pick up a copy of the most recent board of realtors approved real estate contract.

The Board of Realtors contracts are drafted and approved by the state or other local bar association members and is designed to take into consideration all the factors that govern real estate matters specific to the laws of the state and the peculiarities of that region.

Having a contract that is generic but totally comprehensive is important because it will speed up the formal contract stage of any purchase or sale. It is a good idea, however, to make sure that the terms and conditions within this standard contract are exactly to your liking. Just because the contract is standard does not mean that you must agree with the terms and conditions it contains. If you are the buyer, then you can dictate what you want to offer and the terms and conditions you want to be obligated to or expect the seller to live up to.

Having your own lawyer make suggestions to changes or additions to this standard form is good advice, and as the changes to the standard contract will be minimal, so should your cost.

Warning: Not all standard forms are standard. With the advent of modern computers has come the ability to print out forms that look to be standard, but in these forms the originator has altered a few words here and there that can change the meaning of whole paragraphs, for example, one simple change is to replace the word *not* with the word *now*. Every contract you sign should be read aloud by you. If there is anything you do not understand or that sounds strange, then do not sign that agreement until you have a full and comprehensive understanding of what is written and you accept and agree with everything.

153. What is the Best Investment Technique I Can Use to Reduce Risk?

The best single technique any real estate investor can learn to use is the *option*. The option is a very flexible technique that is used in many creative transactions. The basic option is a simple promise from a prospective buyer that if that buyer is allowed to buy (or lease or exchange) a property owned by a prospective seller, then in payment for that option the prospective buyer will give up some valuable consideration.

The advantage of using the option is that you have 100 percent control of the outcome of the situation. For example, if you pay a property owner $1,000 for the option to buy his or her lot at the end of twelve months, the property owner has given you the right to buy that property and cannot sell it to anyone else (except subject to your option). If the value of the property goes up within that year, then you will get the benefit of that value increase.

The option can give you time, and in real estate time can be the best factor to have on your side. Within the time of your option you may be able to cause something to happen, such as get new zoning, fix up the property, or build next door, or something favorable may or occur, such as the proposal of a new highway, a new hospital to be built a block away, etc. Options give the informed investor the advantage to leverage up on a very small amount of money with a very limited risk to the end result of great gains.

154. How Can I Use *Sweat Equity* to Acquire Real Estate with Zero Cash Down?

Sweat equity is the value you create whenever you buy a property. At times you can capitalize on that value by using it as all or part of the down payment to acquire the very property where you create the value. There are five key steps to follow to maximize your chances on using sweat equity as a tool to buy property.

The Five Key Steps for Achieving Maximum Results with Sweat Equity

1. Know your sweat equity talents.
2. Find goal-oriented situations where those talents fit.
3. Have a plan to implement your talents quickly.
4. Be confident when you make your presentation to the owner.
5. Present a *win–win* plan to the owner.

Know Your Sweat Equity Talents.   First of all, you may have talents that you never thought you had, so the first step is to find what those might be.

Start by reviewing everything that can be done to increase the value of a property. If you have no talent with a hammer, a paint brush, or in the garden you should not give up looking because your real forte might be in doing the paperwork needed to get a property rezoned. Keep in mind, too, that sweat equity need not be limited to effort specifically oriented to real estate—it can also be effort that the seller will find valuable and satisfactory as a down payment. If you install swimming pools for a living, for example, you could offer the seller a swimming pool for his house.

Find Goal-Oriented Situations Where Those Talents Fit.   Look for property that will work to move you toward your goal, and at the same time allow you the opportunity to use your sweat equity talents. This does not mean that you buy *only* this kind of property, because other opportunities will come up that do not require sweat equity.

Have a Plan to Implement Your Talents Quickly.   Stress the areas that give sudden and quick results and are positive value producers. These generally will be centered around *economic conversions* but are by no means limited to that technique. Simple fix ups, new paint, a new front door, minor but quality repairs, new or redesigned landscaping, a new rental theme, a zoning change, a building variance, etc., can give overnight boosts in value.

Be Confident When You Make Your Presentation to the Owner. Selling your sweat equity talents can require you to be a good salesperson, but even if you are not, be sure that you are confident in what you are doing. Often the low-key approach works well, and if you have examples of your work, then show it off. Use photographs of homes you have painted, pools you have installed, landscaping you have cut or planted, etc., even if the work was not done for properties you were buying, the end result is to show the seller that he or she can have confidence in your abilities because *you* do.

Present a *Win–Win* Plan to the Owner.   If you agree to fix up the seller's apartment building, redo the landscaping, paint the walls and so on, and all the seller has to do is supply the material and give you an option to buy the property at the end of 18 months at today's price, what does the seller have to lose? The seller loses nothing except some time, and he or she is getting well paid for that time by the effort you are going to expend. This is just one way to show a "no lose" situation to the seller; each situation will vary but each can be a positive experience for both sides. You show that you are ready to risk your time and effort to increase the value of the property.

When you increase the value of the property, you are doing so because you want to borrow ultimately the needed funds to buy the property or to warrant the seller holding 100 percent of the financing. When the situation fits, anything is possible.

155. How Can I Use My New *Sweat Equity* to Acquire Other Property?

Sweat equity works well when combined with one or more creative deal-making techniques. One of the best of these other techniques is the *option*, mentioned earlier. The following is an example of how one investor used sweat equity to start her real estate investment portfolio.

Jan owned a small garden shop that also had a team of landscapers who took care of yards around the neighborhood. She had never thought of using these talents and facilities as a base to acquire real estate until it was suggested to her by a realtor friend that presented her such an opportunity.

The property was a large old home that was well located near the center of town. It was on a large lot that was zoned such that in addition to single-family use, professional offices were permitted. One of the best features, and the original reason the realtor had thought of Jan in the first place, was that around the house were several dozen large Canary Island date palm trees. These trees, plus other mature landscaping around the home, had all but overgrown the lot and nearly hid the house completely from the street.

But with one look at the lot, the trees, and the neighborhood, Jan realized she was looking at a good opportunity, if she could manage it.

The talent matched. She knew that she could sell most of the mature landscaping around the lot, retaining a few of the Canary Island palms but moving off virtually everything else. What she would get from the sale of that plant material she could spend on fixing up the building and its conversion to law offices.

The situation was ideal for her talent, so all that she needed was a plan that would enable her to convince the owner to sell her the property—with nothing down.

Together with her realtor friend she formulated the following offer:

1. A price was agreed to that was fair for both parties.

2. She developed a plan for fixing up and remodeling of the lot and the home that would involve a complete new landscaping plan, painting, and restructuring of the home into large office suites that could also, if the rental market shifted, be used as residential apartments.

3. The seller was to grant her a lease–option on the home that would give her 24 months free rent based on the fact that she would do all the work outlined in the plan. At the end of that period she would have the option to buy the property at the agreed-upon price. If she did not buy the property for any reason, she could continue her lease, but this time paying the monthly rent, plus an increase based on the cost of living.

Jan was risking her time and effort but little else. After a few months into the project she moved into one of the first suites that had been remodeled, and that saved her the rent she had been paying for an apartment across town. The sale of the Canary Island palms and some of the other mature landscaping more than paid for the painting of the building and the other repair costs, and before the end of the first year the property was finished.

The building turned out to be beautiful once the old matured landscaping had been opened up. Shortly thereafter, several law firms were interested in taking the whole building.

At that point Jan could have simply sold her option at a big profit. She had more than doubled the value of the property because a dark, gloomy unrentable old house had become a well-located stately site for the headquarters of a local law firm. However, selling her option was not in her plans, and instead she negotiated a great long-term lease with one of the interested law firms. With the lease as the basis for her collateral, and the newly improved property as the security, she obtained a first mortgage that more than paid the full purchase price she had negotiated a year earlier.

One added bonus to this deal was that while all the work was going on at the old house, she had a large sign out front advertising her landscape business as the company doing the work. That sign brought added work to her business. The combination of the work and extra business added reputation to her firm, and the solid experience of using sweat equity to acquire property lead Jan into other similar transactions.

156.   Why Do Real Estate Exchanges Work?

Real estate exchanges are "hot" items in any market because they enable a buyer or seller to deal without the need for money. This is important, not because the seller shuns money, but because the seller can actually *get* money in the exchange, but not always from the buyer. Exchanges function in both small and enormous transactions all the time, and they do so because of one or more of the following reasons.

The Four Reasons Real Estate Exchanges Work

1. Tax savings
2. Way to move you closer to your goals
3. "Face-Saving" Transaction
4. Accommodation to the Deal

Tax Savings.   The IRS allows certain real estate exchanges to be *tax-free* and other kinds of transactions that involve a swap or change from one property to another to have tax-saving opportunities. A review of the IRS 1031 and the Section 1034 exchange discussed in this book is suggested.

Way to Move You Closer to Your Goals. Any exchange that moves you closer to your goal is a good exchange. Notice that I did not say *the best exchange*, but it is important to understand that you should make decisions based on your available options, not wishful thinking. Many sellers overlook the difference between these two factors and hold out for that unattainable desire rather than taking a positive move in the right direction, even though that move has not taken them *all* the way they wanted to go.

Face-Saving Transaction. Some real estate exchanges work only because it enables the seller or the buyer to finalize the deal. When the seller is highly motivated, an exchange property added to the offer as a sweetener by the "buyer" might be that "mystery box behind the curtain" that allows the seller to save face and the deal at the same time.

Because many real estate exchanges do not show values of either property, but only the differences (mortgages assumed or given, cash paid, etc.) there is the added face-saving attribute of an exchange in that the sellers need not admit (even to themselves) that they took a loss on the deal.

Accommodation to the Deal. Often a big deal or an important transaction is closed on an exchange. This might come following a long negotiating process where the buyer offers something as a counter to a seller's proposal. If the main goal is attained, many sellers will accept something they actually do not want and would not buy to make the bigger deal. Of course, they may turn around and exchange that same property or item in another deal or give it to the broker as part of the commission owned.

157. How Can I Use Exchanges to Invest in Real Estate?

There are two basic approaches to real estate exchanges that work well for investors. All investors should be aware of these approaches and should strive to learn how to use real estate exchanges as a method to build wealth.

The Two Basic Approaches to Using Real Estate Exchanges

1. Exchange as an aggressive buyer.

2. Use exchange as a tool to attract buyers.

Exchange as an Aggressive Buyer. Every seller should look at their situation and determine if they can use the property they have for sale as a stepping stone to move into another real estate investment. For example, Marilyn has two apartments in New York City. The one she lives in has a $100,000 mortgage while the other is free and clear. She has decided to sell the mortgaged property and move into the unmortgaged apartment. However, the market is a "buyer's market," and the few offers she has had on the mortgaged apartment have been way below her bottom line.

Marilyn should consider exchanging *up* to a better investment. In fact, she might discover that by using both apartments in the deal she can move her equity into a truly meaningful real estate investment that could change her life by giving her the income to become financially independent.

Best of all, by becoming an aggressive seller she can actually turn the market around. She now is not really a seller at all; she is a buyer in a strong buyer's market.

Use Exchange as a Tool to Attract Buyers. When no decent offers are coming in, sellers can offer their property out for exchange or at least partial exchange. This aspect may entice a buyer to show interest who otherwise may have avoided that property.

Many sellers do not offer exchanges because they think, "If I exchange, I won't get the cash I need...." First, it is possible to exchange and get cash, as the following example will indicate, but more important, what do you need the cash for? If the answer is to buy something else, to move to Chicago, or to go on a trip around the world, then the exchange might produce that end result just as easy as or even easier than a sale that has yet to happen.

Oscar has a mountain cabin for sale. He has not used it for five years and is tired of renting it out and having to deal with the problems of owning rental property a full day's drive away from home. The cabin is offered for sale and is free and clear. Oscar wants $70,000 cash.

What is he going to do with the money? At least $40,000 is going to go to pay off the first mortgage on his existing home. But the problem is that no buyers are interested.

Oscar runs an advertisement in the local paper saying he will accept an exchange for up to $20,000 in value. He gets several offers from out of the blue—a late model car, a boat, a vacant lot nearby, and so on—and in each case the potential buyers want to pay the balance over a period of time at a good interest rate.

In the end Oscar realizes that his original goal of paying off his home loan is not exactly reached, but he does end up with a nice vacant lot that he thinks will go up in value, and a first mortgage on the cabin that is at a higher interest rate than what he owes on his home. The payments made to him by the new owner of the cabin give him more than enough to meet his mortgage payments, and he has some cash left over. His exchange moved him closer to his goal.

158. How Can I Use Barter to Acquire Real Estate?

Barter is the oldest known method of commerce. It is also a very active way of doing business in the world today. Countries barter millions of dollars of goods for the goods or services from other countries. Businesses use barter as a way to exchange goods and/or services that would go unused or unsold for items or services that allow the company to expand.

Airlines are just one of the businesses that barter frequently. Some of the businesses that make considerable use of barter are shown below:

Airlines

Art galleries

Cable networks

Cruise lines

High-end fashion clothing

Hotels and motels

Insurance

Jewelry manufacturers

Local newspapers

Magazines

Nonproperty rentals

Printing companies

Radio stations

Restaurants

Special travel programs

Television stations

If you own or work for any of these companies, you are an insider to how to make a deal with them. If you are not, you should not worry; perhaps you will work out a deal to get their services or products, which can be used as a down payment. In return you promise to give them something you will get, such as rent in one of your apartments in your new apartment building.

Barter need not be all there is to any deal, but every time you can incorporate some barter into your transaction you are moving closer to the maximum use of your services. Even the seller who agrees to accept a cruise around the world worth $50,000 in the sale of his $500,000 office building can be the result of a beneficial barter. All you have to do is contact a travel agency, find out which cruise companies pay the most commission, and then offer that cruise as a part of your deal. If your cut of the commission was $10,000 (it could actually be even more), that is only two percent of the purchase price; however, if your purchase price required only $100,000 down, you may have saved a full 10 percent of the down payment.

159. How Can I Use *Pyramiding* as an Investment Tool?

Pyramiding is a technique of acquiring a property by offering debt on another property as the down payment. For example, you own a home in Texas worth

$100,000. There is a first mortgage of $35,000 on that home. You want to buy a small apartment complex in Alabama and offer the seller a $40,000 second mortgage on the Texas home as a down payment. This is the basic form of pyramiding.

One of the advantages of using this technique is that by not adding secondary financing to the property you buy (at least at this stage) it might be possible to generate cash in a short-term refinance of the property once its value has been increased.

To make more elaborate use of the technique, it is helpful to understand the five key steps that make this interesting tool work.

The Five Key Steps to Real Estate Pyramiding

1. *Understand the "greener grass" syndrome.*   It is natural for people to look across the fence and think the grass is greener on the other side. It is much the same with real estate. Many sellers will be more inclined to hold a mortgage on another property than they will on their own property. This factor can be used successfully by investors who want to use pyramids to increase their real estate holdings.

2. *Get control over property 1 before you move to property 2.*   It is essential that before you can offer a mortgage against one property as the down payment on another, you should either own the first or have it firmly in your control.

3. *Use your knowledge of the area to demonstrate value.*   This is where your *comfort zone* pays off. You should already have done the homework to back you up on the values and on how to increase the values further.

4. *Move the other party closer to his or her goals.*   This is just logical negotiating. Whenever you can help the other party in the transaction move closer to his or her goals, you have also moved closer to finalizing a deal.

5. *Never let anyone question your success.*   Your research and your facts should speak for themselves, and your confidence should be unshaken. The seller does not have to take your deal; that is the seller's right. But one of the pitfalls with the pyramid technique is that the buyer is put on the defensive about the value of the property being offered as security. Always be willing to support any statement you make, but in the end, suggest that the seller is welcome to make an independent study or appraisal to justify your values and leave it at that.

160.   How Can I Form a Real Estate Syndication?

A real estate syndication is an investment technique or program where one person, the syndicator, finds a property to buy, ties it up, and then offers that property to other investors to share in the investment. Because this type of investing is often governed by state and federal laws, you should be knowledgeable of those laws prior to embarking on this kind of venture. However, syndications can be very profitable to both the syndicator and to the investor, so if this thought is interesting to you, make an effort to learn more about it. One of the best sources is a lawyer in your area who has put together the legal documentation for syndicators. The local Board of Realtors should be able to give you the names of several such lawyers.

Until that situation arises, take a look at the fourteen most important steps to successful syndications.

The 14 Key Steps to Successful Syndications

1. Look for property you want to own.
2. Get control of the property.
3. Have your ownership format ready to use.
4. Demonstrate why the property is a good investment.
5. Know what the state and federal laws will allow you to do.
6. Have strict investment rules with hefty penalties for backsliders.
7. Offer the opportunity to others.
8. Limit the time for their response.
9. Take "backup" applications.
10. Check out every prospective investor carefully.
11. Chose the investors you want.
12. After a short wait, offer their money back.
13. Close on the deal.
14. Enforce your investment rules with an iron fist.

161. How Can a Syndication Be Used to Acquire Property?

A syndication is a very flexible use of OPM. Not only are you using OPM to buy what you want to own, but you can actually get paid for doing it.

Consider that you find a 50-unit apartment building that is worth $1,950,000. You know that if you can offer a down payment of $500,000, you can buy the property for around $1,500,000. In your opinion this is a great buy. Why? Because you have been looking around for smaller apartment buildings (the size you could afford), and you know what is on the market, the rents that can be charged, and the trends. You know and you recognize this opportunity. All you have to do is get some other people to agree with you and to put up the cash. How much cash—why not the whole $500,000?

But first, you should tie up the property, and then proceed with the steps outlined in the answer to the previous question (160).

162.   What is the Secret to Land Speculation?

The answer is keeping your eyes open. Does that sound too simple? The key to profit through land speculation is to buy or tie up land that is destined to go up in value. Land goes up in value because of what is happening around it. Almost everything positive that happens in real estate does so with a long lead time, if you know where to find that lead.

So, by keeping your eyes open all you have to do is be observant of all those events that are taking place within your comfort zone that may affect the long-term values of land. The following are some of those events to look for.

New highways

Road expansions

New turnpike or expressway exits and entrances

New public works

Increases in commercial or industrial infrastructure

Expanded public utilities to new areas

A negative impact in another area

When any of the above events are in the talking stage at the local planning office or presented before the city council or county commissioners, that is the time to start looking for land that will get the benefit of this proposed event. You can even start to talk to prospective sellers about their property.

The idea is to get into a position to make a move on property in the areas likely to go up in value as soon as you can pinpoint where the positive impact is to take place.

163.   How Can the *Land Lease Technique* Be Used to Acquire Property?

A land lease is the leasing of land by its owners to someone else. In its most basic form, for example, the owner of a vacant lot leases you that lot so you can turn it into a parking lot for the adjoining restaurant you own.

However, in a more creative approach, it could be that your real interest in the vacant lot was to build an office building with a five-story parking garage as a part of the structure. You lease the land, but you own the building. If the land owner agrees to subordinate the lease to financing, you may be able to obtain all the money necessary to construct the building without investing any of your own money. However, if the property owner were to subordinate the financing, he or she would be in a secondary position behind the mortgage, a situation that could be very risky.

Some lenders will lend money, both construction and permanent loans, on land that is leased, without the need for subordination. They do this when the lease terms are so attractive that a lease-hold equity has been created that supports the needed "equity" behind the loan. For example, if you were leasing a lot for $30,000 a year, but the real value today was $800,000 the lender would calculate that your lease-hold equity was around $500,000. They find this by capitalizing your rent cost (at 10 percent in this example, but it could range from 8 to 12 percent), and then deducting that from the real value:

Lease rent capitalized at 10 percent is $300,000

($30,000 ÷ 10 percent = $300,000)

Lease-hold equity = $500,000

Value:	$800,000
Less capitalized lease payments:	− 300,000
Total	$500,000

If the lender was satisfied with a $500,000 equity, then the subordination may not matter.

Using the Land Lease as a Technique to Acquire the Property. Often the structure of the transaction comes down to the overall structure of the financing. Because the land lease has several attractive features for the seller, these aspects can be used by the buyer to an advantage. The two main benefits to a seller are tax benefits and the intrinsic nature of land.

By Not Selling the Land, There Is No Capital Gain. If there is no capital gain, then there is no tax to pay. This can be a great benefit to the seller who has a low tax basis in the property, and who would have a high tax to pay in the event of a sale. Whenever this kind of situation is present, the seller should consider the land lease as an alternative to an outright sale. Buyers may want to propose the land lease as a buyer's tool to increase the overall amount of financing.

Ownership of Land Is One of the Most Fundamental and Intrinsic of All Values. Because of this, it is often easier to get a property owner to hold a land lease at a lower cost than a second mortgage for the same principal amount. For example, if the land under a building was valued at $200,000, the seller may be better off taking a land lease at $14,000 per year rather than a second mortgage at $16,000 a year in a direct sale. Why? Because the seller may have a large gains tax to report over the life of the payback of the second mortgage, whereas the lease payment does not trigger a capital gain. The seller may, in fact, be so motivated by the land lease that he or she would rather hold a land lease than get $200,000 in cash (if the gains tax was only 30 percent the seller would be left with only $140,000 after tax and would have to find a better return than the $14,000 a year).

164. How Does the Lease–Option Technique Work?

The lease–option technique is widely used in the acquisition of many different kinds of properties. A basic example follows.

Using a Lease–Option

You are interested in buying a vacant lot on which you would like to build an office building. The seller has fairly priced the land at $200,000 but you do not want to buy it right now, mainly because you do not have the $200,000. You know that once you have the building preleased you will be able to obtain the needed financing to acquire the land and build the building, so you need to buy time.

You offer to *lease* the lot for a period of 10 years at an annual rent that begins at $5,000 for the first year and increases every year thereafter by an additional $1,000 per year. You make your initial offer using a letter of intent, which gives you the freedom of making an offer that is not binding. By using this nonbinding approach, you are able to negotiate the major elements of the ultimate deal without resorting to long legal documents now. These will be used later, but they are not effective in preliminary discussions. Depending on the situation you may elect to make no mention of an option to buy in the initial offer, saving it as an afterthought in a counterproposal when the seller reacts to your original "offer."

Eventually you will propose that the lease contain a provision that enables you to buy the property. This is your option, and allows you the right to buy or not to buy.

The seller of this lot may very well accept a short-term lease of his land even though he is very interested in selling it. So, he might propose a counteroffer to you that he would lease the lot but only for a two- or three-year period. If this occurred (you hoped it would), you then counteroffer with your option provisions.

As long as the option price is satisfactory to the seller and he does not view the lease as a hinderance to the ultimate sale of the lot (if you do not buy it), this kind of deal should be quite workable.

The advantage to you is that you tie up the lot for a small amount, have absolute control over the lot for a sufficient time to prelease your building, and are in a good position to close on the land long before the lease term expires. Your cost will be the rent you have to pay and the other costs that may be incurred as a part of the lease.

165. What Should I Know before Getting Involved with a Joint Venture?

Joint venture proposals can work well for certain real estate investors. However, there are five simple factors you must weigh prior to getting into business with anyone as a joint venture partner.

The Five-Item Prejoint Venture Checklist

1. How do your goals differ from those of the other partners?
2. Where are the weak links in the partnership?
3. What will your liability be?
4. Who will be in control?
5. Do you trust the person in control?

How Do Your Goals Differ From Those of Other Partners?   This is important because if everyone has greatly different goals, it may be very difficult to fit the investment to these diverse goals. Decisions that are motivated because of income-oriented goals, for example, may not fit the results desired by growth-oriented goals.

Where Are the Weak Links in the Partnership?   Is it you or the mechanics of the operation or venture? Look around and make sure that if there are any weak links that there will be a solution to circumvent the difficulties bound to occur—or stay out of the deal from the beginning.

What Will Your Liability Be?   Your liability may be limited to your investment, but not always. If there is any possibility for personal liability because of an accident or other loss, make sure that the venture has provided insurance for each partner.

Who Will Be in Control?   Control should be decided before the venture partners put up their money. However, be aware that control can change along the way, and if there is a change, it may go against your wishes.

Do You Trust the Person in Control?   Trust is a relative factor and is often tied into risk. However, how well do you know the person in control? Have you checked their background? Have they been honest with you? You may never know until you do check them out. Once you do you may have a different idea about your trust.

166. How Does the "Keep Some, Sell Some" Technique Work?

The idea of contracting for something, and then keeping part of it as you sell off the rest can be a very easy way to build wealth in a hurry. Here is how it works: You find a property you would like to own, say a golf course–front villa in Hilton Head, North Carolina. The villa would be ideal as a weekend or holiday home. The problem is that it costs more than you can afford.

However, if you could get several friends together who would like to get in on a good deal, you can use their money to buy your interest in the property.

This is a type of private timeshare in that you take a residence and break up the use between several owners. To compensate for your expense and effort in putting the deal together, you would be entitled to an interest in the deal. No one will object to that as long as you follow the usual rules of the game. Take a good look at the answer to question number 160 and follow those suggestions.

167. How Can I Exchange Something I Do Not Own for Something I Want to Acquire?

The *future exchange* is an interesting approach to a problem that can occur when you want to exchange something you do own for another property and the other owner has turned you down. So you ask that property owner, "What would you take?"

When you have a "shopping list" of other property available from a property owner, it is possible that you can enter into a three-way exchange to achieve your desired goal. The following is an example of a three-way exchange.

How to Use a Three-Way Exchange

Assume that you have offered Donna a condominium apartment you own as a down payment for a villa she has. She is asking $150,000, and the villa is free and clear of any debt. Your condo is also free and clear (or you plan to make it that way) and is worth $75,000. You want to pay her cash for the balance, which you plan to get from a new first mortgage on the villa.

She responds to your offer with a big fat *no*. So, you step back and ask her what she would take in an exchange. She tells you she does not want anything that would cause headaches. She does not want management problems and would consider some nice mountain land in New England. She does not need so much cash out of her deal and would, in fact, take $50,000 in cash and the balance in land, if it was where she wanted. Great, only you don't own anything there.

You call a few brokers in the area she said she would like and start networking your condominium. You offer your condo plus some cash for the right vacant land. It would not take very long for a prospective land owner to be attracted to owning your condo and getting some cash out of the deal.

A deal might be put together that results in Donna getting $100,000 in land plus $50,000 cash. The land owner gets your condo plus $50,000 in cash, and you get the villa and owe $100,000 in a new mortgage that you pledge for the first mortgage with a local lender. Everyone ends up with something closer to what they wanted, or something they would rather have than what they owned.

168. What is the Quickest Way for Me to Become an *Insider?*

No matter what your goal is, you will achieve it quicker by association with those people who have already achieved their goals. A student of any trade learns from the professional.

The key in real estate investing is to find the insider and to learn from that person. This is not as hard as it may seem because the real insiders are clearly visible, if you know where to look for them. Take a look at the list below.

Eight Places Where You Find Real Estate Insiders

Planning and zoning meetings

City and county council meetings

Public hearings of proposed zoning changes

Real estate section of the local newspapers

Business section of the local newspapers

Public records showing property ownership

Recommended to you by local VIPs

Recommended to you by local lenders

Once the local insiders are exposed to you, make an effort to meet them. Set a goal that they will *know who you are* by using follow-up techniques. You control this and can quickly get to the point where you and the insiders are professional acquaintances.

Observe what they do in public meetings. Find out why they are there and what they expect to learn. Make sure you learn the same lessons.

By the time you do, you will be well on your way to being an insider yourself.

18

Finding Money for All Your Real Estate Transactions

169. What Is a Mortgage, Who Is the Mortgagor, and Who Is the Mortgagee?

There is a very simple way to remember which of the two parties is the mortgagee or the mortgagor. The key is the last two letters of each word. The *ee* and the *or* establish who is the lender and who is the person who must pay back the loan. However, before giving you this simple method it is important to understand exactly what a mortgage is, because most people use the phrase, "Go to the bank to *get a mortgage*," which is wrong, unless you are going to lend money to the bank.

What Is a Mortgage Anyway?

Real estate financing generally involves a combination of two different financial obligation instruments. The *primary* financing obligation is the promissory note (sometimes called *the bond*). The promissory note describes the details of repayment, such as the amounts due, the method of payment, the interest rate charged, the grace period, etc. The mortgage is the document of the *secondary* financing obligation and is the pledge of property as security to the debt. Each of these two instruments are given to the lender.

Because the person borrowing the money gives the note and mortgage to the lender, you can see that you do not go to a bank to *get a mortgage*, but to *get money* and to *give a mortgage*.

Now, back to the two letters at the end of the words. The *or*, as is found in mortgagor, grantor, lessor, and so on, distinguishes that person as the party who *gives* something. Thus, a mortgagor gives the mortgage document to the lender.

The *ee*, as is found in mortgagee, grantee, lessee, and so on, distinguishes that person as the party who receives the document or item. As the mortgage is the document showing the security pledged, the lender gets the mortgage and gives money.

The actual word *mortgage* is the formation of two Old French terms *mort*, which means dead, and *gage*, which means pledge. I will leave it up to you to decide if the true meaning is "you're as good as dead when you pledge it," or once paid off·"it is a dead pledge."

170. What Are the Most Common Types of Mortgages?

There are many different types of mortgage repayment programs, and each has its own merits to be considered when you are shopping for a loan. However, there are six basic mortgage formats that make up the majority of loans.

The Six Most Common Types of Mortgages

1. Fixed rate mortgages

2. Adjustable rate mortgages

3. Graduated payment mortgages

4. Growing equity mortgages

5. Reverse annuity mortgages

6. Shared appreciation mortgages

Before reviewing each of these six mortgages in detail, keep in mind that interest rates, points, closing costs, and payment schedules can vary from lender to lender based on the total payout term and the period of installments. There is no set standard deal, and each loan offered should be compared only with another loan of the same payout schedule. Monthly, quarterly, semiannually, and yearly payments are the usual periods of installments, but even these can vary within the same document.

Fixed Rate Mortgages. These are mortgages that have a fixed rate of interest for the term of the loan. In general, the loan terms quoted range from 15 to 30 years but may have a balloon payment at an earlier date. A loan of $100,000 to be repaid over a 30-year term at 9 percent interest would have a monthly payment of $804.66. This payment would fully amortize this loan over a full

30-year period. If the loan had a balloon at the end of 10 years, the unpaid principal would become due and payable at that time, although most lenders take this provision as an opportunity to renew the loan at new interest rates.

Adjustable Rate Mortgages.   Adjustable rate mortgages (ARMs) are very popular forms of mortgaging because they gives the lender the opportunity to adjust the mortgage on a frequent basis, usually annually, to keep the return to the lender current with the market. This type of loan repayment schedule can be good for the borrower if interest rates remain unchanged, or even go down, as they did in the early 1990s. However, when interest rates in the market place move up, these loans will become more costly for the borrower. There is usually a maximum interest rate to which an ARM can be adjusted, and adjustments can be tied to one or more of several different "national" rates, such as the average yield on 15-year Treasury Notes over the past twelve months, the prime rate, or the price of gold.

Graduated Payment Mortgages.   Graduated payment mortgages (GPMs) have an adjustment in the monthly payment over a period of time. These mortgages often begin with monthly payments that are less than what interest only would amount to. When this is the situation the total principal owned will grow by the amount of unpaid interest. The $100,000 mortgage mentioned above under the Fixed Rate Mortgages section, at 9 percent interest, may be set up as a GPM at $500 per month for the first two years. Clearly the monthly payment is now less than interest only (9 percent of $100,000 is $750 per month). The result of this mortgage would be that at the end of two years the principal would have increased in value by that shortfall between the $500 payment and the interest due (which would increase slightly every month as the principal was growing).

The mortgage payment could then graduate to a higher amount, say, $800 per month, then $900 per month, and so on. The advantage to the borrower is that the early payments are designed to help a first-time investor by moving the obligation of the debt to later years of the repayment.

Growing Equity Mortgages.   The growing equity mortgages (GEMs) repayment plan is an interesting approach to the repayment of a loan because the monthly payment will increase over the term of the loan, but will increase in such a way that the entire increase is allocated to the *repayment of principal*. In this way what starts out looking like a 30-year schedule (based on a fixed rate method of repayment) can suddenly shorten to around 12 years, depending on the usual increase in payment. This method of repayment is an excellent choice for a buyer who wants to repay the loan in a hurry and knows that he or she can handle monthly payments that may double over the next ten years or so.

Reverse Annuity Mortgages.   This is a very controversial form of "lending" that is not exactly a mortgage. In the reverse annuity mortgage (RAM) the borrower is given a "line of credit" that results in a loan amount that must then be repaid. Instead of the borrower getting the lump sum at the start of the mortgage, the lender pays to the borrower monthly payments until a period of time has passed and the amount paid, plus interest due, has accrued to the maximum line of credit.

Shared Appreciation Mortgages. This type of mortgage is also called a shared equity mortgage. The basic format of this method of mortgage payback relies on the fact that two or more borrowers enter into the mortgage agreement. Generally one of the parties actually lives in at the property. The original shared appreciation mortgages (SAMs) provided that a percentage of any appreciation in value at the time of a sale would be given to the lender. This has changed, however, and new SAMs are far more conservative.

FHA has a SAM program that requires the co-borrowers to be related, which has given this mortgage another title, the CYD (call your dad), as parents are more often than not the co-borrower.

This type of loan differs from a simple co-signer to a note and mortgage because the co-borrower actually shares in the ownership of the property. As it is likely that only one party will actually make the payments (the one living there), then an increase in value would ultimately be earned by the co-borrower who has allowed his or her credit to be used to secure the loan.

171. How Can Wording in the Mortgage Make a Big Difference in How the Mortgage Is Paid Back?

Every note and mortgage should be very carefully read and understood. Even "standard" mortgage forms can contain provisions that can be misleading to professionals, so if you are not fully comfortable in understanding the terms contained in any contract (a mortgage is a very important contract), follow the simple tactic of asking the loan officer or closing agent to go through the agreement step by step.

Take, for example, the following two paragraphs that describe the repayment of a first mortgage of $100,000 over 20 years at 8 percent interest, with monthly payments.

1. Payments are to be 240 equal monthly principal installments together with interest, at 8 percent per annum on all unpaid principal outstanding. This repayment schedule will fully amortize this loan by the 240th month.

2. Repayment of this loan shall be over a term of 20 years in 240 equal monthly installments comprised of principal and interest, at 8 percent per annum. This is a fully amortizing loan.

At first glance many investors and even some smart real estate lawyers will read between the lines and come to the wrong conclusion that each of these paragraphs describe the same monthly payment. How do they differ? See the following calculation.

Paragraph 1.   The loan amount is $100,000. Equal monthly installments, numbering 240, will be $416.67 per month. This is found simply by dividing the loan amount of $100,000 by the number of monthly installments (240).

To this monthly installment the interest on the declining loan principal must be added.

The interest for the first month would be 8 percent times the principal owed with the result divided by 12 to find the monthly equivalent of the annual rate.

$$0.08 \times \$100,000 = \$8,000$$

$$\$8,000 \div 12 \text{ (months)} = \$666.66$$

Principal portion of the monthly repayment:	$ 416.67
Interest portion *of the first month only*:	666.67
Total payment	$1,083.34

Each month, however, the mortgage payment will decline because while the principal portion remains constant, the interest will be less. At the end of 10 years a total of $50,000 will be paid off ($5,000 per year rounded off). So the 121st payment would be $416.67 plus interest on only $50,000 remaining which is $333.33, or a total of $750.00 per month. This payment continues to decline until the final payment is principal plus $2.78 interest.

Paragraph 2.   This is a standard form of repayment based on the same amount each month that is calculated to amortize the loan over the 240 months. Check any amortization schedule and you will find that the yearly payment would be $10,370. Divide that by 12 to get the monthly payment of $864.17. The difference between these two payments of $219.17 at the outset could be more than the buyer anticipated.

Solve the Problem by Including the Exact Amount of the Monthly Payment Part of the Agreement.   This is easy to do—just use a rate constant table and calculate the monthly payment, or let the agent calculate it with his or her computer (if the agent does it, ask for a full amortization schedule that will break down each payment into principal and interest on a calendar basis. The first and last years of the repayment schedule will rarely be a full twelve months, so keep that in mind. This type of printout will be helpful later when you need to calculate your annual tax deductions of interest.

172. How Do You Set Up a Wraparound Mortgage for Maximum Protection of the Mortgagor?

When you are the buyer giving a wraparound mortgage, there will be several important factors to consider and three important steps to take to get the maximum protection on the repayment of the underlying mortgages.

Review Some of the Problems That Can Occur

In the following situation Marilyn owns a triplex that you want to buy. Your plan is to live in one unit and pay off the purchase mortgage(s) partially with rent from the other two units.

You have negotiated a fair price of $180,000, but she has two existing mortgages on the property. One is a first mortgage of $60,000 that pays out in 12 years at 8 percent per year. This mortgage has a monthly payment of $649.45 per month (check a constant rate table for 12 years at 8 percent).

There is a second mortgage of $50,000 that pays out in 10 years at 9 percent per year. This mortgage has a monthly payment of $633.38 per month (check a constant rate table for 10 years at 9 percent).

If you assume the total debt you are obligated to a combined monthly payment of $1,282.83, which seems high for only $110,000 in debt. However, these mortgages are amortizing quickly and will be paid off in 12 and 10 years, respectively. Yet, you have only $30,000 cash to invest, and that means that you have to finance a total of $150,000 or pass up the deal. If you were to give Marilyn a third mortgage of $40,000 at 9.5 percent interest for the 15 years she has said she will take, that would mean an additional monthly payment of $417.70. This added to the first and second payments gives you a grand total of $1,700.53, which may be much more than you can afford, even with rent from two of the units.

A wraparound mortgage is set up to facilitate your down payment and repayment schedule. This mortgage is in the amount of $150,000, with a 28-year amortization schedule at 9.75 percent interest, with equal monthly installments. The payment is $1,304.75 per month or just slightly more than the combined total of the first and second mortgages. Marilyn agrees to this only if you agree to let the wraparound mortgage balloon at the end of the twelfth year. At that time, if you still own the property, you will refinance the loan and pay off the balloon that would total $126,623.53.

The wraparound mortgage is set up so that Marilyn is to be obligated to continue the payments on the first and second mortgage out of the funds you pay her on the wraparound mortgage. Each mortgage is treated as a separate mortgage as far as the amortization schedule is concerned. The important and critical factor to keep track of is that you do not owe $150,000 plus the first and second mortgages. The wraparound mortgage consists of the first mortgage of $60,000 and a second mortgage of $50,000 plus the *new money* or *difference* of $40,000.

Marilyn accepts this deal for any of several good reasons. It might be because she does not need the money now, but can see the benefit of letting the loan build up so that at the end of the 12 years she will have a nice nest egg. Of course, when the first mortgage is paid off at the end of 6 years she will get to keep the money that had been going toward that monthly payment. Another reason she accepts the deal could be because it solves her primary motivation: to sell the triplex.

As the buyer of the triplex, you need to be concerned with these three factors:

1. That Marilyn makes the payments on the first and second mortgages

2. That if she did default on the payment, there would be an immediate opportunity to "step in" to make the payments

3. That failure to meet her obligations on the existing first and second mortgages would constitute a default on Marilyn's part and allow you to recover your cost to protect your rights

Establish a Collection Escrow to Protect Your Rights

All three of the preceding factors can be properly taken care of if, as a part of the contract, or at least, at the closing of the sale, a collection escrow agreement is set up to ensure that all the payments you make on the wraparound mortgage are properly channeled to meet the underlying debt. Only then should any extra funds that may be left over be paid to the seller.

Set Up a "Third Party" as a Collection Agent.   It is important that the collection agent not be your accountant, lawyer, or best friend nor those of the seller. A third party such as the closing agent, a real estate management firm, or other party you and the seller can agree on should be chosen.

Give the Collection Agent Fixed Instructions.   The collection agent must have detailed instructions of what to do with the funds paid in by the wraparound mortgagor. These instructions should require prompt notice to the seller should payments from the mortgagor be late so that the seller can protect his or her rights and interest in the property by making the underlying mortgage payments on time.

Sellers Need Special Provisions to Protect Themselves.   All sellers who take back a wraparound mortgage on a sale will want the collection agreement to contain provisions that allow them to promptly step in when the buyer defaults on any payment. Because the seller relays the payments made by the buyer to meet all underlying mortgage obligations, it is recommended that very short grace periods (if any) be allowed for the buyer to make payments due. Stiff penalties for late payments should correspond to the necessary paperwork and added cost that may be needed to cover late payments on the underlying mortgages.

173. What Provisions Should I Include in the Mortgage When Using a Blanket Mortgage?

A *blanket mortgage* is a mortgage that pledges more than one property as security to the debt. When you give this kind of mortgage there are four key provisions you should include in the mortgage.

The Four Important Blanket Mortgage Provisions

1. Release of security clauses
2. Substitution of security provisions
3. Clear and concise *position of security* defined
4. Repayment terms covered

Release of Security Clauses.   This will enable you to remove some and eventually all of the extra security or property you have pledged to the loan as the loan to value ratio decreases. The change in loan to value ratio can occur through the continual paying of the principal owed, or the increased value of the property securing the loan.

Substitution of Security Provisions.   This will allow you to release one property (that you may want or need to sell or refinance) and to replace that lost security to the blanket mortgage by another property. This flexibility will allow you to deal with your portfolio in a more responsive way than if you were tied into a static situation.

Clear and Concise *Position of Security* Defined.   If there are any limitations to the position you are giving up when you add a property to the security, those limitations must be carefully spelled out in clear and concise terms. For example, if you put up a vacant lot you own as additional security, but want the right to build a home on that lot and to obtain a first mortgage of up to 50 percent of the combined value of the home and the lot, then that limitation should be absolutely clear. For the other party, such a limitation may not actually reduce the value of the security because the 50 percent value remaining could be greater than the value of the original lot.

Repayment Terms Covered.   Repayment schedules of any mortgages should be carefully outlined, but when the mortgage contains releases of security, or substitution of security as often is the case in a blanket mortgage, the mortgagor should have some flexibility in splitting the different segments of the added security. This would require separation of the blanket mortgage into one or more blanket mortgages that would maintain the principal owed, but divide it from one large mortgage to two or more smaller ones.

For example, a developer puts up several vacant lots as security to a $200,000 loan to construct a model home. As sales occur the builder may want to construct a second model home and at the same time start construction on five homes sold. To build the five "sold" homes would require a release of five lots from the blanket mortgage, but in turn the builder agrees to split the original $200,000 into two $150,000 loans on the two models (the original and the new one), and at the same time add $100,000 in cash equity to generate the extra $200,000 needed to build the second model home.

174. What Is *Novation* and Why Is It Important?

How tricky can lenders get? Remember assumption? When a lender allows you to sell a property that has an existing mortgage on it by letting the new buyer assume the mortgage as the seller, you may think that you are completely off the hook for any further liability on that mortgage. Sorry to tell you this, but unless the assumption agreement also contained an agreement of *novation*, you are still tied into the mortgage.

When the lender agrees to execute a novation, the lender is agreeing that the former mortgagor is no longer obligated to the loan and that the new mortgagee (who was approved for assumption) is the party now obligated.

When selling a property that has a FHA mortgage, make sure that the assumption contains novation.

175. What Key Questions Do You Need to Have Answered to Protect You from Random Releases of Property You Sell?

When you hold a mortgage on a property that can be divided into separate parts, such as an apartment complex, vacant land, or an office building, the buyers may want you to give them the right to release portions of the original security from the remaining balance of the mortgage. This situation is most common when an investor buys a rental apartment complex with the idea of conversion to condominium or cooperative apartments, or when a land developer acquires a large tract that is to be subdivided into lots. The land developer may then wish to sell off lots, or to build homes and sell the lot and home together, prior to the repayment of the purchase money mortgage on the purchase of the land.

Before agreeing to a provision like this, there are four questions that you will want to have clear and agreeable answers to.

The Four Questions to Be Answered before You Agree to Releases of Security

1. *Is there* quality control *of the buyer's use of the property*? If the project is to take a 500-acre farm and subdivide it into a residential community, as long as you are holding a mortgage on some of the land, you would want to know what kind of community it is to be. Builders will often paint a far more rosy picture of the desired end result than it may turn out to be, so as soon as that pretty picture has been described, ask the developer to build in some safeguards for you. You can do this easily by putting in *deed restrictions* that restrict or limit what the buyer (and subsequent buyers) can do on the land. You can, for example, establish the minimum lot size, minimum building size, indicate that all residential construc-

tion contain an enclosed two-car (or three-car) garage, not have flat roofs, not have black asphalt driveways, have setbacks greater than the local rules would allow, and on and on. Naturally you do not want to be so repressive that you tie the hands of the developer, but most of the truly magnificent residential subdivisions in America have very strict deed restrictions that some thoughtful land owner or developer agreed would have a beneficial long-term effect.

2. *Have you established* release prices *and* minimums *to ensure the buyer's equity?* When you agree to releases, the actual release price should be greater than par. For example, if you are holding a mortgage of $500,000 on a 50-acre tract of land that a developer plans to construct a "manufactured housing project" (the new name for a trailer park), par would be $10,000 per acre. Your release price to the developer should be a greater percentage than that, often 125 to 150 percent of the par rate. At 125 percent the release price per acre would be $12,500 per acre.

When the developer needs to have land released from your mortgage (to sell it, for example), you can require a minimum amount of land be released at any time. This is a negotiable factor, of course, but it should be established according to the type of development the builder anticipates. In the case of a trailer park the release may be in 5-acre minimums. An important factor to consider is to keep all the land in each release package in one block. In essence, if the developer must take at least 5 acres at a time, all of those acres would be within one boundary. Most developers will want purely random releases, that is, releases that can be scattered all around the development. This gives them the maximum salability of the product, but can be the least attractive method of release from your point of view. Sellers generally want to provide a release pattern that starts with the least valuable of the land and works toward the more valuable (such as at the rear working toward the road frontage). In the final contract there is apt to be some give and take to allow the pattern to fit the project while giving the seller some protection. A random release provision with minimum sizes that must be together can be a good compromise.

If the release provision is at 150 percent of par, it is easy to see that as the land is released the amount of land remaining is at a lower loan to value ratio, which increases the seller's security.

A word of warning to sellers: Read the wording of any release provision very carefully to see how the release value is calculated. For example, you sell 500 acres of land for $1,000 per acre. You get $100,000 down and are holding a first mortgage for the balance, which is $400,000. Your intention is to allow the buyer to release land from the mortgage on the basis of 150 percent of par in 5-acre minimums. Par would be found by dividing the $400,000 by the acreage (500 acres).

Thus $400,000 ÷ 500 = $800 per acre. 150 percent of that would be $1,200 per acre. As you have established a minimum of 5 acres per release you believe the buyer must reduce the mortgage by $60,000 (5 × $1,200 = $60,000) for every 5 acres.

The buyer's lawyer or agent draws an agreement that has the following provision:

...and it is further agreed that the Buyer shall be entitled to releases from the purchase money mortgage (originally set at $400,000) for every principal payment of $60,000 toward the purchase price. Releases need not be taken on each payment, and Buyer may accumulate credits toward releases, which may be taken only in increments of 5 acres or more.

This might sound like it did the trick, but if you caught the buyer's slick wording you will realize that as the original down payment is a principal payment toward the purchase price (not the purchase money mortgage), the buyer would already have credit for more than 5 acres. With an additional payment of $20,000 of principal, the buyer's total payment to you would be $120,000, which would give the buyer a full 10 acres to be released from the mortgage.

Your understanding of the agreement between you and the buyer was that by the time the buyer got 10 acres you would have gotten the original down payment of $100,000 plus $120,000 for the two 5-acre releases, or a total of $220,000 and not just the $120,000.

3. *Is the remaining security adequate for the balance of the loan?* As was mentioned in the preceding paragraph, the remaining security can be increasing due to an above-par release payment. If there was a $100,000 mortgage on a 5-acre tract of land, and the developer wanted to build warehouses on half-acre lots, each half acre would be at $10,000 par (an equal share of the mortgage). If the release price was 150 percent of par, the developer would have to pay down the mortgage $15,000 per lot to have them released. By the time five lots were released, a total of $75,000 would have been paid off, leaving only $25,000 to cover the remaining half of the land. The seller's situation would be improving if the release pattern did not leave undesirable lots remaining.

4. *In a foreclosure would you be satisfied with what you get back?* Random releases or ill-advised release patterns can use up the desirable property and leave the lender with property that may appear to be above par in value but in fact be well below it. Such would be the case if the property was released in a way that used up all the road frontage first. When you agree to a release pattern, it is critical that you determine the absolute maximum situations under which you would be willing to hold a mortgage. You can limit or hold back road frontage until the final release, for example. Other provisions to increase your security would include:

- No unreleased land can be surrounded by released land.
- No unreleased land track can be less than a specific size.
- Developer infrastructure (water, sewers, roads, etc.) must be brought to all property prior to releases.

176. How Does *Subordination* Affect the Security of a Mortgage?

There was a time when less than ethical developers would contract to buy your property subject to your agreement to subordinate a large purchase money mortgage to new financing. For example, you would sell a hotel for $1,000,000 and agree to hold a second mortgage of $500,000 behind the existing first mortgage of $300,000. This gives the developers an equity at this point of $200,000 (they paid you that amount, exchanged something else, or whatever). You subordinate your interest to a new first mortgage because they say they want to remodel the property and return it to excellent condition and income potential.

What happens if a big mortgage is slapped on the property and the developers walk away from it? This does not sound too good, does it? The buyer goes out and borrows $2,500,000 on the property and pledges the property as the security—ahead of your second mortgage, and then they promptly stop making any payments. In essence, they walk away from that loan (so it may appear), and the lender calls you up and says the property will be foreclosed, do you want to protect your $500,000 interest by paying off the new first mortgage?

A superior mortgage can "wipe out" your second mortgage. Bad news can get worse. Not only did the buyer walk from the mortgage, the improvements that were to be made from the mortgage funds were never finished (or even started). As the buyer did not do anything to the property, there is no reason to expect additional income, so it will clearly not support that kind of debt presently on it. You stand to lose your interest in the hotel because you are behind a first mortgage that is greater than the value of the property. You do not want to start making payments, so in the end your second mortgage is wiped out and the lender then takes over the hotel (deed in lieu or foreclosure). Later, if you are lucky, you may discover that the original buyer and the lender who took the property over were actually the same person, only dealing under different corporate names. Why did they do this? They acquire the property with only $500,000 invested instead of $1,000,000.

Subordination is the act of moving behind an existing or future lien. Whenever you agree to step aside in this way, you are at risk of losing your entire position. There are ways to protect yourself to some degree. The following are examples of things you can do to increase your security in the advent of subordination. You should use combinations of these protections rather than just use one or two of them.

- Get co-signers
- Get assignment of rents from other properties
- Have a *letter of credit* as additional security
- Insist on advance principal payments during subordination
- Insist on a completion bond in the advent of new construction
- Limit subordination to a specific period of time
- Limit new loan amounts
- Limit subordination to clearly defined institutional financing
- Require personal guarantees

177. What Is *Substitution of Collateral* and Why Is It Considered an Insider Technique?

A *substitution of collateral* is a provision that creates a very flexible situation for the mortgagor because the mortgagee agrees to accept, at a future date, another property as a substitute collateral or security to the loan. The lender may agree to a specific property or a formula of value replacement. The following are two different provisions as examples.

1. The lender agrees that anytime following the first anniversary of the mortgage, provided the mortgage is current, the mortgagor may replace the security to the mortgage, described as *the site* herein, by either of the two properties described in exhibit A hereto attached.
2. In substitution for the all or part of the security pledged to this mortgage, as described in paragraph A of this document, the mortgagee agrees to accept any property that meets the following criteria:
   a. Is free of any debt or liens
   b. Has a recent certified appraisal showing its value to be equal to no less than two times the outstanding balance of the loan at the time of the replacement
   c. Is located within Dade County, Florida
   d. Is not under any moratorium of use, subject to impacts or assessments for use
   e. Is not in violation of any code or ordinance

As restrictive as the second paragraph might sound, it still provides considerable flexibility to the property owner. Why would the owner want such flexibility? Take a look at the following example.

Frank's Substitution of Collateral

Frank has acquired a large apartment complex that consists of 48 apartment units. The complex is comprised of eight six-unit buildings in a beautiful garden setting. The price was $2,00,000.

There is a first mortgage of only $200,000 and the seller agreed to a second mortgage of $1,700,000 based on the agreement by Frank to pay to the seller $100,000 down and spend another $250,000 for immediate repair of the property. The seller-held mortgage amounts to just over $35,000 per unit.

The seller also agreed to allow substitution in all or part, along the provisions of paragraph 2 in the example shown above. In addition, the seller agreed to *release* each building from the second mortgage for every principal payment or substitution of $240,000. This allows Frank to make some major restructuring of the project to free up some units to sell off. Here are just a few of the things Frank can do.

- Give the seller a substitution of collateral of $480,000 to release two buildings from the second mortgage, or 12 units in all.

- Sell condo units in the buildings, and with the proceeds from a few of the sales pay off the existing first mortgage and pay down the second mortgage to get more releases.

- Get releases for the remaining units by substitution of collateral by pledging the newly remodeled units from the first four buildings that have been released, but as individual units. This can actually make it easier for Frank to sell the units, as financing will not be in place for a buyer to assume.

These are insider techniques and are part of what makes real estate interesting. There are many ways to make deals work that are all ethical, above board, and exciting.

178. When Is a First Mortgage *Not* a First Lien?

The fact that the document may say *first mortgage* does not make it so. Loans are ranked in the position of their lien on the property that is pledged as security to the loan (in the mortgage document). The mortgage and the mortgage note must be recorded in the proper jurisdiction to be set as a lien against the property for anyone to see. If the mortgage and mortgage note are not recorded in a timely fashion, or are recorded in the wrong property records (say in California instead of Florida, or in the wrong county), then any subsequent mortgage that gets recorded will be ahead of what was intended to be a first mortgage. Such would be the case if the buyer took out a second mortgage to help pay for closing costs and down payment, and this second mortgage got recorded ahead of the first mortgage. Guess what? The second mortgage is really the first mortgage and the first mortgage (but only if recorded) is a second mortgage.

Closing agents know all about this and generally insist that prior to releasing funds at closing, they run a postclosing title check to make sure that the seller did not actually take out another loan (and not tell anyone) the day or so before the closing. Then, after the documents have been recorded, some closing agents double check again to make sure that the loans were properly recorded in the right order.

This is critical for obvious reasons and points out a very good reason to use qualified closing agents, whether they are lawyers or title insurance or escrow agents who are professionals in this task.

If you are contemplating buying a first or second mortgage at a discount, you must double check to ensure that the mortgage is exactly what it is supposed to be. Some investors make big returns by buying "second" mortgages at a discount once they discover that the recorded first mortgage has actually been paid off, or is at such a low loan to value ratio that for all practical purposes the second mortgage will soon be a first mortgage. Keep in mind that unless the mortgage has a subordination provision that would allow new financing to be placed ahead of it even after superior mortgages have been paid off, all mortgage positions move up in their lien position when superior mortgages are paid off, e.g., a second mortgage becomes a first when the previous first is paid off.

179. Which Lender Almost Always Gives the Best Terms on a Loan?

The seller is usually the best source for a purchase money mortgage or other, more creative financing techniques. After all, the seller has other motivations that need to be satisfied, and if you can pinpoint the goals the seller needs to achieve and can show the seller how your proposal will move the seller closer to those goals, then the other aspects of the contract to sell become secondary.

Dwell on benefits they get. The key to this is not to stress the mortgage terms but to dwell on the benefits the overall agreement achieves. This may require some creative thought on your part or at least proper orientation to focus the seller on creative options available to them.

For example, a seller is anxious to sell his or her home in order to move to Texas where a new job awaits. The seller may be convinced that to achieve this move his or her property must be sold for cash so the cash can be put towards a new place to live. The reality is that the seller need only obtain something that can be used as a down payment for a new place to live. Cash works fine, but if that is not available, then a buyer who offers a well-secured second mortgage (co-signers, blanket mortgage, and so on) may be able to show the seller that there will be other sellers in Texas who would be glad to allow a pyramid to work (sellers hold the mortgage on another property when they sell theirs).

Sound complicated? Not really—all it takes is the simple understanding that when people need to sell, the reason they need to sell is what you should solve, not what they believe to be the solution.

180. How Do I Shop around for a Lender?

There are both private and institutional lenders who are worth shopping around for. Start with the institutional lenders, as they are easier to find: banks, savings and loan institutions, thrift institutions, credit unions, insurance companies, mortgage real estate investment trusts, and pension funds are the major institutional sources. Some of these, mainly the first four in this list, can be approached by you. Alternatively, you can seek out a mortgage broker who will be found an ample supply in most communities in the *Yellow Pages* of the phone book under Mortgages or Mortgage Bankers and Brokers.

You want to avoid putting up nonrefundable deposits, and when dealing with mortgage brokers and bankers, make sure you have checked their references.

Feel free to mention loan quotes to the lenders. Often the best approach is an honest face and a straightforward statement: "You know, First Federal offered me $20,000 more without any closing costs. Can you beat that?"

181. What Is the Key to Getting a Loan?

Look confident, act confident, and be confident about what you are doing. This rubs off not only on the loan officer, but on yourself as well. But above all, have a goal that you work toward. Goal-oriented people are able to focus on the end result and are less likely to become emotional about the interim step. At least, that is the way you should think about it. If you find that you are more emotional about getting to the destination than the destination itself, then it is likely you do not have a clearly defined goal or destination in your mind. Work on that.

182. What Is a FHA Mortgage and Where Do I Get One?

In 1934 the Federal Housing Administration (FHA) was formed out of the Department of Housing and Urban Development (HUD) of the federal government. FHA is primarily a loan insurance program that works through institutional lenders. This insurance guarantees the upper portion of the loan made, which increases the security to the lender and allows the loan to be made at a competitive market rate, even though the required down payment may be well below the conventional market.

The low down payment allowed may be as low as 3 percent for an acquisition of $50,000 or less, and only an additional 5 percent for purchase prices above the first $50,000.

As FHA does not actually make loans, their programs are made through local lenders that specialize in FHA programs. The easiest way to find who these lenders or their representatives are is to call the nearest FHA office to where you want to invest. Check with your phone company for the listing of the Federal Housing Administration.

A quick glance of the *Yellow Pages* under Mortgage Companies, Brokers and Bankers, may show large ads for companies that advertise their specialty in FHA and VA loans.

183. Who Can Qualify for a FHA Loan?

There are over 15 different types of FHA loan programs and each program has slight variations that can affect qualification. However, the good news is that *all* FHA programs are designed to *help* first-time buyers acquire their own property.

Once you find a lender in your area who is experienced in making FHA loans, sit down with that person to discover which of the FHA programs may best suit you and exactly what you would qualify for in the way of price and type of property. Keep in mind that FHA loans are not limited to homes or apartments, as small income-producing residential properties can also be purchased if you or at least a shared appreciation mortgagor will live there.

The loan officer or mortgage agent will want to know the following information:

1. Your and your spouse's combined earnings

2. Type of job and tenure

3. Total debts

4. Scheduled monthly payments for that debt

5. Rental payments (car, furniture, but not living quarters)

6. Court-ordered payments for outside support

7. Outside expenses you pay for others (parents, children, etc.)

The loan officer will review these items with you and will establish the levels that FHA will insure. There are some guidelines and "rules of thumb," but there are also exceptions to those rules so it is best for your specific circumstances to be reviewed to ascertain exactly what you can qualify for.

184. What Is a *GI Loan* and How Do I Get One?

At the end of World War II, Congress approved the Serviceman's Readjustment Act of 1944. The common term for this new program was, and still is, "the GI Bill of Rights."

The purpose was to give the hundreds of thousands of GIs (general infantrymen) a new start and to ease their expenses in civilian life by providing them with a variety of medical benefits, bonuses, and low interest loans. Title II (one of six sections of the original bill) was dedicated to giving the GIs an opportunity to buy their own home or other real estate.

These loans are not directly made by the Veterans Administration but are insured by them, and they work much the same as do FHA loans. However, GI or veterans loans can be 100 percent of the purchase price.

One of the most misunderstood areas of the GI loans is finding out who qualifies. The following are the basic qualifications, but as with most anything that has to do with the government, if you seem to qualify but are not sure, then contact the nearest VA office by checking with the local phone directory or calling phone information and asking for the Veterans Administration nearest you. Mortgage brokers and bankers advertising in the *Yellow Pages* may also announce themselves as specialists in VA or GI loans, and these sources should also be able to help you. In general the qualifications are as follows.

Veteran Loan (GI Loans) Qualifications

1. Served on active duty during the following periods for the number of days indicated.

September 16, 1940, to July 25, 1947	90 days
July 26, 1947, to June 26, 1950	181 days
June 27, 1950, to January 31, 1955	90 days
February 1, 1955, to August 4, 1964	181 days
August 5, 1964, to May 7, 1975	90 days
May 8, 1975 to present	191 days

2. Discharged for service related injury during service with no minimum time needed. If entered service after September 7, 1980 discharge for any disability, whether service connected or not.

3. If enlisted after September 7, 1980 or entered active duty after October 16, 1981 a full 24 months of active duty or the full time of the original enlistment may be needed, but there are many exceptions to this.

4. Spouses of service personnel missing in action or prisoners of war for at least 90 days may be eligible for one VA home loan.

5. Unmarried surviving spouses may be eligible for VA home loan if the veteran's death was service-connected. Previous eligibility used by the veteran will not be deducted from the full guarantee allowed the surviving spouse.

6. Any U.S. citizen who was in the service of the armed forces of a country allied with the United States in World War II.

185. What Are the Most Asked Questions about Veterans Administration Loans?

1. *What if I was in the reserves and not in active duty of the regular army or other service?* The VA or GI loan is not for you, but FHA has a program that is called the FHA/VA loan [203(v)]. This is similar to other FHA programs that are available, but for the qualifying reservist the down payment requirements would be lower.

2. *How does the VA guarantee to the lender work?* The current maximum the VA will insure is $36,000 (subject to periodic increases). As this is an amount of the loan that the VA guarantees to the lender, it acts as a protection for the lender in making the loan. The actual amount of the loan is not tied to this guarantee but is a function of what the lender is willing to do. One exception to this would be loans that the lender would sell to the Government National Mortgage Association (GNMA or Ginnie Mae). GNMA limits these loans to a maximum of $144,000.

3. *Can you get a GI loan on a manufactured home?* Yes, although the maximum loan guarantee will be less, resulting in lower loan maximums.

4. *If the entitlement was already used, can a qualified veteran get requalified for a VA loan?* Yes. The entitlement for the full $36,000 (or whatever the current maximum would be) can be used again, even if the original entitlement was much less. When a loan is paid off you will qualify for renewed entitlement *only when you sell the property*. However, if you sell your property and the buyer assumes the loan you must have the buyer qualify as a veteran and submit their *Certificate of Eligibility* to the lender or you must obtain a *release of liability* from the lender. If the buyer cannot qualify as a veteran, you will not get a release of liability and the amount of your entitlement that is used as a guarantee to that loan will be tied into that loan until it is eventually paid off.

5. *What is the biggest danger when a veteran sells his or her property and the buyer assumes the loan?* The problem is that unless you get a release of liability not only is your entitlement locked into the loan, but you are also the primary guarantor to the loan. If there were a default in the future (even years in the future), the lender would look to the VA for coverage, and either the lender or VA could look to you for recovery of any deficiency in a foreclosure.

6. *How long is a VA entitlement good for?* Once you qualify, that qualification lasts as long as you or your surviving spouse lives or until that rule is changed.

186. What Can You Do to Increase Your Chances of Getting a Loan?

The following "secret" steps work wonders for many different situations. The criterion is simply that whenever you are to meet with someone who will have some control (even the very slightest control) over something you want, follow these steps.

The Five Secret Steps to Increase Your Chances at Nearly Everything

1. Meet the head person.
2. Meet the head person's secretary.
3. Have the secretary set up your next appointment.
4. Have the secretary remind the person of your appointment.
5. Let the secretary prod the person for you later on.

Meet the Head Person. This is not difficult to do and will pay off. In the situation involving a mortgage the head person would be the president of the bank or lending institution. To meet this person you simply drop a nicely written letter on your own quality letterhead and ask for an appointment in the relatively near future. You mention that you are planning on making some investments in the area and would like to discuss several items of mutual benefit.

Prior to the appointment you will want to make sure that you have spoken with the head person's secretary. You might call one day to double-check the address, ask which floor their office is located, or ask some other "intelligent" question. Ask for his or her name, and thank him or her by name (but never use the first name by itself no matter how many times he or she says you can do it).

Meet the Head Person's Secretary.   By now you already know the secretary, but have not met face to face. You can save this for the day of the appointment, or if convenient, drop by the office a few days before the appointment and introduce yourself. Be sure you are dressed with your most successful looking business type apparel. A good approach is to have an envelope that has a clipping about the institution that you saw in the newspaper. Best would be to mention something about the head person. Least effective and what you should avoid would be mentioning something about yourself.

Have the Secretary Set Up Your Next Appointment.   Here is how you work this. You have the appointment with the head person and you keep it very brief. You do not ask for anything, but spend the whole time asking about the bank or institution. How long are they in business, how did the head person get started, what is the future for the company, and so on. The idea is to make the head person *sell* their services to you. You are there as a prospective client of the bank, not as some guy off the street who wants a loan.

During the appointment you tell the head person you are going to be in touch. The head person might suggest that you talk to someone important, like the mayor or some other person. You say that you will, and you will let the head person know how it turns out.

A few days later you drop the head person a note, and let him or her know what happened. Even if nothing positive occurred, you have established a small seed of truth or integrity in that you did what you said you were going to do, and you did it right away.

The moment you drop this note in the mail, call the secretary and ask him or her to tell the head person that you have followed up with the head person's suggestion, and would he or she thank the head person for you. Do not tell the secretary what the suggestion was. You are setting the stage that you and the head person share information that the secretary may not be privileged to.

If the conversation goes well, or on the next day, mention that you would like to talk to the "best" loan officer to discuss some business with the bank regarding single-family homes (or apartment buildings or the type of property you want to deal with). Make sure you make it plural, as in homes, apartments, buildings, and so on.

The secretary will suggest someone. Ask about that person, just to get an idea and some background information. How long has this person been with the bank, what kind of loans is he or she experienced in—again, you put the onus on them to *sell* you on their people and service.

Now you ask the secretary, almost as an afterthought, if it would be possible for him or her to set up an appointment for you...and oh yes, what would be the best day next week? You can suddenly be rushed: "Oh, I have a call from London...Please set it up for me, I'll check with you in the morning, and absolutely any time Thursday or Friday next week is fine. Bye."

The secretary will call the loan officer (or employment director, or head of the purchasing department, whoever is important for your call). The person getting the call from the secretary of the head person will assume that the call was directed by the head person, and another subtle seed is being planted.

Have the Secretary Remind the Person of Your Appointment.   When you call to check the details on the appointment, thank the secretary. Then, write a quick note, thanking him or her again, and in the last part of the note ask if the secretary would mention to the person that you will try to be a few minutes early just in case they could see you early, but there is no need to get back to you, however.

Be sure to show up a few minutes earlier than you mentioned. By now the person you are meeting with may think you are the head person's brother or someone even more important.

Let the Secretary Prod the Person for You Later On.   If the person you met with needs a subtle push, as in the case of a loan officer and your pending loan, look again to the head person's secretary. Call the secretary and suggest he or she let that person know you will stop by the next day to see how things are going. Be very sparing in this, and do not use it unless necessary.

All this might seem to be "overkill" and in some situations it could be. However, the effort is not hard, and if you are establishing yourself as a potential real estate investor you will want to be making contacts with head persons (and their secretaries) all over town.

187.   Do the Mortgage Reduction Plans Really Save Me Money?

Sure, but is the saving worth the cost? Does this sound redundant? First take a look at the way most mortgage reduction plans work.

The plan: If you pay down the principal of a mortgage faster than the scheduled repayment, you will shorten the repayment time. This statement is the basis for the repayment program and is the simple fact for which someone is apt to pay several hundred dollars to learn when this plan and fact are packaged in a "sold on TV" financial program with the title *How to Save Over $100,000 in the Repayment of a $120,000 Loan.*

Assume that you have a 30-year repayment on this $120,000 loan at 9 percent interest. The monthly payment in a typical mortgage would be $965.60 for the full 30-year term. In essence, 360 months times $965.60 gives a total (add up all 360 months) of $347,616 over the 30 years.

If you add only $100 per month extra (and have it apply just to the principal owed), this same mortgage will be paid off in about 20 years and seven months, which is 247 months. As the original loan schedule still has 113 months to go, you might say (correctly at that) that by following the

"Cummings Prepayment Plan," you would save having to pay $109,112.80 (113 months times $965.60).

So far so good. Now, by paying an additional $100.00 per month for 247 months you paid in $24,700 earlier than you needed to. At first this might seem that if you deducted that amount from the $109,112.80 you would come up with the real savings of this plan, or $84,412.80. Is this your real savings? No. Based on the information at hand not only have you not saved anything, this plan may have cost you money. How so?

This mortgage is at 9 percent interest. If you can get more benefit from the $100 per month than 9 percent, then you would be better off not making the principal payments. Notice I used the word benefit rather than return. Many people have consumer loans or credit card charges that cost them a great deal more than 9 percent interest per year. Some of these charges can exceed 20 percent.

On the other hand, if you have money in the savings that you do not need as a security blanket and is earning you less than 9 percent, the faster you pay off the loan the better you might be. But even here there is something else to consider.

What is your plan for this property? If the plan is to keep the property for a few years, then sell it, then the mortgage in place can be an important factor to help you sell this property.

It is certain that the gimmick of saving money simply by paying off a mortgage early is not true. As this example shows, it can cost you money on one hand, and even if there is a positive effect due to interest rate differences, the overall disadvantage of building equity in a property you plan to sell may not be to your advantage.

As with every investment, look hard at your goals before you take any short-cut that leads you to a dead end.

188. What Are the Insider Tips for Negotiating the Best Mortgage Terms?

In general, lenders seek to reduce their risk wherever possible. However, as risk goes down, it is an accepted financial reality that so does the yield on the investment. Because of this, lenders seek a balance where they can leverage their deposits up to a portfolio of loans that create a blended return for an acceptable risk.

The blending comes from a mix of high-return, but high-risk loans such as automobile, aircraft, boat, credit-card, and other similar financial transactions. The lower-risk loans are the high-equity real estate transactions given to proven risk-free clients.

There are three things you can do to increase your chances of getting the best loan terms possible.

1. Have a professional loan presentation.

2. Show a proven track record.

3. Decrease the loan to value ratio.

Have a Professional Loan Presentation. Keep in mind that each lender will have their own loan application and format that they like to follow. You will want to adhere to that format, but you should also be creative in adding other material to the package that enables them to make a decision based on the assumption that they had material in their hands to support that decision.

Loan officers are, after all, not giving you their money. They are giving you the *bank's* money. This means that although they might take a risk with their own cash, they are now caught between a rock and a hard place. On one hand, the bank depends on them to make loans, and to make a lot of loans every week to ensure that the needed revenue to keep the bank in business is coming in. On the other hand, the bank also demands that the loan officers not make mistakes. One of the worst mistakes a loan officer can make is to recommend or push for a loan, and then have that loan fail. That results in big red marks against that loan officer in his or her personnel file. If there are too many marks, the loan officer can be terminated.

So, provide more than enough material that supports these three elements: the value of the property, you and your ability to do everything you say you will do (including meet the repayment terms of the loan), and demonstrating that their approval of the loan you have requested is a sound move on their part.

Show a Proven Track Record. If this is your first loan for your first real estate investment you may have to be creative about your track record, but always be honest. Look to success you have had in anything else you may have done. Your job and your personal life can do if there is nothing else to use as evidence of success. Remember that it is not what you say you did that is really important, it is what you do that is. To prove this, make demands on yourself and then live up to them. Even doing this for a very short period of time can have a major impact on your self-confidence. Be prompt for appointments, and have everything the loan officer asks for, on time or early, and you will build the loan officer's confidence in you, too.

Decrease the Loan to Value Ratio. If you can show that the value of the property is even greater than the price you are paying, then you can show the lender that what might look like a 110 percent loan to value ratio is really closer to a 70 percent loan to value ratio. For example, if you have a contract to buy a vacant warehouse for $300,000 and want to borrow $325,000, the loan officer might tell you that your chances are zero. However, if you can show that the real value of the property is $460,000, you are in good shape. I was involved in a situation exactly like this, where the buyer got a bargain price from the seller because the buyer was the sole tenant who planned to move if he could not buy the property for $300,000. All the buyer had to do was show that because his own company would agree to pay rent, the value was clearly established at $460,000. He substantiated that with some independent opinions and got enough money to pay off the seller plus some extra cash to cover legal and closing costs.

189. As a Buyer Just How Creative Can I Get with Mortgages?

Short of usury and being involved in some other illegal act, you can be very creative with mortgages in a contract. Taking into consideration honesty and ethical dealing, a contract between two people that is discussed openly can be very flexible and creative. When it comes to real estate transactions there are many different ways to solve problems. The following are just a few of the techniques that can be incorporated into mortgages to give you the edge, to help make the deal, to save on taxes, to increase cash flow, to shift income, or just to help out a relative in their first real estate purchase. All of the following can be used in various combinations to create an endless supply of creative opportunities.

Twenty-five Creative Mortgage Techniques

Adjustable rate mortgage

Assignment of payments for benefits you relieve

Balloon payment

Blanket mortgage

Co-signer

Deed in lieu of foreclosure

Discounted mortgage

Friendly foreclosure

Gift of interest in the mortgage

Graduated payment mortgage

Interest-only payment

Lease–option conversion

Moratorium of interest

Pyramid mortgage

Release of security

Repayment by barter

Repayment by return of benefits

Selling of an interest in the mortgage

Shared appreciation mortgage

Subordination of interest

Substitution of security

Unsecured note

Use of mortgage as security for a loan

Wraparound mortgage

Zero coupon payment plan

190.   What Can I Do to Get around a *Nonassumable Mortgage*?

Many mortgages have provisions that make them nonassumable, or even when they appear to be assumable they have the same restrictions on the new mortgagor as on a buyer taking out an application for a new loan. Because of this, many buyers want to avoid this situation and cost. However, the nonassumable provision is often very clear and precise about what the seller can and cannot do that might trigger the lender, causing the borrower to be in default, and attempting to stop the sale of the property.

191.   What Is a "Starker" Exchange and What Are the Pitfalls I Need to Watch Out for?

Once upon a time there was a tax case involving an a delayed 1031 exchange. The defendant to the tax case was named Starker, and thus the historic case that has resulted in a host of rules and regulations that govern exchanges that start as a sale and end up as an exchange.

What is a *Starker?* A very simple example is as follows: Alice owns a vacant lot she wants to dispose of so she can invest the proceeds into a small motel she would like to own. She has tried to effect a 1031 exchange where she would swap her equity for that of a motel and, if the accounting worked out right, avoid any gain on the lot. Her problem, after all, is that the vacant lot is worth $500,000 but she paid only $50,000 for it 20 years ago. A taxable gain of $450,000 is not a pleasant event when it comes to tax payment time.

However, no direct exchange seemed possible, yet several buyers were ready and willing to pay her price. What should she do? She should follow the rules and guides of a "Starker" and beat the IRS at their own game.

Here's how it works. As long as Alice meets the IRS guidelines, she can enter into a contract to sell her lot. She must set aside the cash she will get from the sale within very strict rules that do not allow her to use the money, but which permit her to look for and contract for another property of her liking which she can purchase (providing it meets the rules of a 1031 exchange). If she meets all the IRS rules and regulations, she will not have to pay any capital gains tax that might have resulted on the sale of her lot.

In essence, this is a 1031 exchange as described earlier in this book, but with one major and very important twist. It is not really an exchange. It is a sale, and with the proceeds of the sale it becomes a purchase.

Keep in mind the true importance of this statement. If Alice sold her lot for $500,000 and paid the tax on the capital gain of $450,000 (which could be $150,000 or more), she might end up with only $350,000 to reinvest. However, if she can meet the requirements of a Starker exchange, she can reinvest the entire amount (less commissions and cost of the deal) into another property.

Warning: When it comes to actually doing this kind of transaction you are advised to seek the advice of professionals who can clue you in on the latest information, tax rules, and legal ramifications as they apply to this type of real estate deal. This is not something you should try to learn from this or any other book. When it comes to the IRS, you had best stick with those professionals who are 100 percent current, which no book can be.

Remember that a 1031 exchange must be a like-kind exchange, and therefore a Starker exchange must also meet that rule. Like for like does not mean farm for farm, or office building for office building. Like for like is based on the intent of ownership. What we are talking about is investment real estate. If what you want to dispose of is investment real estate, then it will qualify for a 1031, and also a Starker exchange, provided that you acquire investment real estate.

The key factors in the Starker are the exact documentation of the transaction. You must follow some very strict rules that will, in their finality, allow you to close on a sale of your property only as long as you do not have use of or get your hands on the proceeds of the sale. Any cash must be tied into the acquisition of the replacement property or you will face a failure of the 1031 tax benefits.

The rules of the delayed exchange require that within 45 days of the date you close on the sale of your property (the day someone else takes title to your property), you must identify a property you will take in its place. Fortunately you can identify more than one property (because you do not know if you can actually take title or close on any single property at that time).

The rules also require that you take title to your new property no more than 180 days from the date you close on the sale of your property, or the due date of your tax return for that year, whichever comes first. It is within this paragraph that problems start to arise, and one of the reasons that you should be well represented with current tax and legal consultation because whenever you mess with the IRS, you flirt with the devil.

There are many pitfalls with the Starker, and the most common is falling into a trap that only one property need be identified. As you have only the first 45 days following the closing of title on your property to identify what you want, if you fail to locate more than one property you may be locked out of a successful 1031 tax treatment if the single property you select cannot be delivered. Real estate titles are often hard to transfer, sellers sometimes lie about their situations, and many transactions fail at the closing table due to undisclosed problems. A simple problem that might be cleared up a year from now will not help you because you will have run out of time under the rules of this kind of tax deferment.

192. What Critical Factors Should You Be Aware of before You Take Back a Mortgage on a Property You Sell?

It is possible that there will be unique situations that can make other factors even more important than those shown below, but for the most part the following are essential in all cases.

1. *What is the value of the security?*   The real value is what is important, not the price. You have to consider that there will be cost in the event of a foreclosure and that the property may be ultimately returned to you in a distressed situation and a lower value than at present. You have to start with adequate real market values and discount those.

2. *What is the track record of the mortgagor?*   This can be simple to discover, but not without some effort and willingness to make personal calls. References are a start but are only truly effective if they give you leads to other people or places to contact. If you come across something strange or anything that leaves you with an uncomfortable feeling, then dig deeper.

3. *Can the loan be reasonably repaid?*   Some sellers take pride in selling property they know they are going to get back. If you do not want to ever get the property back (this is the *right* approach), then you should never take a mortgage that is clearly a burden to the mortgagee of the property.

4. *Can you get notice of default from superior mortgagees?*   Remember that to foreclose on your mortgage you must either have a direct default made on your mortgage or have the right to call your loan in default when superior or inferior loans are in default. The first mortgagee may be six months in arrears and you may not know about it because this mortgage does not even know about you. One step to solve this is to have periodic *estoppel agreements* from the other lenders as to the status of the loans. Keeping track of this may be difficult and time consuming but could be worth the effort.

Another way to stay on top of this is to have the buyer send you copies of cancelled checks from the lender, or receipts of payments made. If this is an obligation of the buyer and a part of the contract and the mortgage the buyer signed with you, then failure to send you this proof of payment would be evidence of possible default.

5. *Can you reasonably serve notice to the mortgagor?*   Take, for example, the mortgagor who lives outside the United States and whose address is unknown. If you cannot get service to that person, then you may have a problem with any legal action. One way to solve this problem partially is to make sure that the mortgagor must designate a local agent for such service. Make sure that your lawyer sets this into both the contract and the mortgage and that the local agent has the authority and power to act as the legal agent for the mortgagee.

6. *Can you reasonably collect on a judgment?* Getting a judgment and collecting on one are two different matters. Even if you can serve the person's local agent, that person may now live in another state, or even in Rio, and your ultimate cost to get a judgment may not be worth the effort.

The bottom line is that you must be sure that whenever you hold a mortgage your homework has been done to ensure that the person obligated to repay the loan is likely to do so. If you are comfortable in that, then be satisfied that the equity in the deal is adequate and keep on top of the repayment.

19

Reducing Cost and Avoiding Problems at Closings and Deed Transfers

193. What Happens at the Real Estate Closing?

The term *real estate closing* refers to the actual event when the title transfers hands. This occurs when all the documentation is completed, papers, affidavits, mortgages and mortgage notes, deeds, bills of sale, and so on are all signed and executed, and the mechanics of the transfer of title or other real property interest takes place. This "moment" can be a simple, very smooth noneventful happening, or it can be a traumatic, emotion-filled episode. In either case, it is sure to be something you will remember for a very long time.

To increase the chances that the closing will be simple and smooth, review the following series of events of a transaction that has only a few snags, none of which threaten the deal.

The Steps That Lead to a Real Estate Closing

1. The property is offered for sale. Property owners meet with a real estate agent and sign an exclusive listing agreement, and later that day a "For Sale" sign goes up on the lawn.

2. Time goes by and despite some action and a few offers that were too low, the property remains unsold.

3. The sellers reduce the price.

4. The sellers reduce the price again.

5. You come along and make an offer below the newly listed price.

6. The sellers reject the offer, saying they are "insulted" at such a low regard for their property value.

7. Their agent gets them to counteroffer back to you.

8. You counteroffer, accepting their price, but making a change in the terms, asking them to include the furniture.

9. A final counteroffer is proposed, as the sellers agree to include some of the furniture but not all. You accept.

10. You have the right to inspections that (as usual) allow you to check for termites and structural, electrical, plumbing, roof, pool, retaining wall, and environmental problems, review contracts, leases, and other property problems including the status of the title. The contract has a provision that the seller is to correct any problems up to 3 percent of the price of the property.

11. The inspectors discover that there is termite damage and active infestation, that there are roof leaks, and that other minor repairs are needed. An estimate for repairs is obtained.

12. The sellers object to your inspector's results and hire their own inspectors, and there is some back and forth arguments about the actual extent of the termite problem and the cause of the leaks.

13. In the meantime you apply for a new mortgage to refinance the sellers' old financing.

14. You shop around at three lending institutions, fill out the necessary papers, meet with the loan officers and now wait.

15. Two weeks go by and you are contacted by one of the lenders who offers you a loan commitment that spells out the terms of the loan from that lender.

16. By the end of another week all three lenders have responded.

17. You go to the other two lenders and ask if they can better what you have been offered.

18. One of the other lenders comes up with a slightly better loan package for you and you accept.

19. Both buyer and sellers have agreed to the cost of repairs according to the inspections.

20. It is agreed to "set the funds aside" to cover the cost of repairs rather than to actually do the repairs now because you want to close and move in.

21. A closing date one week away is set; you fly back to Toronto and have the movers pack up everything in your rented apartment in Canada, and the vans start for Arizona and your new home.

22. The closing agent (your lawyer or title insurance company) discovers there is a problem with the title. There had been an improper deed transfer several transactions earlier, and apparently had been overlooked when the current owner purchased the property. The sellers may not have a clear title to pass on to you.

23. The closing is postponed while the lawyers work on the problem.

24. You have to find storage for your furniture.

25. You move into a motel.

26. The lawyers discover several more problems with the title.

27. After a week, and the sellers running up a "cost to clear title" of several thousand dollars, everything is set to close.

28. The lender says "wait just a minute. Where are the financial reports you promised to send?"

29. You call your accountant in Toronto..."Sorry," he says, he forgot to send them, but does so that same day.

30. The morning of the closing you wake up with a migraine.

31. The morning of the closing one of the sellers is in a serious car accident and the closing is postponed for three weeks or until the accident victim recovers.

32. You have to return to Toronto, but go to the closing agent's office and sign everything you need to sign, put up the balance of the money, and execute the loan papers. All of the money and paperwork is to be held by the closing agent in escrow pending the sellers' delivery of the title.

33. While you are in Toronto the sellers complete their part of the deal and it closes.

34. The closing agent now takes all the documents that must be recorded (mortgage documentation, deed, bill of sale, and other items that may be related to the transaction and required to be recorded or that either party wants to be recorded) to the proper authorities so they can be recorded.

35. The closing agent will check the title just prior to the recording and then following the recording to make sure that nothing else was recorded that would cause a change in the intended order of the transaction.

36. Several days following the actual date the documents were executed by both the buyer and sellers, the recording will have been accomplished and the closing agent will release the funds to the seller and deliver the deed to the buyer.

37. For a period of time following the closing, the sellers may be obligated to certain warranties that were specific to the contract, such as "all appliances are guaranteed to be in good working order for a period of X months," or to certain warranties that are controlled by state law. Both the buyer and sellers should know what these warranties are.

The important aspect of the steps that lead up to the actual closing is that you should anticipate that there will be snags. It is rare for everything to run without any kind of a hitch, so anticipate them and allow yourself ample time to deal with them. The buyer or seller that sets the closing date six weeks in advance and expects it to occur without any problems is overly optimistic.

194. Should I Use a Lawyer at the Closing?

First of all, every buyer and seller should either be an expert in real estate procedures for their own representation, or they should seek out professional help in dealing with the potential problems that can occur.

If one side is represented and the other is not, then it is possible that things can occur that will not be in the best interest of the unrepresented party.

However, representation at a real estate closing need not be through a lawyer. Many buyers look to other professionals to represent them at the closing. In some states, such as California, escrow agencies are designed to function as closing agents for both buyer and seller. Around the country there are title insurance companies that provide title insurance and at the same time take care of all the paperwork and recording, etc., that are required.

So, why would you use a lawyer? The answer is easy. The closing of the title transfer is apt to be the single most important financial transaction that most people will ever make. Your lawyer should be involved right from the very start to ensure that the contract has been properly executed and that it contains all the provisions necessary to protect you. It does not make any difference if you are the buyer or seller, you should make sure you are properly protected.

In the final analysis there are no disadvantages to using a lawyer providing you have one who understands your goals, financial abilities, and is competent in dealing with real estate in the area where the property is located. The cost difference between using a lawyer or a title insurance company should be minor as long as you do not have a very complicated contract, and if you do, then the lawyer is needed anyway. But be sure that you have a good relationship with your lawyer and other professional advisors. They should be there to advise you, not make decisions for you.

195. As a Buyer, How Do I Keep My Closing Costs to a Minimum?

The first step to keeping cost down is to know what the "normal costs" are for a similar closing. This is information you will want to shop around for *before you make an offer*. How do you find this out? Simple—you make a few phone calls, and you also ask the real estate agent to get you several price quotes.

As title insurance companies and or escrow agencies may offer services similar to those of lawyers for closing, these would be the first source for the needed price comparisons. Armed with these data you can then ask your lawyer or several different lawyers what they will charge for a package deal: That deal should include the following.

- To review and make suggestions on the actual offer to purchase
- To provide title insurance
- To handle all the closing documentation and recording

Because nearly every lawyer who practices in real estate law is associated with an insurance company to "sell" title insurance, it is likely that they will match or nearly match the prices of the title insurance companies. But you may have to ask them to do that.

Most insurance companies that insure title give a price break on policies that are issued on properties that have had previous insurance. This insurance need not have been with the same insurer, but because it did exist, the discount can save you as much as 25 percent of the cost of new insurance. You must make sure that you find out if the sellers had obtained title insurance when they acquired the property, even though that may have been dozens of years ago, you can still save now.

196. What Are the Key Steps to Keep the Seller's Closing Costs to a Minimum?

There is an adage: "If you *buy* right, you can *sell* right." This can apply to just about every aspect of a real estate transaction, including the closing costs. Take a look at the four steps below that illustrate that point.

The Four Key Steps to Keeping the Seller's Closing Cost at a Minimum

1. *Keep meticulous documentation and title insurance when buying.*   If you are really tough as a buyer and insist on getting all the documentation you should have, your cost when you go to sell can be reduced. The most important items to get as a buyer are

   - Property boundary and building surveys
   - Title insurance and/or detailed title searches
   - Removal (when purchased) of all possible title insurance exclusions
   - Detailed legal description
   - Building plans
   - Several past years of real estate tax bills marked PAID
   - Warranty agreements
   - Contracts and leases
   - Casualty insurance policies

   Add to those items everything that you change or alter or add to the property as you own it. As a real estate investor you should have a file that contains every important document that has anything to do with the property you own.

2. *Keep up with continual property maintenance.* Keeping property in good maintenance will not only help you get a higher price for it when you go to sell it, but it will help you have a smoother closing. One approach is to look at your property from time to time as would a property inspection team. Find the problems that are developing and get them fixed.

3. *Contract for the buyer to pay some or all of the cost.* One of the best ways to cut your closing cost is to have the contract provide that the buyer is to pay all or part of those costs. This is legal with some limitation to FHA and VA loans, and the buyer may simply agree to this in exchange for some other offsetting term or condition that may not matter to you.

4. *Promptly solve preclosing problems.* One of the keys to keeping small problems from growing into big problems is to tackle them right away and solve them. This is very important because it is a matter of attitude more than anything else. First, anticipate that there will be problems, then have the mental attitude that when they come up you tackle them with both feet and solve them. Sometimes you cannot easily solve the problem, but the very fact that you are promptly and diligently making an attempt to do so can smooth rough waters.

Be very cautious about "getting bogged down" with a problem. Often the closing agent takes a far more lax attitude about problems that are so common they sometimes forget that your motivation is to get the deal closed. Keep on top of everything that is going on, and while there is no need to hyperventilate when something comes up (because it will), deal with it when it does.

197. What Are the Dos and Don'ts I Should Know When I Am Getting Ready for the Closing?

There are many things that you should be aware of that can happen in between the moment you sign a contract to the actual moment of the closing. Of these there are nine that seem common enough so that you should become specifically aware of them. They are listed below.

The Nine Preclosing Nightmares and How to Deal with Them

Personality conflict between the parties

"Coldfeetitus," the seller's remorse

"Backoutitus," the buyer's nightly cold sweats

Confusing advice

"I've been suckered" syndrome

Termite delight

Legal problems

Money problems

Renegotiation time

Personality Conflict between the Parties.   It is not uncommon for the buyer and seller to be at odds somewhere along the route from contract to closing. The deal may start out that way the very first time the prospective buyer walks into the house and says "My goodness, who in the world picked out the hideous color of that carpet?" Who? The seller, that's who. The seller who is standing right in front of the prospective buyer. This is "bite your tongue" time if you are the seller.

Of all the problems to deal with, personality conflicts are the most difficult because it is emotion, not logic, that causes people to react. No seller should ever be "insulted" by any buyer's offer. After all, at least the buyer likes the property enough to make an offer.

However, because emotion can get in the way of a contract being signed, or a smooth closing, all experienced real estate agents know that sometimes it is much better if the buyer and seller never even meet face to face. It is possible, in fact, to go all the way to closing and never have the two parties come together in the same room.

"Coldfeetitus," the Seller's Remorse.   This is an event that almost always happens. The usual situation occurs a few days following the signing of the contract when the seller tells a friend, neighbor, real estate agent (not the one involved in the deal), or some other party (hairdresser, bartender, etc.), about the sale. "You idiot," is the reply, "you got taken."

From that little seed "coldfeetitus" starts to grow and in a few days the seller is thinking of ways to get out of the deal. Fortunately this often passes. There is little a buyer can do to deal with this problem, and usually it is up to the agents involved to satisfy the seller that the original decision to accept the contract was the right move.

"Backoutitus," The Buyer's Nightly Cold Sweats.   I do not know any buyer who has not had second thoughts about the deal. In this case "backoutitus" often starts with a comment from someone (it could even be the seller), who indicates something like this: "Why, if you'd held out one more day, I'd have accepted $50,000 less." The nightly sweats begin.

Buyers often need to be reinforced that they also made the right decision, and often the only person that can do this is the real estate agent that participated in the sale.

Confusing Advice.   Both parties can become confused by advice that begins to filter in as the closing nears. Sometimes the buyer is setting up the seller for the final problem or the renegotiation of the contract, or the seller could be playing mind games to pressure the buyer to speed up approvals of inspections.

When one party or both parties become confused by the situation, usually all they need is to slow down and meet with someone who can fully explain what is going on and what can be done about the "problem," and then they should relax. Often the advice has come from a misinformed advisor—sometimes your own lawyer.

"I've Been Suckered" Syndrome.   This is almost exclusively an exchange problem. It is similar to the seller's remorse or the buyer's "backoutitus," and when it occurs the deal is doomed unless some major renegotiation can put the transaction back on track.

In an exchange one or more parties swap properties, often in a three- or four-way deal where no one actually gets the property of the person who gets theirs. In this kind of transaction the parties may have painted an inaccurate picture of what they were offering, and that information got embellished along the way. In the end it is like a rumor that goes around a circle of people ending up being so far from the original statement that the property is not what the taker believed it to be.

I have known people to take property in an exchange without ever looking at it, accepting the giver's word, and then to exchange it with someone else, and so on, with no one ever looking at what finally ends up on the table of a deal where the final taker actually goes and tries to find that beautiful wooded mountain paradise.

In the real estate game you try to learn who to trust, but make sure you double-check everything.

Termite Delight.   That is what I call this problem in Florida and other termite-prone areas. In your area it might be something else, like swamp gas or sinkholes. This is any problem that the present owner most likely knew about but did not mention. You may never prove it, and it may matter only a little. But it matters nonetheless, and like any untruth that seeps through the crack of integrity, it may just be enough to cast doubt about all the other statements that are behind the dam.

Legal Problems.   Real estate is a sea of legalities: deeds, mortgages, satisfactions, liens, judgements, foreclosures, *lis pendens*, leases, notices of eviction, and so on, all of which can cause anything from a minor headache to a major (and expensive) day in court.

This does not mean you need to lose sleep over these problems, but that you should make sure that you have a very good lawyers and other professionals to deal with these legal situations.

Fortunately when a legal problem does arise, it can be dealt with promptly, and most of the time you may never know about the steps the closing agent took to solve those problems.

Money Problems.   The biggest money problem occurs when the buyer cannot get the mortgage on time (or at all) that is needed to buy the property. The loan commitment does not come through as quickly as everyone thought (or was told) it would. This might be because the buyer may not have filled out all the necessary forms and submitted documents to the lender, or just that the lender is dragging its heels on the loan request.

One way to solve this problem is to be prequalified for a loan. Many buyers understand this procedure and take the steps to build their contacts with lenders early in their investment career. Some lenders will even process your material to ascertain just how much of a loan they would make to you before you present the application for a specific home or other property.

Renegotiation Time.   This is the point when the buyer has finished the inspections and now wants to sit down and fine-tune the deal. In essence the buyer will attempt to renegotiate the price and/or terms, because, according to the buyer, the property needs more attention, does not have the income promised, has deferred maintenance, requires painting, or whatever. All of this may be true, but then perhaps it is not and the buyer is just testing the water to see what the seller will do.

If you are the seller and you want to find out if the buyer is just attempting to renegotiate a better deal, but will close on the old one, see if the buyer will commit to walking from the deal. Ask the question in writing and request a written answer: "If we cannot agree to a modification in the agreement, do we understand that you are electing to cancel the agreement under the provisions in the contract?"

If there are other buyers, then the seller may be more difficult in these renegotiations. On the other hand, if the present buyer is the only buyer the seller should not let the deal slip away without an effort to close it. It may be possible that the buyer wants minor, unimportant changes in the agreement and that they would be acceptable to the seller. On the other hand, if major revisions are suggested, then every factor needs to be looked at all over again.

One good tactic is to be willing to entertain new contract proposals but only if the buyer agrees to cancel the first contract completely.

198.   How Can the Seller Legally Back Out of the Deal?

One of the best provisions a seller can include in the contract to sell is the seller's right to approve of the buyer's credit. This would be a reasonable request anytime the seller is holding a purchase money mortgage or continues to be at risk on any existing financing. The buyer may logically want to limit the seller's rights to disapprove of the deal by giving the seller a very short time period to make that determination. Clearly the buyer does not want to pack up and move from Toronto expecting to relocate if the seller is going to use that provision to back out of the deal.

The term *legally back out* can be misleading, however, so all buyers should be aware that if a seller is determined to "get out of the deal," it can become very expensive on the part of the buyer to "force" the seller to a closing. Even though the buyer may have every right to compensation for damages or for cost and even to sue for specific performance (where the court would ultimately order the seller to transfer title according to the terms of the contract), such legal actions are rare. Why? Because buyers generally move on to something else rather than be tied down to a long battle over a property they now no longer want because of the bad taste in their mouths from the deal.

Why would a seller want to back out? There can be as many answers to that question as there are dollars in the next offer.

199. Can the Buyer Legally Back Out of the Deal?

Because of the multitude of problems that can be latent in any property every buyer should make sure that they have an inspection period that gives them one or both of the following options:

1. That if for any reason the buyer does not approve of any of the inspections to be accomplished, then the buyer may elect to withdraw from the agreement and promptly have refunded any and all deposits.

2. If any damage is found in the building, fixtures, or structure, if any manual electrical or mechanical device or apparatus is not in good working order or in need of repair or maintenance, if any violation is found of current or soon-to-be-enacted building codes, city, or other governing ordinances, or if any defect, cloud, or other problem with the title occurs, then the seller shall promptly correct said findings, or at closing credit the buyer with sufficient funds to correct the same.

Naturally, the buyer can simply elect not to close. In this event the seller may have some rights to legal actions against the buyer to recover damages and costs; however, in reality such legal actions can prove to be very costly and drawn out. Generally the only source of pressure to the buyer comes from the *at risk money* the buyer has placed in escrow pending the closing. This is the deposit monies that generally are put up and that become at risk (buyers lose it if they do not close) when the inspections have been completed.

A buyer determined to get out of a deal may reach that point the day of the closing when something new comes to light that changes the whole picture of the transaction. This might be something relatively simple that was overlooked during the inspections, such as an addendum to a lease from tenants in the property that gave those tenants the right to extend their lease for another 99 years. Ouch—that means the buyer cannot move in to the property. Or the reason the buyer now wants out is because he or she discovered that the seller (or anyone else for that matter) knew something very important and damaging about the property and was required by law or at least by ethics, to disclose that fact to the buyer, but did not.

Many situations occur where the agents are blamed, and often they are at fault by misrepresenting the property. "Why, Mr. and Mrs. Buyer, you can rent out this vacant space for $12.00 per square foot any time you want." However, the agent forgot to say that to get this kind of rent you would first have to build a 500-bed hospital across the street.

200.   What Can I Do If the Property I Bought Is Not Everything the Sellers Told Me It Would Be?

The term *caveat emptor*, means "let the buyer beware." In many parts of the world it is the rule that governs most transactions between two or more people. But with real estate transactions in the United States (at least), buyers have many different safeguards working for them to ensure that the property purchased is exactly what has been presented.

Yet, every day dissatisfied buyers wake up to realize that the property they now own is less than they expected it to be. What happened in between the moment that the seller signed the deed to the buyer and the distasteful moment? Well, many things could have gone wrong. Take a look at some of the problems that can arise and their possible solutions.

Twelve Not So Unusual Problems

1. You purchased the wrong property.
2. The lot size is different than reported.
3. The survey is very, very, wrong.
4. The barn belongs to someone else.
5. The tenant has a 50-year lease at $35.00 per month.
6. There is a second mortgage no one told you about.
7. There are no "live termites," only 500 million dead ones.
8. The seller's "dead" wife shows up and moves into "her" home.
9. Other people claim they paid the tax so they own the property.
10. The rental potential is half what you were told.
11. The sellers dig up the landscaping and take it with them.
12. The property was built in 1891, not 1981.

The Solutions to Most Pre- and Postclosing Problems

The real solution is to check and double-check everything. This does not mean that you have to do all the work yourself, because if you are using a professional closing agent they should do it as a part of their normal closing procedure. Note the words *should do it*. Often there are big cracks in the procedure, so the following checklist will help you close them up.

The Buyer's Pre- and Postclosing Checklist

1. *Make sure you have an approved contract executed by all the legal owners.*   Just because the home "seems" to have only one occupant, that does not mean there

is just one owner. The only way to be sure is to check the title in the property records. One quick check is to ask for the past real estate tax bills (go back a couple of years at least). If several names show up as owners then you know you may need other people to execute the contract. Divorces, separations, and murders can account for confusion in this problem. By the way, proof of who has been paying the tax can help remove the risk of any possible "squatter's rights" from people who may claim title by adverse possession.

2. *Get a copy of the seller's title insurance policy.*   This will give you a lot of important information and can provide you with a discount off the title insurance when you close. Some of the important information contained in the seller's policy would be possible exclusions to the policy, which would be specific situations or items that the insurer (when the seller purchased the property) would not insure. These situations or items may still exist and while they were acceptable to the buyer then, they may not be acceptable to you now. Make sure that they are cleared up by the seller.

3. *Obtain a recent property boundary and building survey.*   Often in a title insurance policy there is a simple statement such as this: "no item or situation shall be covered by this insurance that would have been disclosed by a recent property survey." Some of the problems that can come back to haunt you years after you close could be that the property had and still has latent legal problems such as encroachment of buildings onto neighboring property, easements, or rights-of-way that exist even though no one has used them yet, but plan to (new train track down the middle of the land, high tension power lines, road to the back 40 acres, and so on). One of the worst problems is that when you see the recent survey you discover that the property is not actually what you thought it was, or even where you thought it was.

Having a survey is great, but one of the most important things you can do is to take it and walk the boundaries of the property. Find the corner markers, be sure the buildings are well clear of any setbacks, and so on. Most closing agents never actually go to the property, so looking at the survey in a closing office 10 miles away is little help for those kinds of problems.

4. *Get every lease, contract, mortgage, and other document that has anything to do with the property from the seller.*   Be sure that the seller signs a statement that the documents given to you constitute all of such documentation. Then, double-check the property records to make sure that there are no other documents recorded that would prove otherwise. Leases, mortgages, judgements, tax liens, etc., may exist, even without the seller knowing about them.

5. *Make sure that there is a detailed inventory of all items you are to acquire.* Often this inventory list is a part of the buyer's approval process, as sellers rarely will have such a list ready the moment they sign a contract. When the list is made, make sure that a phrase is included along the lines of the following. "...in addition to the items mentioned above, all landscaping material, underground and aboveground sprinkling equipment, and other items that are affixed to the buildings or other structures, or embedded in the ground

shall be a part of those items being acquired by the buyer." When there are many different valuable items that are to be included, sometimes it is important to take photographs of those items, and rather than mention the ones that are included specify those items that are not included.

6. *Be specific about times for inspections and rights to withdraw.*   This works for both parties and can help solve problems that occur simply because people drag out the inspection process.

7. *Be there when the inspections are made.*   Actually this is good advice for both the buyer and the seller. This is important because the inspectors will be far more careful to do a thorough inspection under the watchful eyes of at least one of the parties to the contract. The more important reason, however, is to be able to question every problem that the inspector finds. Get the inspector to probe a little deeper into the problem to see if it can be fixed easily or if more comprehensive and expensive repairs are needed.

8. *Give yourself ample time to accomplish the preclosing things you need to do.* Remember, you do not want to limit your cost until you are absolutely sure you approve of all the items that are being inspected. This means that if it takes three weeks to get financing approved, and if it takes three weeks to do and review the inspections, then to have a six-week period to close might be too tight of a schedule.

20

Planning Your Real Estate Insurance Needs

201. Do I Need to Insure My Real Estate?

One of the costs to owning real estate is the insurance you should carry. You generally have several options when dealing with insurance. The first to consider: *Is insurance a must*? The answer to this question is determined by your own circumstances, and another question: What do you stand to lose if you do not carry insurance?

Insurance covers you against a casualty or liability loss. There are many different points of view in the discussion about insurance, but there are five key factors that demand you insure your real estate.

The Five Key Factors That Demand You Insure Your Real Estate

1. Many lenders insist on it.
2. People are quick to sue.
3. Defense can be very expensive.
4. Repairs may not be allowed.
5. The more you have, the more you risk.

Many Lenders Insist on It. It is logical that a mortgagee of a large first mortgage is going to insist that you carry ample insurance to protect the asset that secures the mortgage. Some lenders build this insurance into the mortgage payments and float the insurance through their own "in house" insurance company. If this is the situation with any mortgage you currently are obligated to, find out if you can buy your own insurance. If you can, then shop around for a better price. Often you can lump all your coverage with one company and get a break on the annual premium.

People Are Quick to Sue.   If no one ever sued, would there be need for insurance? Yes, there would. After all, there will still be storms and other casualty damage. But, just the thought of having some "hot shot" just-out-of-law-school advocate ready to take you for every dime you own, can give you some sleepless nights. Sue? Sure they do.

Worse than that, they win, and they can win big. Juries have been known to return awards that can make the value of the property you own seem insignificant.

Defense Can Be Very Expensive.   Even if you are 100 percent in the right, the very act of having to defend yourself can be the single expense of a lifetime that wipes out savings. Lawyers know this; if they are defending you, they will recommend an early settlement, and if they are opposing you, they strike for the jugular.

Even when you have insurance, your insurance company will seek to settle whenever that is more practical than winning an expensive battle.

Repairs May Not Be Allowed.   Some property owners take the posture that they will "self-insure." This often is a rationalization of not wanting to pay high insurance costs, but they overlook a growing problem with casualty damage. Will the local building codes allow the property to be repaired at all?

Many cities have a ratio of damage to value that can cause the property to be reevaluated to see if it will meet the codes as though it were a brand new building. Many older properties no longer meet the current codes, and if the property sustains damage sufficient to require full compliance to the current building regulations, major remodeling or even complete demolition and 100 percent new construction may be required. Self-insurance under these situations can prove to be the wrong choice.

The More You Have, the More You Risk.   This is a fact that saddens the richest of people. The people who have the most also have the most to lose. Worst of all is that when there is a liability claim, the amount of the claim demanded may be determined by how deep your pockets are. If you have nothing (including no insurance), then your risk is greatly limited.

Many wealthy investors seek ways to limit their own exposure to any claim. For this reason there are lawyers and accountants who specialize in finding ways to shelter wealth, not only from taxes but from liability claims from others.

Corporations, limited partnerships, trusts, and so on each have some advantage to some people. If you have what you consider to be a valuable portfolio now and anticipate that it will be growing, it would be a good idea for you to spend an hour with a professional dedicated to reducing exposure to such risks. Insurance is an alternative approach.

202. What Is Casualty Insurance, and How Much Should I Buy?

There are two basic categories of property insurance: casualty and liability. Casualty insurance is the kind of insurance that will insure you against a loss due to a variety of different calamities, both natural and artificial. In each situation the insurance is tailored to repay you for some or all of a loss you may have as a result of a specific event. Every insurance policy is written so that not every item is covered, and not every *cause of loss* is a covered cause. If this sounds redundant it is not. What this means is that it is possible for a policy that appears to cover everything will not, and there will be some event (such as an act of war, or flood, or some other situation the insurance company excludes) that can occur for which you have zero coverage no matter what your loss.

When it comes to casualty coverage you should weigh the risk against the cost. To cover 100 percent of the cost to replace what you have for every possible insurable cause of loss can be very expensive.

How Much Insurance Should You Get?   Take a five-unit apartment building, for example. The current market value is $180,000, which can be divided as follows: land = $25,000; building = $135,000; fixtures and appliances = $20,000.

In a total loss of the building and contents of the building, you would lose $155,000 in value. But is it likely that you would have a 100 percent loss? You can insure for that possibility, but you might save a lot of money by taking a small risk that your actual loss would never be that great. Because of this, most people insure their real estate against casualty loss below the full replacement value. However, the insurance company may set a level below which you cannot insure. To make this decision you need to review your needs with your insurance agent. The agent will have data that will show the probable risks.

Your Insurance Agents Can Help You Decide.   Once your insurance agents know your situation, they have guides that can help you establish the percent of value you need to insure, as well as suggest some of the extra kinds of insurance that may be important because of the high risk for your part of the country or location in town.

Some Insurance May Be Available Only in a "Pool."   If your property is in a high-risk area for certain coverage, such as a flood or earthquake area, your only chance of insurance may be through an expensive "pool" set up by the state insurance commission. While expensive, at least you *can* get the insurance if you feel you need it.

203. What Are Some of the Special Types of Insurance Available for Real Estate?

If it can happen, then you probably can insure against it. This is the rational that allows boxers to insure their fists, movie stars their smiles (and other parts of their body), and ships at sea their cargo. Insurance is all a matter of risk and cost.

When there are no massive insurance claims the insurance companies ride a crest of easy profits…but nature has a way of turning around very suddenly, as the end of the 1980s and beginning of the 1990s proved. But heavy claims that require enormous amounts of cash payments get lots of press, and increased media attention draws attention to the need for insurance. This has advantages and disadvantages for the insurance companies. On one hand, they hate to pay out such great sums of money, but on the other they can now raise their insurance rates. The heavy coverage of the catastrophes in television and other media actually encourage and promote more people buying more insurance. Fear is one of the strongest of all motivations.

What are some of the kinds of insurance you can get for your real estate? Take a look at the following *partial* list of items that may be necessary or available in your area.

Twenty-Five Things You Can Insure against

1. "All perils"
2. Airborne ash
3. Aircraft
4. Avalanche
5. Dishonesty
6. Drought
7. Earthquake
8. Electrical surges
9. Explosion
10. Fire and smoke
11. Flood
12. Freezes
13. Hail
14. Lava flow
15. Lightening
16. Mud slide

17. Negligent work
18. Riot or civil commotion
19. Seeping water
20. Sinkhole
21. Theft
22. Tornado
23. Vandals
24. Volcanic eruption
25. Windstorm

Remember, this is only a partial list.

Warning: It is not unusual for an insurance policy to exclude some of the above 25 events. To get coverage for *excluded coverage* you may have to purchase specific and special insurance to cover the possibility of such an occurrence. Specific limitations to coverage may also exist for different events to the extent that while you think you are covered 100 percent, you are not. It is a good idea to *read* a sample policy of what your coverage will be *before* you buy it. By shopping around for insurance companies you may discover more coverage with less restrictions and exclusions for less money.

204. Why Do I Need Liability Insurance for Real Estate and How Much Should I Buy?

You may be liable for any body injury and property damage that occurs on your property or as a result of your actions. If you own anything or expect to, some amount of liability insurance may be needed. If you own real estate, then liability insurance would be a must.

Liability insurance may be an included coverage with a general "all perils" policy, or it can be a separate form of insurance. Generally the maximum coverage you can get is $1 million, but by obtaining an umbrella policy (expanded coverage), you can increase the amount virtually as far as you want to pay.

The most important aspect of liability insurance is that the insurance company will pay for the defense of a claim. This can be misleading, however, because they are really defending themselves and not necessarily you. Most insurance policies allow the insurance company to settle a claim and pay off the claimant even though you are in the right. Also, once the amount of coverage you are allowed according to your policy has been reached, the insurance company will no longer represent you. Because of this you should obtain your own lawyer aside from any help the insurance company provides whenever a claim is to be decided in a court of law.

205. What Is Title Insurance, What Does It Protect, and When Can It Be Dangerous?

Title insurance is supposed to insure that the title you have taken in a real estate transaction is good. This insurance is much like a liability insurance in that it will pay your cost to clear some title problem that is covered when it occurs. However, when you have a problem you may find that the insurer has a loophole to escape through, so watch out.

To ensure that the title insurance company does not have an escape clause, be sure that you have removed all the exclusions to the clause. One such provision common to a title insurance policy is a phrase that reads something like the following:

> ...and any other claim, cloud on the title, or title defect, as a result of any action prior to the issuance of this insurance policy shall be excluded and not covered if the basis for the claim, cloud on the title, or the title defect would have been disclosed by a recent boundary survey and building location survey at the time this insurance policy was issued.

Many people do not get a recent survey at the time they close on a property. However, if you put a provision in the offer to purchase that the seller is to provide this survey, and that all property boundaries and building corners are to be marked on the survey, with iron pipes in concrete at property corners, you will have a document that can be updated cheaply in the future when you plan to sell.

206. If I Rent, What Insurance Do I Need to Carry?

This may depend on the type of property you are renting. This can be important because you may overpay for insurance that is a duplication of insurance already in existence. Review the following five steps to get the most out of your renter's insurance.

The Five Steps to Buying the Best Renter's Insurance Possible for Maximum Coverage

1. *Get a copy of the existing property insurance policy.*   There may be more than one policy that covers the property. For example, if the building is a condominium or cooperative, there will be an association policy that covers certain elements of the building and sometimes some of the contents. This is often a function of state law. The owner of the specific space (condo or coop) may also have interior insurance that would cover items not covered by the association policy.

2. *Have a qualified insurance agent explain the state law.*   Often the state law will require the insurance company to insure certain items or parts of the property even though the insurance policy may not specifically indicate it.

Often there are very fine lines that occur when laws change in the middle of a policy term, so each situation and each policy need to be reviewed. You cannot assume that a situation last month with another unit in the same complex also applies to the property you are anticipating renting.

3. *Make a list of everything important you plan to have in the apartment or space.* This is important regardless of what kind of rental you have. If this is a business or residence, be sure you have an up-to-date list of items that you add or replace during your term as a tenant.

4. *Shop around with several different insurance companies for the best deal.* If you have insurance on other property (cars and/or other real estate), one of the best places to go for a quote will be your current insurers.

5. *Get a quote every year from other insurance companies.* This is not difficult to do and can save you money. It is not unusual for a different insurance company to quote you a lower premium. First-year premiums are often the lowest you will ever see, so make a change from time to time whenever you can save money. *Warning*: If you ask for a quote from another company, make sure they have quoted on the same amounts of coverage you now have. An overzealous insurance agent may want to get your business so much that they leave out a few "risks" in your coverage (after all, your building is not going to be hit by a flood).

207.   Should I Keep All My Insurance with the Same Insurer?

Yes, unless you can save sufficient money by dividing your coverage between companies to make it worthwhile.

One hazard with more than one insurance company is that you are apt to have some overlapping insurance, or worse, you may have some gaps that expose you to some risk you could have covered at a small added cost or no cost at all by staying with one company.

208.   How Do I Determine My Insurance Needs before I Buy the Policy?

Before you sit down with insurance agents it is a good idea to be ready to answer their questions, and to have an idea of the values you may want to insure. The following steps will help you prepare for that task.

The Seven Steps to Adequate Insurance Coverage

1. *Make a detailed list of items to be covered.* A simple chart that groups items together is okay, such as furniture, clothing, and so on. Do not overlook any

contents of your residence or office. Homeowner's policies generally cover your personal property even if it is not at your home at the time of a loss.

2. *Assess the* new replacement value *of each item.* In many cases you will not be able to prove the actual cost of an item, so put down your estimate of replacement cost.

3. *Determine if you would replace the item.* This is for your own eyes only. This will help you determine if the coverage is necessary. If the item is automatically covered, then in the event of a loss you can keep the cash settlement and not replace the item at all.

4. *Take detailed still and video photographs and show scale.* This is important both to give the agent an idea of what you want to insure, as well as to prove you actually had the items in the event of a loss. When taking photographs (still or video) have some reference that will indicate the size of the items. A ruler is the best way to establish the approximate size.

5. *Review different coverages available to you.* The cost of insurance can vary much more than you might realize. Often the coverage within the same company can vary greatly depending on the actual location, elevation, type of construction, age of the construction, intended use, proximity of fire-fighting services (including hydrants), and so on. The deductible you accept can mean great savings to you if your interest is to cover the major loss and self-insure minor losses.

6. *Be sure you* ask *what is* not *covered, and what limitations are there to what* is *covered.* When you are making comparisons of two or more policies, be sure that you know how they differ. It is unlikely that two standard policies (from two different companies) will be identical in coverage, exclusions, and limitations.

7. *Find out what additional coverage you can add.* This is something for the future and can make a difference if you plan on adding additional property or want to build onto the existing structure. Know what you are buying, and where you can go with it.

209. What Steps Can I Take *after* a Fire or Other Casualty Loss to Get the Maximum Insurance Benefits?

1. *Call the insurance agent as soon as possible.* This is important, but actually takes second priority to the next step. If the casualty has been a major one that affects other people as well as you, anticipate that it may take some time before you can get your insurance agent on the phone. The disaster of Hurricane Andrew in 1992 taught the insurance companies many lessons about such problems. You may have seen the plight of people whose homes were destroyed. Many such homeowners were so frustrated in their attempts to reach an insurance adjuster that they painted the company name and policy number on the side of the house in hopes that someone would see it. *Do not do that*, as some

very dishonest people wrote down those numbers and collected "cash on the spot" money from claims adjusters who were trying to help their insured get over the worst of the storm's aftermath.

2. *Salvage whatever you can.* You should make every effort to save whatever you can, but do not do so at further risk to yourself or your property.

3. *Take photographs of damage.* If you cannot take photographs or do not have a camera, then make detailed notes of all the damage.

4. *The first chance you get, read your policy.* This may give you some additional steps to follow that are peculiar to your insurance.

5. *Have your agent explain to you all the "recoverable" damage or loss you may have prior to the adjuster's appointment.* When you eventually get your agent on the phone, an appointment will be set up for the adjuster to inspect the damage. It is a good idea to know ahead of time exactly what your policy will cover.

6. *Get a second opinion of the "amount" of the loss.* The adjuster may give you his or her estimate, but remember, it is only an estimate and not something that is etched in stone. No matter what you think the repairs or loss should cost to fix or replace, get another estimate from a professional who will actually do the work or replace the items. Usually the adjuster will increase the amount of the award on the claim if you can support the additional amount.

7. *Get advice from your lawyer prior to signing a release.* It may be unusual to have a continued dispute over the amount of the loss, but if you are at all uncomfortable that the insurance company is still pushing for you to "sign a release" for an amount less than what you feel is right, then see your lawyer.

8. *Consider an "outside adjuster" to review the insurance companies adjuster's estimate.* In the case of a major loss, it is a good idea to get an "outside adjuster" or a company that specializes in acting as your intermediary with the insurance company. These people know how insurance companies work, and how to get the most of what your policy allows. These people also know the state insurance laws extremely well. This is important because the state law may require the insurance company to provide you coverage that is not specifically outlined in your policy.

9. *Take more photographs during the follow-up repairs.* This gives you a record of what is going on. Date the photographs by having them processed quickly, then marking the date on each photograph, or have someone in the photograph hold a card with the actual date marked on it. The card and the person provide proof and a witness of the date.

10. *Do not sign a release until all loss and cost has been covered.* You need to wait until everything that could show up does. Some damage is latent and may not actually appear for several weeks after the damage. Mildew is a good example of such a delayed fuse. Water-soaked walls can look like they have been fixed. After all, the hole in the roof has been patched, and the walls repainted. "Oh, but what is that smell?" "Mildew!"

11. *Review your insurance coverage for future needs.*   Now that you have experienced a loss, and the problems that can come with such a problem, take immediate steps to shop around for new coverage. If you can find the same coverage from another insurance company (the same agent may represent several companies, or shop around and see other agents too), then you may want to switch. Why? One very good reason is now that you have had a claim with your existing company, you may be on the "raise their rate" list at the first opportunity. Worse, you might be on the company's "cancel" list, and you will want to jump the gun and leave them before they brand you as having to answer *yes* to the question: "Have your ever been denied insurance for any reason?"

21

Avoiding the Major Pitfalls in Real Estate Investing

210. Can Being Overly Demanding or Too Soft Kill a Deal?

One of the most difficult problems to overcome in contract negotiations is how to walk the fine line between being overly demanding and too conciliatory. Each of these postures may kill the deal because they can send wrong signals to the other side.

What Happens When You Are Overly Demanding? When buyers push for every inch they can get, the final straw will eventually be reached. When that happens the other side may throw in the towel and walk away from the bargaining table. Granted, all buyers want to get all they can for as little as possible, but when there is too much pushing for everything, sellers may eventually get the idea that the buyers are just playing around and not serious. Or, worst of all, the sellers will act in such a way to lock out the buyers for future dealing, even to the extent of dealing with someone else at a lower price, just to keep the first buyer from getting the property.

To play "hard ball" effectively in any contract negotiation, the buyer runs the risk of killing the deal. This tactic is not an incorrect method of negotiation if the buyer does not care if the deal blows up. The posture, "I'll buy it on my terms or not at all" does occasionally produce a deal, but rarely if there are other qualified buyers in the bidding for the property.

In any circumstance, it is counterproductive for buyers to give the impression that any "hard ball" tactics originate directly from themselves. On the other hand, buyers can still push...as long as there is an impression or feeling of genuine cooperation evident in the negotiations.

Top negotiators know from experience that reaching a satisfactory conclusion in any negotiation depends on the parties satisfying the maximum of their goals but not necessarily all their goals. The key to this statement is that it is not necessary that they satisfy *all* their goals.

Get the Tough Decisions over with Early.   A major error that many buyers make is to leave the really tough decisions to the end. This occurs when the buyer continues to push for more, making it harder for the seller to see a reasonable solution to his or her own goals. The deal ultimately explodes in everyone's face when the buyer asks for one thing too much, and often that "one more thing" is a major concession on the part of the seller. Transactions should be closed on small items and not big ones. A good salesperson knows the question to ask is not the following: "The buyer rejects your counteroffer of $500,000 and wants you to drop the price another $50,000; will you do it?" Instead the better approach is: "The buyer accepted every condition of your counteroffer with a modification of the price to $450,000, and she says she will close next week if that is okay. Do you agree to close by the end of next week?"

What about Being Too Soft in the Deal?   Either side can become too agreeable. If the mood is too conciliatory too soon, it can undermine the credibility of the party. A buyer who is too eager to please may give the impression that he or she is not sincere or is just shopping around. On the other hand, a seller who is too eager to please may invite an offer that is too low to ever move to realistic values.

Pick the Middle of the Road as the Best Approach.   As a buyer, the best approach is to be candid with the seller, or at least, as candid as you can without giving away unique ideas about the property. Clearly you would not let the seller know that you wanted to convert the old home into stately offices for an insurance company, or some other great idea that would tip your hand and the price you might have to pay.

Complement the Property Owners for What They Have, and Let Them Know You Would Like to Own It.   This approach is based on the understanding that most sellers want to sell their property to someone who appreciates what they have to sell. Buyers whose attitude is "This is crap, but for a price I'll take it off your hands," may end up with a deal here and there (usually because it was crap).

Flattery Works in Any Seduction.   Take a look at the buyer who approaches every deal with a positive approach designed to make the seller feel good: "I think your property is absolutely ideal for my needs. You should be commended on the wonderful landscaping (or some other clearly seller-caused value point)—that was one of the features that sold me on this property over all the others I've been looking at this week." Did you notice that there are some very subtle and very positive elements in that statement? The "absolutely ideal for my needs" lets the seller know that the buyer is unique.

Not every buyer's needs may be suited by that property. There is the clear buying signal "sold me," with the caveat "over all the others I've been looking at," which indicates there are other properties out there. The clincher is "this week," which lets the seller know that there have been and will be other weeks and other properties. Despite these messages the buyer and seller relationship can progress in a positive manor to the final stages of agreement. "Mr. Seller, I love your property and my wife loves your property and I know this home is just the right place for our five children to grow up and you have sold me right down to the core. Gosh, if you and I can just work out a way for me to buy this wonderful property, why, why, my wife June and I will name our next child after you." That is overkill, but the right idea.

Learn That the Other Side of the Table Is Not the Enemy and Deal Accordingly.   The real key to continued success in buying and selling real estate is to keep reminding yourself that the other side of the table is not your enemy. They are, after all, the very vehicle that will help you reach your goal. You want to buy or sell, and they want to be on the other end of that action. If you are selling a property that they *want*, the major battle has been won. While you can still lose the war, your task is not to sell anymore, but to close the transaction.

A Buyer in Hand Is Worth...Something at Least.   As a buyer your task is to convince the seller that you are worth holding onto, that your immediate value of being there, and in a position to close, is worth some ultimate concession. However, you should not let that ego trip stand in the way of losing a property you would truly like to own.

Use an Intermediary to Absorb the Heat of the Deal.   Both buyers and sellers can benefit by using someone that can maintain contact with the other side of the transaction without giving the wrong buying or selling signal. A broker or other negotiating partner in the transaction can be worth their weight in gold in closed transactions.

211. What Should I Do If Someone Claims to Own My Property?

"Squatter's rights" occur when someone has acquired title by adverse possession (also called *title by prescription*). In the broadest use of this right, a person who has no original legal claim to a property can enter it, even though illegal, and take possession of the land. If this possession meets certain criteria prescribed in state law, then the actual title to that land or property can ultimately be vested to the interloper.

The law of squatter's rights exists for the benefit of a community, or at least originally so. When a property is owned by someone who never uses it or hardly knows it exists, the community may benefit by having someone there on the property who will use it. This encourages the use of the land.

Conditions Thay May Lead to Adverse Possession

There are certain conditions that most states require to be met for title to be acquired by adverse possession:

1. There must be *actual* possession that is *open* and *visible*. Possession should occur in such a way that the owner would reasonably be able to see the possession. A fence, a sign "Jack's Place," rows of cultivation, buildings, or other structures are all such evidence.

2. Possession should be *hostile* to the owner's rights. This would be usual in just about every such case except where there was some relationship between the parties that would indicate there was not an adverse event taking place.

3. The claim to title should be *notorious*. This means that the claim should be made public. One simple way to do this is to run an ad in the local legal section of the newspaper. What are the odds you would see such an ad for a property you own?

4. A *continuous* claim of possession should be evidenced. This does not mean 100 percent of the time, nor does it mean that the squatter must live on the property. If the property is a seasonal property or if some other part time use would be reasonable for any owner, then such part time use, when maintained for a period of time set by the state law, will qualify this aspect of the claim.

5. Possession must be *exclusive*. This means the claimant must preclude the use to anyone else, even the rightful owner.

How Do You Defend Yourself against a Squatter?

First, make sure there are none when you buy a property. This is done by having a recent survey, checking title, obtaining verification that recent real estate taxes are current and that the past bills have been paid by the rightful owner, and ordering a detailed inspection of the property to question each use of the property, such as, "Whose crops are those?"

212. What Are the Most Common Pitfalls to Avoid When Investing in Vacant Land?

Vacant land can be one of the best sources for ultimate wealth. Many of the richest people in the world owe their wealth to the vacant land that they once owned. Often that land is now the sites for shopping centers and other commercial or residential projects. This fact does not automatically mean that the guaranteed path to wealth is through vacant land. There are many pitfalls you will want to be aware of when contemplating the acquisition of vacant land. Some of the most critical are shown below.

The Eight Most Common Pitfalls When Buying Vacant Land

1. Negative future already planned

2. Moratoriums prevent advancement

3. Negative community attitude toward development

4. Hidden problems underground

5. Deed restrictions that stop you cold

6. Fees with a heavy impact

7. No municipal services planned

8. Not having an interim use for the land

Negative Future Already Planned.   Most events that can affect the value of real estate are public knowledge long before they actually take place. A new highway, for example, does not happen overnight; it has been in planning stages for months, even years. This event can increase some property values and decrease others. Road widening can take away needed frontage, limited access can make it hard to get to a site, and new noise levels turn a beautifully quiet residential zone into a nightmare of "For Sale" signs.

Even though most of these future events are known well in advance, knowing they are in the works is not always as simple as opening the morning paper and reading about them. This is where the buyer's effort of becoming an insider pays off. No property should be purchased until the buyer has found out what, if anything, is planned that is likely to have an impact on the area.

Moratoriums Prevent Advancement.   Any kind of community moratorium can have the effect of stopping development. This can cause buyer interest to dry up overnight. Moratoriums can be put into effect rather suddenly and can appear to come out of the blue, but they do not. They are the communities' reaction to a festering problem. Too much demand on utilities and too little capacity to serve that demand can force the water department to put a moratorium on new hookups. The same can be said for sewers, fire protection, and so on. Every public service department has some influence on a governing body to call a halt to new proceedings while the matter can be studied. Often the study takes years.

So how do you deal with this kind of a problem? One way is to look at the basic services and question each department to see if there is a problem now or in the near future that could cause a moratorium that would affect an area of interest. The following items are the basic services or departments that should be on the due diligence list. Often there are several levels of service that need to reviewed: city, county, state, and federal.

- Road
- Traffic
- Bridges

- Rail crossings
- Water
- Sewer
- Fire protection
- Garbage and trash
- Police protection
- Schools and education
- Parks and recreation

Negative Community Attitude toward Development.   Some communities develop an attitude that is anti-new-development. These communities may be "old money" areas that have grown stately and do not want any change to occur, or they can be relatively new areas that still have a lot of growth potential through vacant land in the area, but the residents living in the community do not want any one else to enjoy what they currently have. Either of these two communities can present many headaches to the investor looking to make a fortune, or even just a living, by investing in vacant land.

Fortunately the mood of a community is easy to test. Attend one building and zoning meeting and one city council meeting, and you will get the picture. If there is still doubt, then talk to some of the architects in the area—they will know which cities in their work area are easy to deal with or "tough as nails." Avoid "tough as nails" communities if you have a choice.

Hidden Problems Underground.   That beautiful pasture or strawberry patch may look very picturesque, and can be right in the path of every thing good and wonderful. But what might lurk under those ripe berries? What could those cows be treading over?

A host of problems can lay underground that need to be known about *prior* to becoming the owner. Farmers have been known to store drums of fuel oil and gasoline for their tractors in the fields, and those drums could have been leaking for years. Other pollutants and waste can be there, giving those strawberries a bright red glow (in the dark!) and a large hole in your pocket when, as the new owner, you must have tons of soil dug up and sent 1,000 miles away to be dealt with properly.

The solution is have the land tested and inspected by qualified experts. If there is reason to believe there might be a problem, or if the present use suggests that a problem could be likely, make sure that the seller pays for the test.

Deed Restrictions That Stop You Cold.   Any seller can lace a deed with restrictions that can establish a higher level of restrictions than those of the local ordinances. It is possible that a deed that is several transfers back has the restrictions that everyone forgot about—after all, the land is just a vacant lot. Why is it a vacant lot? It could be that someone put in a restriction that effectively has prohibited a use that would be warranted for the area. A detailed review of the chain of deeds will reveal what deed restrictions, if any, may still be in effect.

Some states have enacted laws that limit the time a deed restriction will still be in effect, even if the deed restriction uses terms such as *forever* or *99 years*.

Courts have also taken a more practical approach when dealing with illogical deed restrictions that no longer serve the area as intended or that are out of date to the current needs. However, many deed restrictions or *restrictive covenants* may be in place that are legally enforceable and highly restrictive to the use of the property.

Fees with a Heavy Impact.   Many communities have approached their lack of services with a novel approach to pay for the needed or expanding service: make developers pay for it.

They do this with impact fees that can be very expensive. These fees can be administered at several government levels, too, making them all the more costly. The following are just some of the possible impact fees or costs that can come with development.

- Utility impact fees to hook up to water or sewer lines.

- Donation to parks and recreation for the added impact on those services from people who may live or use the newly developed property.

- Cost or donation to relieve traffic congestion. This can be the most expensive of all. Not only can the government take part of the land (without payment to you), but they can require you to build new roads, bridges, or contribute to a fund for such works.

- Schools fund. You can be forced to pay a fee to a general fund, or if your project is big enough, set aside land for public schools.

- Pay to other funds such as fire, police, public health, water management, environmental studies, wildlife areas, and so on.

What can you do about all this? Know what it is that you will be asked to pay prior to buying the land. Once you own land you must become active in local affairs to make sure that the local residents do not shift the cost for their added infrastructure onto you.

No Municipal Services Planned.   If you buy too far ahead of development, you might own farmland for a 100 more years. This is okay for farmers. The septic tank or outhouse works fine, the windmill pumps up plenty of nice clean water, and the 100-amp electrical service that just barely makes it from the main line a mile away runs all the electrical appliances at the farm, only not all at once. But forget the new housing project unless you plan on putting in your own public services. By the way, new cities are often formed by developers doing exactly that.

Not Having an Interim Use for the Land.   If the land is costly and expensive to hold on to, then an interim use for the land is essential. It is always a good idea, and when possible it can be a criteria to consider when deciding between two or more properties.

Back to the great wealth of the world: many of the wealthy families of the world got their riches from land, but not always because of the original purpose to which the land was put to use. Farmland became oil fields; oil fields became cities, and later shopping centers and residential subdivisions.

Modern investors should seek to find some use for the land they have to help pay for the cost of taxes, insurance, and mortgage payments. "U-Pick-It" farms, landscape growing and sales yards, flea markets, boat yards, used car lots, storage lots, and so on are several good examples of such use.

213.   What Can Go Wrong with My Zoning and How Can I Be Affected?

1. *An adverse change to different zoning.*   This can happen anytime the local city or county decides a master plan needs to be revised or that zoning for a specific area needs to be changed for some other reason. The change of zoning can destroy years of plans by creating restrictions for intended development. For example, you have a restaurant and have saved up to buy a beautiful site where you hope to build a new restaurant. Then, after 15 years of paying off an expensive mortgage, the city changes the zoning to a category that prohibits any commercial activity.

2. *More restrictive use of your existing zoning.*   The continual tightening of restrictions is the more common adjustment that is made to zoning. Take multifamily zoning as an example. The usual adjustments are to reduce the number of units that can be constructed on a site. The original zoning might have allowed 25 units per acre, but the city changes all zoning of that category now to be limited to 10 units per acre. Commercial zoning may also have more restrictive changes as well. Sometimes the changes are more subtle, and at first may not appear to have the ultimate economic impact that they do. For example, a zoning that previously allowed for a building to be constructed no more than 70 feet in height is changed to reduce the height to no more than 50 feet. This difference of two stories of construction can mean a loss of gross building area, which may reflect a reduced income potential from the building. It is important that you be aware of this, but if the highest and best economic use would be a two-story building, then the reduction of height would have no effect. This is critical because the present owner may have had his own dreams squelched if he had purchased the property with the idea of building a seven-story apartment building, and five floors just will not do. From his point of view the property no longer has its investment potential, so the land is put up for sale. Along you come, ready to buy the land because two floors is ample for your restaurant.

3. *Moratorium of use in your category of zoning.*   Moratoriums that halt building are an obvious disadvantage to increased value of property. The long-term

effect may be that the moratorium benefits the community as it gives the city leaders and their employees time to rethink, replan, or just catch up to the level at which the community service should be. However, in the short term, there is no development, and there are no buyers.

214. Can a Building Moratorium Really Destroy the Value of My Vacant Property?

Yes. Building moratoriums are usually imposed by local authorities as a step to stop any development. This can be the result of several different events. The two most common are to give time to review changes in zoning and to allow public services time to catch up with demands created by overdevelopment.

In any event, the moratorium can have the effect of cooling off a prospective buyer who is interested in building now, not at some yet-to-be-determined date.

Remember, There May Be Exceptions to Every Rule. If a moratorium has been put into effect that seems to have stopped development in your area, there may still be hope. Sit down with the local building officials and have them explain the exact details of the moratorium. Enquire as to the possible avenues you can follow to obtain building permits despite the moratorium. Will a change in zoning help? It might, as the moratorium may be directed at a type of development. To solve problems like these, you can call on your newly found insider friends. If you do not have any yet, ask the head of the building department to recommend you a good lawyer who deals with these kinds of problems.

215. What Is *Grandfathered Use* and Why Is That So Dangerous?

A *grandfathered use* is a nonconforming use that does not meet the current codes or zoning regulations but is allowed because it existed prior to the current rules and regulations. This does not mean that every prior situation is allowed to continue when a zoning rule or other law is changed, because many are not; but when they are allowed it is critical that you understand the dangers of acquiring a property with a *grandfathered use*.

Review several examples of an allowed nonconforming use.

- Buildings that have less than current setbacks from property lines
- Type of business activity a recent zoning change now prohibits
- Building height taller than current building codes allow
- Hallways too narrow to meet new construction codes
- No handicapped facilities
- Less parking spots than current code demands

- "Green area" less than the current ratio of building to lot allows
- Number of apartment units on site greater than current code allows

Where the Dangers Lurk

When you buy a property with a nonconforming use that has been *grandfathered in*, you run the risk of not being able to make major repairs in the event of a major casualty loss. Even worse, your casualty insurance may not cover you for such loss.

If you want to make any changes to the structure, the local building department may require you to conform to all the current building codes and restrictions. This may be a task that is very costly to do and that would greatly reduce the value of the property.

216. What Are the Major Pitfalls to Mortgage Financing?

The use of other people's money (OPM) is one of the great advantages of real estate investment. Investors who could not even qualify for a car loan are able to buy property worth hundreds of thousands of dollars and owe mortgages equal to 80 or 90 percent of that amount. How? Because they either assume an existing mortgage, or the sellers hold the paper themselves. But not every cloud has a silver lining. The following are five pitfalls that await the mortgagor.

The Five Pitfalls in Taking Out Mortgages

1. *Paying for mortgage commitments that do not come.*   The Bank of Stark (no reflection on any real bank of that same name), was a great place to get a "throwaway" loan commitment back in the early 1970s. What made this bank attractive was that the officers would commit to an end loan that would ultimately be used by the borrower to replace a construction loan. The *end loan* is very important because there are many lenders who like to make construction loans, since the yield is higher than long-term loans and the term of years is relatively short. If a project will take two years to build, the construction loan may be for a maximum of three years. Construction lenders get in and out of deals all the time, but not the end loan lender, who makes a long-term loan that may have a 15- to 30-year payback schedule.

When the construction lender sees that there is an end loan commitment already in place, they relax and make the construction loan.

Enter the Bank of Stark (and other mythical banks and bankers). Pay them $50,000 and they will grant you a $2,000,000 end loan commitment. Sure the interest rate looked high—prime plus 6 points, or more—but this was just a throwaway commitment. The borrower only wanted to get the construction loan to build the building and sell the building without ever needing the end loan, or hope that the lending market would improve so much and the building look so valuable (all rented, of course) that the expensive to get and more expensive to keep Bank of Stark end loan would not be necessary.

The success of the Bank of Stark and other lenders like it was that most of its loans never had to be made. The mortgagors were able to sell or find other financing—until one could not. That is when the walls came tumbling down—there was no Bank of Stark.

The moral of this is to be very leery of paying up front commitment funds to mortgage brokers, bankers, and other lenders who promise something that they later cannot deliver on. Ask and get and then check their references.

2. *Getting low ARMs that have no caps for interest increases.*   Many lenders offer very low "entry" interest rates for ARMs. This entry interest may be in place for a few months, even the first year, or however long the competition to make loans drives the lender to offer. However, after that entry period the interest starts to go up, and like 4th of July fireworks, it reaches a point of economic explosion. This does not mean that ARMs are to be avoided—quite the opposite, in fact. ARMs can be a great way to take advantage of adjustments in the interest rates when they look like they are already high and headed down. As for the early 1990s it looks as though the rates are not going down but up. And up they will go, until they level off, and even go down again. All of this requires some mathematical thought to work out the probable interest rate over a period of time. If the lender will hold the increases to levels that will not allow the interest rate to climb above the market rate for fixed rate mortgages, then ARMs can still be attractive.

3. *Balloon mortgage payments.*   A balloon payment has the tendency of sneaking up on you and hitting you right in the wallet when you least expect it. The advantage of a balloon mortgage is that it usually allows you to schedule a softer payback schedule that leads up to the balloon. Some mortgages are scheduled on a 25-year amortization, for example, but balloon at the end of the first seven years. The problem is, what do you do at the end of seven years? Go out and get a new mortgage? What if you cannot due to a tight mortgage market, or a situation where interest rates have gone through the roof? This can be a very difficult situation.

The answer is simply to avoid any balloon mortgage unless you have some insurance that you will be able to deal with the debt obligation when it comes due.

4. *Mortgages that are not assumable.*   Unfortunately most institutional loans are either not assumable, or are assumable with full qualification (almost the same as unassumable). Generally only private mortgages held by the seller (purchase money mortgages) can be negotiated to be fully assumable.

When you buy a property and end up with a mortgage that will not be assumable by a buyer you want to sell to, then you suddenly have a balloon mortgage when you do not want one. The only way you can effectively deal with this is to either pass on buying property with nonassumable mortgages or to anticipate the consequence well in advance of your need to sell.

5. *Lenders not approving a "buyer" to assume your mortgage.*   Even when your mortgage is "assumable," it may not be, as has been mentioned above. Why? Because the lender turns down your buyer. This is an everyday occurrence in the industry, and many buyers seek to use creative techniques to hold their deals together.

More than one seller has had their hair turn gray after having a buyer turned down by the mortgagee. Some sellers are able to hold the deal together by staying on the paper (in essence, stay at risk on the loan as a co-signer to the debt), or by getting the buyer to put up other security as additional collateral to the loan. But many buyers simply walk away from the deal when this occurs.

217. Is There Any "Easy" Way to Avoid All the Possible Pitfalls That Await Real Estate Investors?

No. Avoiding pitfalls in any endeavor requires a wide-awake approach to everything you do. It takes effort and dedication to the task. It demands that you learn to do and understand the things you cannot do and do not fully comprehend. It insists that you learn from your mistakes and attempt to build on what you have learned.

The positive aspect of real estate investing is that virtually everything that can happen has happened before. You can follow historical trends because similar events in the past have produced similar results to what is going on now.

218. What Is a *Quitclaim Deed* and Why Can It Be a Very Risky Form of Title Transfer for the Buyer?

A *quitclaim* deed (not quick claim) is a deed to convey only a present interest a person may have in a property, whether or not such an interest actually existed. Famous quitclaim deeds have included such deeds in the Empire State Building, the London Bridge, and so on. They are all valid deeds, but only as valuable as the interest they actually transfer.

When a quitclaim deed is given, there is no representation or warranty of title made. This kind of deed is helpful in clearing up clouds on title or other problems that can arise.

Danger—be wary: Because the quitclaim deed does not represent nor warranty title, taking such a deed as payment or security for something may prove to be a mistake.

219. What Is a *Trustee's Deed* and What Are the Limitations in Protection It Gives the Buyer?

A *trustee's deed* is a conveyance of a property by a trustee of a property. This can result from several different situations, the most common of which is when a property owner establishes a trust to hold title to property. In so doing, the title is placed in the name of a trustee. The actual trustee may be the same person or another party depending on the type of trust established and the laws governing that kind of entity. When the property is sold or otherwise disposed of, the trustee would execute a deed in favor of the new owner. This deed would be a trustee's deed.

The problem with a trustee's deed is that it transfers only that title that the trustee has rights to. If the beneficiaries of the trust have reason and rights to contest the transfer, or if the trustee violated the trust agreement, then a cloud on the title can appear.

Read the trust agreement and obtain ratification of the transfer by the beneficiaries. One sure way of dealing with a future problem is to nip it in the bud. Even though the trustee has a legal right to give the buyer a deed, the buyer can insist on verification and assurance that the deed is going to meet the qualifications of a general warranty deed.

220. What or Who Are Phantom Deal Makers and How Do I Deal with Them?

Phantom deal makers are like the little ghosts in the comic strip who are all named "Not Me." In essence, a phantom deal maker is your adversary that in reality does not exist.

The seller looks you in the face and says, "A couple came by yesterday and said they would offer $400,000. That makes your offer for $250,000 look silly, don't you think?"

A buyer looks you in the face and says, "Yeah, well see that bigger house across the street? The owner said she would sell it to me for $245,000."

Dealing with the phantom. Whenever I am told about some phantom I shift into a two-step process. You can do the same.

1. Ask the other party if he or she would be more comfortable if you withdrew from the negotiations so he or she can work with the other interested parties.

2. Continue with your negotiations as though you never heard anything about the phantom and that you had never even asked the question in the first step.

221. How Can I Know If a Property I Want to Buy Has a Defective Title and Why Is That So Important?

It is unlikely that you would know if a property has a defective title without a detailed check of the chain of title transfers. As every legal judgment against a person and their property will eventually become a matter of record, a review of the property records and other public documents should resolve the matter. However, judgments are not the only item that has to be checked to verify that title has transferred correctly from one party to another along the way.

If there has been an improperly prepared document in the chain of title, it is possible that a document can create a cloud on the title. For example, a property owned jointly by a large family may convey title, but for some reason the wife of one of the members did not sign the deed, or there was no witness, or the deed was not dated. Even if that event took place several owners ago, the problem can just now surface and the heirs of that woman now cause a problem.

Every title should be checked and verified by qualified professionals trained to perform that task. Most buyers add to that by purchasing title insurance to defend their rights should a cloud or claim appear in the future. When you buy property and are shown that the present property owner acquired title insurance when the property was purchased, that does not guarantee that there are no possible problems; however, it does give you a good starting point that, if there are any problems, they may show up in what the title policy excluded. Pay close attention to any exception or exclusion of coverage and seek to have those problem areas removed prior to your taking title.

222.   What Is an Encroachment and How Does It Affect Title?

An encroachment is when some improvement or object from one property crosses the boundary of another adjoining tract. There are two kinds of encroachment: visible and hidden. A visible encroachment would be one that was obvious to the eye, whereas a hidden encroachment is underground or not clearly visible because of some other obstruction.

When there is an encroachment and appropriate and timely steps are not taken by the property owner whose boundary has been encroached upon to remove the encroachment, an easement by prescription may develop. It is possible that in some instances the actual boundary of the properties may change in favor of the encroaching party.

The innocent party can seek legal remedy the moment the encroachment is discovered to have the encroaching object removed. In such cases the court generally reviews the cost and benefit of such removal and may rule that the encroaching party must pay damages, but does not have to remove the object.

On the other hand, there are examples where people have constructed a building in the wrong place to the extent that the building was completely on another property, which amounts to being a gift to the other property owner.

Hidden encroachments usually occur underground; basements, water, electric, sewer, and other such connections, and septic tanks all have been known to encroach below the ground onto adjoining property. These encroachments can be the most damaging because they may not show up in a survey. As most title insurance policies will not defend a claim against a title where the problem would have been discovered by a recent survey, the decision then is whether the survey should disclose both aboveground and belowground encroachments.

Not all "clearly visible" encroachments are ever noticed. This happens because the property boundary is not clearly marked or is assumed to be somewhere other than it really is. This can be the result of negligence on the part of the surveyor or a simple lack of a survey and the reliance on the statements of a previous seller. Some metes and bound descriptions that are measured by distances to an Old Oak, or the a meander of a river or stream, can be altered by removal of one old oak and the planting of another, or the physical engineered change of a river's flow.

An encroachment does affect title, and if there is an easement by prescription or the taking of some of the land because of adverse possession, property values can be greatly affected.

223. What Are the Most Important Steps I Should Take *before* I Ever Buy Real Estate?

1. *Establish attainable and measurable goals.*   Ask 1000 people if they are goal oriented, and most will say they are. However, their goals are usually misdirected and rarely clearly attainable within a timetable, and no measure of progress is possible. The goal "to be rich" is such an example. It sounds great but is like starting a journey for Anatolia and having no idea where it is or how to get there. Only by having a well-defined goal that is attainable can success be reached, and ultimate success is reached only by working down a path of attaining one goal after another. Success breeds contempt for failure.

2. *Review your abilities and limitations.*   Now that you have a target, that ultimate goal, take stock of what you have to do to get you there. In every endeavor, having the right tools is important, and if your tools need to be enhanced, then take steps to do that. This might require an adjustment in your goals or the need to establish some intermediate stepping stones, like an adult education class in bookkeeping, hotel management, or landscaping to help build depth in your future dealings in real property.

3. *Establish a plan that builds on your abilities and strengthens your limitations.* Only you and your partners need to know about this plan, or for that matter, what your abilities and limitations really are. The only thing that is important is for you to work to improve. Many people are complacent about their abilities and limitations and get into a rut when they are functioning at the maximum of their abilities because they are walled in by their limitations. Escape that trap by expanding your abilities.

4. *Begin to build your comfort zone.*   The area you chose to invest in is your comfort zone. All you need to do is to know it as well as anyone can to become the real expert about what is going on in that area.

5. *Establish yourself as a local real estate insider.*   This task is obtainable by anyone who has the determination to learn, some time to devote to the task, and the ability and willingness to play the role.

6. *Open your eyes to the opportunities in your comfort zone.*   As you learn what is going on and start to see how past trends are a guide to future events, opportunities that escape most people will suddenly jump right out of the neighborhood. At first you will assume that everyone else sees them too–but soon you begin to realize that the average person in a neighborhood does not even know the name of the people who live around them, much less see real opportunities.

7. *Make offers.*   One of the secrets to success in buying real estate is making offers. You make offers to learn how to deal with people, you make offers to learn about the property you might like to own, you make offers because that puts you in contact with other insiders, but most importantly, you make offers because no seller knows what they will do until presented with a written offer.

8. *Periodically adjust your goals.*   Your long-range goal should rarely change. That focus can be fine-tuned, and once in a while, as you get closer to it, you may more clearly define it. But the intermediate goals, those short-range stepping stones, need to be constantly adjusted. This is important and necessary because events around you change and you must be flexible so that you can adjust with them. New technology is developed and new techniques are found that are better than old ones, and this demands that you continually expand your opportunities by being able to see them when they appear.

9. *Learn from your failures.*   After all, failure is nature's way of telling you that you are doing something wrong and that corrections need to be made to your plan. However, most people fail because they have no plan, and by lacking a focus and an original direction there is no clear way to know what should be changed. One of the very first failures to learn from is the frustration that comes from continually batting your head up against a wall trying to get over it, when in reality that wall is blocking a path you should not have even tried to follow in the first place. By looking at yourself and trying to be objective, you may discover that what you really want to get is different than what you thought you needed. Learn to take all your failures seriously, and examine what went wrong, and why. Always ask yourself these two questions:

- Did I have my heart in what I was trying to do?
- Was my attitude primed for success?

Often the turnaround from failure to success is to answer these questions honestly, then either do everything you can to change your own approach to the task or find a different task to which you have a more positive approach.

10. *Build on your successes.*   There is nothing sweeter than overcoming adversity and achieving success. Even a small success can start a growing process where other successful ventures seem to fall into place. This is not *luck*; this is the way a well-thought-out plan that is carefully implemented should work. This is the fruit of your efforts and the demonstration to yourself that you can do it.

224. To Be Continually Successful as a Real Estate Investor, What Should I Do Every Day?

To maintain a successful career as a real estate investor there are things you should do every day.

1. Read your written-down goals. Do not rely on a memory of what you are looking for. When you look at your goals daily, you keep yourself tuned in to your future.

2. Check your actual progress against your earlier planned and estimated timetable. Time is the most important factor, and only experience in its allotment will give you a mastery over it.

3. Make adjustments in your plans that will allow you to keep your original goals firmly in sight and as your direction.

4. Adjust your goals only when you have already achieved them, or if your goals were too optimistic for your abilities. Be cautious about downgrading your goals simply because you have not obtained them. First ask yourself, "Have I done everything I can or could to achieve what I started out to do?" If the honest reply is "no," then find out why and correct that situation.

Key Word and Subject Index

by Question Numbers

How to Use: Locate the key word or subject you wish to research and turn to the **QUESTION NUMBERS** indicated. This will provide you with answers designed to give you information on that word or subject. When more than one question number is shown, you should read each question indicated to obtain the maximum data on that word or subject.

Absolute auction, 127, 129
Accelerate the mortgage, 122
Acquisition of real estate, 6
Action of foreclosure, 122
Ad valorem tax reduction, 139
Adjustable rate mortgages, 141, 148, 170, 216
Adversarial buyer vs. seller relationship, 31
Adverse effect of infrastructure, 8
Adverse possession, 211
Agents absorb the heat, 31
All items index (COLA), 15
Amortization tables, 137
Analyzing property, 79
Animal smells, 38, 106
Annual assessments for condos and coops, 54
Appeal to your greed, 88
Appliances in rental property, 16
Appreciation factors of raw land, 77
Association interviews, 57
Attitude and becoming an insider, 5
Auction strategies, 127, 129, 136
Auctioneer selection, 135
Authority to make a lease, 16
Available options when selling, 44
Average daily rate, 89
Avoid saying "no," 31

"Backoutitus," 197
Bad checks, 100
Balloon mortgage payments, 216
Barter concession, 20
Barter techniques, 158
Basis, 32, 109
Benefits gained in deal, 31
Benefits given up in deal, 31
Blanket mortgages, 173
Book value of real estate, 32
Bottom line, 7

Bounced checks, 106
Boundary survey, 200
Breached mortgage, 122
Broken items in rentals, 18
Building moratoriums, 83, 212, 214
Building permit regulations, 83
Building permits, 7
Building rule or regulation, 15, 16
Building rules at condos and coops, 57
Business expenses and vacation homes, 59
Buy-out provisions for syndications, 66
Buyer negotiating strategies, 150
Buyer's agents, 27
Buyer's goals, 41
Buyer's negative comments, 33
Buyer's negotiating offers, 30
Buyer's preclosing checklist, 52
Buyer's prepurchase steps, 41
Buyer's property inspections, 41
Buyer's "time bombs," 43
Buying factors for condos or coops, 54
Buying property in foreclosure, 124
Buying signals, 34
Buying vacation properties, 59

CAM, 15, 106
Capital gain $125,000 exclusion, 107
Capital gains tax strategies, 51, 110
Capital improvements, 7
Cash on cash return, 138
Caveat emptor, 200
Check sheet for 1034 home swap, 51
Checklist for joint ventures, 165
Checklist for the closing, 200
Closing cost reduction, 195, 196
Closing preparation, 197
CMR (competitive market report), 46
Co-signatories to mortgages, 148

Code violations, 43
COLA (cost of living adjustment), 15, 143
"Coldfeetitus," 197
Comfort zone and your goals, 6
Comfort zone and vacation properties, 60
Comfort zone investing method, 2, 223, 224
Comfort zone limitations, 2, 4
Commission, what is common, 29
Common management problems, 106
Common mortgages, 170
Communications improve negotiations, 30
Compound interest and annuity tables, 137
Condo and coop annual assessments, 54
Condo and coop association interview, 57
Condo and coop balance sheet, 54
Condo and coop building management, 54
Condo and coop building regulations, 57
Condo and coop buying factors, 54
Condo and coop forms of ownership, 53
Condo and coop land leases, 54
Condo and coop life style, 58
Condo and coop maintenance charges, 55
Condo and coop mortgage obligations, 54
Condo and coop neighbors, 54
Condo and coop reason to buy, 56
Condo and coop rules and regulations, 54
Condo and coop security, 58
Condo and coop selling strategies, 58
Constant payment mortgages, 141
Contract factors for landlords, 15
Contract factors for tenants, 15
Contract renegotiations, 197
Cooperative apartment ownership forms,
    53
Copper plumbing, 42
Cost of living, 15
Cost of living adjustments, 143
Cost of living statistics, 143
Court-ordered auctions, 131
Crawl spaces, 42
Creative financing, 189
Crime and its effect, 13
Cross-collaterized, 149
Customs department auctions, 130

Damage at vacation property, 62
Dealing with late rent payments, 99
Decline in rental rates, 8
Decline of neighborhoods, 8
Declines in values, 13
Deed restrictions, 175, 212
Defaults in rental contracts, 15
Defective title, 221
Deferred exchanges, 191

Deferred maintenace, 7, 8, 88, 126
Deficiency judgment, 122
Depletion allowance, 144
Depreciation, 93, 107, 112, 113
Depreciation calculation, 144
Desperate owners, 8
Discharged liens, 43
Dog smells, 38
DOT officials, 78, 79
Dual agents, 27
Due diligence, 30, 145

Ease of access to property, 79
Economic conversion, 3, 4, 11, 139, 154
Economic obsolescence, 8,12
Encroachments, 43, 222
Environmental standards, 7
Equity kickers, 148
Estate considerations, 72
Estoppel letters, 88
Excessive debt, 97
Exchange strategies, 107, 111, 115, 156, 157,
    167
Exchange title for life residency, 70
Existing leases, 87

FHA foreclosed property, 125
FHA mortgage qualification, 183
FHA mortgages, 182
Financial ceilings, 30
Finding foreclosure property, 125
Finding lenders, 180
Fire hazards, 106
Fire or other loss, 209
Fix-up increases value, 11
Fix-up list, 45
Fixed rate mortgages, 170
Fleas, 106
Floating time at time-share resorts, 63
"For rent" signs, 15
"For sale" signs and values, 13
Foreclosed property pitfalls, 126
Foreclosure after releases, 175
Foreclosure avoidance, 123
Foreclosure sales, 122, 124
Fortunes by good investment timing, 9
Furniture and fixtures, 16
Future exchange, 167

Garbage collection at rentals, 16
Geographies to a comfort zone, 2
"Get rich quick" scams, 146

Getting out of the deal, 198, 199
GI loans, 184, 185
Gifts of title, 70
Goals, 5, 6, 30, 41, 44, 62, 95, 97, 223, 224
Good, marketable and insurable title, 43
Good memory smells, 67
Government auctions, 130
Governmental controls, 8
Graduated payment mortgages, 170
Graduated rate mortgage, 141
Grandfathered-in zoning, 82, 215
Green area, 215
Greener grass syndrome, 159
Growing equity mortgages, 170

Hidden costs in rental contracts, 15
Hidden gems, 42
Hidden lease terms to avoid, 88
Hidden time bombs for condos or coops, 43,
    55, 87
Hidden underground problems, 212
High-constant-payment mortgage pitfalls, 75
Home office depreciation, 114
Home sellers, 44
Homestead exemption provision, 71
Homework, 30
Housing starts, 12

I'll pay your price, 32
Illegal use of rented space, 106
Impact fees, 212
Important factors in vacation properties, 61
Improved infrastructure, 7, 83
Improvements to rented property, 15
Income from vacant land, 84
Income-producing property advantages, 94
Income-producing-property at peak value, 12
Income-producing-property selection, 92
Income projections, 93, 145
Income tax reduction, 107
Increase property values, 11
Increases in income, 3
Increases in value, 3
Inexpensive fix-ups, 45
Inflation, 1, 7
Infrastructure and adverse effects, 7, 8, 83
Inheritance and the senior citizen, 68
Insider, become one, 2, 5, 168
Insider tips for senior citizens, 76
Insider tips to mortgage negotiations, 188
Inspections of rental properties, 87
Installment sale rules, 74, 107
Insurance amount to carry, 202

Insurance and what to carry, 203
Insurance claims, 209
Insurance coverage, 208
Insurance factors, 201
Insurance for a leased property, 15
Insurance for the tenant, 206
Insurance strategies, 207
Interval time at time-share resorts, 63
Inventory checks for vacation rentals, 62
Inventory for vacation property, 62
Investing goals, 80, 92, 95, 96, 146, 223, 224
Investing in raw land, 77, 78
Investing in rentals, 87
Investing strategies, 210, 223, 224
Investing strategies for rentals, 96
Investment pitfalls, 96, 97, 217
Investment return on rentals, 87
Investment techniques, 153, 154
Investor's four key elements, 5
IRS capital gain exclusion ($125,000), 71
IRS gift rules, 73
IRS intimidation, 108
IRS Section 1031 Starker exchange, 191
IRS Section 1031 strategies, 107, 111, 115, 156,
    157, 167, 191
IRS Section 1034 check sheet, 51, 73, 107, 114
IRS tax audit, 108

Joint ventures, 165
Judgements and collections, 192

"Keep some, sell some" technique of invest-
    ing, 166

Lack of good management, 8
Lack of instant market, 1
Land lease techniques, 163
Land leases under condos and coops, 54
Land speculation, 162
Landlord-tenant laws, 19
Landscaping, 36
Late rent payment penalty, 15, 99
Lease concessions, 17, 20, 22
Lease form to use, 105
Lease-option techniques, 164
Lease renewals, 15
Lease restrictions, 16
Lease violations, 106
Leases, getting the most favorable, 17
Legal description, 52
Legal notices to evict a tenant, 103
Legal representation or not, 194

Lender's preferences, 4
Letter of credit with subordination, 176
Letter of intent, 151
Levels of acceptable risk, 145
Leverage negotiations, 149
Liability insurance, 204
Liens, 43
Like-kind exchange, 107
Like-kind exchange deferred, 191
Lis pendens, 122
List of hidden gems, 42
List of memory smells, 40
Listing agreements with agents, 26
Listing term, 26
Loan approval steps, 186
Loan prequalification, 41
Loan presentation, 188
Loan strategies, 181
Loan to value ratio, 140, 188
Local indicators, 7, 12
Location vs. important location, 79
Lost market potential, 126

Maintenance cost, 12, 55
Maintenance log, 90
Make your property value go up, 11
Marketing brochure, 86
Master plan, 82
Maximize benefits from agents, 25
Maximize sales price, 45
Memory smells, 40
Mental ownership, 31
Mental transformation to "owner," 86
Midnight moves, 102, 106
Mildew, 35
MLS (Multiple Listing Service), 24, 26
Moratorium of use, 213
Moratorium on building construction, 8
Mortgage assumption, 174
Mortgage commitments, 216
Mortgage foreclosure, 122
Mortgage language, 171
Mortgage over basis, 111
Mortgage payment calculation, 137
Mortgage payment methods, 141
Mortgage pitfalls, 148, 178, 192
Mortgage position, 178
Mortgage reduction plans, 187
Mortgage strategies, 148, 188
Mortgage terms, 179
Mortgagee's rights, 121
Mortgages that are nonassumable, 190
Mortgages with substitution of collateral, 177
Mortgagor vs. mortgagee, 169

Most favorable lease, 17
Motivation that make sellers act, 30

National Association of Realtors, 24
National statistics, 12
Negative comments, 33
Negative community attitude, 212
Negotiate favorable leases, 17
Negotiating strategies, 149, 150
Negotiating strategies for rentals, 87
Negotiation checklist, 31
Negotiation deadlines, 30
Negotiation of offers, 30
Net commission, 29
Net operating income, 7, 139
Never be insulted, 31
New roadways effect on values, 8
Nitpicking buyers, 34
Nonassumable mortgages, 190, 216
Nonsufficient funds, 100
Novation, 174

OPM (other people's money), 1, 3, 8, 147, 148
Opportunities and recognizing them, 2
Option to buy real estate, 66, 153
Overbuilt situations, 8
Overly estimated income, 97
Own vs. rent, 14
Owner must sell, 8
Ownership options for seniors, 70
Ownership pitfalls of vacation property, 60
Ownership tips for senior citizens, 76

Paint increases value, 11
Peaking property values, 12
Pending assessments, 43
Pest control at rentals, 16
Phantom deal makers, 220
Pitfalls at the closing, 52
Pitfalls before and during the closing, 197
Pitfalls in financing, 148
Pitfalls in investing, 200
Pitfalls in land investing, 83, 212
Pitfalls of high-constant-payment mortgages, 75
Pitfalls of time-share ownership, 63
Pitfalls of vacation property ownership, 60
Pitfalls to mortgages, 216
Pitfalls with foreclosed property, 126
Plumbing in rental property, 16
Poor management, 8
Positive attitude, 30

Prebidding steps at auctions, 129
Preclosing checklist, 200
Predebt questions, 148
Predicting value increases, 9
Prelisting agreement factors, 26
Prequalified loans, 41
Price paid for a property, 10
Prime lenders, 179
Pro forma income projections, 93
Profit and loss statements, 93
Property basis calculation form, 109
Property encroachments, 43
Property information, 10
Property inspections, 15, 39, 52
Property insurance, 15, 201
Property landscaping, 36
Property maintenance, 13
Property management, 98
Property ownership and senior citizens, 68
Property survey, 52, 222
Property tax, 116
Property tax nonpayment, 119
Property tax reduction, 117, 139
Property values, 7, 8, 13
Public documents and records, 10
Purchase contracts, 152
Pyramiding as an investment tool, 159

Quitclaim deed dangers, 218

Random releases of property, 175
RCI (time-share exchanges), 63
Real estate agency types, 27
Real estate agent selection, 48
Real estate agent's energy zones, 25
Real estate agent's obligations, 27
Real estate as fundamental of wealth, 1
Real estate auctions, 127
Real estate brokers, 23
Real estate closings, 193
Real estate commission paid, 26, 29
Real estate firms, 26
Real estate insider, 223
Real estate insurance, 201
Real estate investor's criteria, 5
Real estate owned (REO) in foreclosure, 125
Real estate ownership, 1
Realtor vs. licensed broker, 24
Reasons people buy, 9
Reduction of housing cost for seniors, 71
Regulatory changes, 8
Relandscape increases value, 11
Release of security to mortgages, 173, 175

Removing animal smells, 38
Removing mildew smells, 35
Rent security deposits, 15
Rent vs. ownership, 114
Rent your vacatin property, 62
Rental agreement key factors, 15
Rental contracts, 15
Rental deposits for vacation properties, 62
Rental income and expense norms, 87
Rental property sales strategies, 90
Rental rates, 91
Rental rates and their decline, 8
Rental rules for vacation homes, 62
Rental standards and enforcement, 90
Renters insurance, 206
Repairs to rented property, 15
Replacement cost, 12
Resolution Trust Corporation, 133
Resorts Condominiums International, 63
Retirement and amount to afford, 69
Reverse annuity mortgages, 170
Rezone for profit, 78
Rezoning increases value, 9
Right to redeem after foreclosure, 122
Right to renew your lease, 15
Risk, 147
Risk enhancers in rental, 88
RTC auctions, 134

Sales steps to buyer inspections, 39
Sales tax reports, 88
Seasonal vs. annual rentals, 89
Security at rentals, 16
Security deposits on rentals, 15
Selecting real estate brokers, 26
Seller's agents, 27
Seller's checklist, 47
Seller's negotiation checklist, 31
Selling furnished property, 37
Selling rental property, 90
Selling strategies for condo or coop owners, 58
Selling techniques, 49
Selling the benefits of condo or coop living, 58
Selling tips for vacation homes, 67
Selling unfurnished property, 37
Selling vacant land, 85
Selling vacation properties, 59
Senior citizen, amount to own or rent, 69
Senior citizen and inheritance, 68
Senior citizen housing cost reductions, 71
Senior citizen money saving strategies, 75
Senior citizen selling strategies, 74

Senior citizen tax planning, 68, 71
Senior citizen using an installment sale, 74
Senior citizen with large capital gain, 74
Senior citizens and property ownership, 68
Senior citizens and rentals, 21
Senior citizens and their wills, 76
Senior citizen's estate consideration, 72
Senior citizen's ownership options, 70
Seniors vs. younger owners, 68
Setback lines, 43
Setting a price for your home, 46
Shared appreciation mortgages, 170
Short-term payback financing, 96
Short-term speculation, 9
Showing buyers your home, 39
Single agents, 27
Small claims court, 104
Smart money and where its found, 4
Smell test at rentals, 16
Space bank for time-share ownership, 63, 64
Special assessments, 43
Special assets, 125
Speculation on a short term, 9
Spendable cash flow, 139
Squatter's rights, 211
Stages of a property auction, 127
Standard deposit receipt contract, 152
Starker exchanges, 191
Steps, preinvestment, 223
Steps for buyers, 41
Steps for insurance loss, 209
Steps leading to a foreclosure sale, 122
Steps leading to the closing, 193
Steps to acquisition of income properties, 96
Steps to adequate insurance, 208
Steps to avoid a foreclosure, 123
Steps to buyer negotiating, 150
Steps to buying raw land, 78
Steps to buying residential rentals, 87
Steps to calculate yield, 138
Steps to contract negotiations, 30
Steps to evict a tenant, 103
Steps to getting a loan, 186
Steps to increase cash flow, 139
Steps to meaningful projections, 145
Steps to pyramiding, 159
Steps to reduce property tax, 117
Steps to reduction of the seller's closing cost, 196
Steps to renters insurance, 206
Steps to select an auctioneer, 135
Steps to sell vacant land, 86
Steps to seller negotiating, 149
Steps to successful syndications, 160
Steps to survive tax audits, 108

Steps to use sweat equity, 154, 155
Storm damage, 106
Strategies to sell vacation property, 67
Strategies using a letter of intent, 151
Strategies when holding a mortgage, 192
Subagent, 27
Subordination, 148, 176
Substitute security, 148, 177
Supply and demand economics, 1, 7, 8
Sweat equity, 154, 155
Sweat equity concession, 20
Syndication, 160
Syndication buy-out provisions, 22
Syndication of your own property, 66
Syndication to acquire property, 161

Tax and the senior citizen, 68
Tax assessor's office, 10
Tax audit survival, 108
Tax basis, 109
Tax basis calculation form, 109
Tax certificates, 119, 120
Tax deductions for vacation properties, 59
Tax deed, 119
Tax-free exchange strategies, 111
Tax records for vacation property, 60
Tax reduction strategies, 73, 74, 118
Tax shelter, 93, 94
Tax strategies, 51
Tax strategies for senior citizens, 71
Tax write-offs for vacation properties, 59
Tenant complaints, 101
Tenant data for vacation properties, 62
Tenant evictions, 103
Tenant improvements, 106
Tenant rights, 19
Tenant selection, 91
Termite problems, 43, 197
Third party collection agents for wraps, 172
Three-way exchange, 167
Time as a negotiation tool, 32, 34
Time bombs, 43, 55, 87
Time-share resorts, 63
Time-share space bank, 63, 64
Time-share vs. 100 percent owned, 64
Timetable when selling, 44
Timing acquisition, 9
Timing and how to handle it, 30
Tips on selling vacation homes, 67
Title by prescription, 211
Title check, 52
Title closing pitfalls, 52
Title encroachments, 222
Title insurance problems, 205

Title policy, 221
Title problems, 43
Title transfers for senior citizens, 73
Tongue-and-groove paneling, 42
Trustee's deed, 219

Undercapitalization, 97
Underestimating expenses and costs, 97
Untaxed appreciation, 107
Untaxed benefits, 107
Urban renewal projects, 8
Urgency to sell, 8
U.S. Civil Rights Act of 1968, 91
U.S. Department of Labor, 15, 143
U.S. Marshall's Auction, 130, 132
Using different insurance agents, 28
Utility charges for vacation property, 62
Utility cost when you rent, 15

VA foreclosed property, 125
VA loan entitlement, 71
Vacancy factors, 13
Vacant land as an income producer, 84
Vacant land checklist, 80

Vacant land sales, 85, 86
Vacation property rental factors, 61, 62, 65, 66
Vacation property tax deductions, 59
Vacation rental rules and enforcement, 62
Values reaching their peak, 12
Variance can increase values, 11
Veteran loan qualification, 184
Veteran loan questions most asked, 185

Water bills for rented properties, 15
Wealth by economic conversion, 3
What to buy, 92, 96
Why people buy, 9
Win-win situations, 31
Wraparound mortgage, 142
Wraparound mortgage problems, 172

Yield on income properties, 138
You accept my terms, 32

Zero payment mortgages, 141
Zoning laws and ordinances, 3, 7, 78, 79, 81, 83, 213

About the Author

Jack Cummings is one of the nation's most successful and distinguished real estate investors and writers. He is active as a broker, exchanger, investment counselor, newsletter publisher, and lecturer. Among his many books are *The Real Estate Financing Manual*, *The Complete Guide to Real Estate Financing*, *Successful Real Estate Investing for the Single Person*, *The Guide to Real Estate Exchanging*, and *McGraw-Hill 36-Hour Real Estate Course*.